CW01660509

International Prai

Tough...witty...in the best tradition of suspense fiction.

New Yorker

Super skilled graft of fiction onto history...an authentic winner.

Sunday Times

Unusual, exotic and tantalising.

Irish Times

Has the rancid strength of a distillation of the best of Le Carré and Deighton: an authentic winner.

Sunday Times

In the top flight of thriller writers.

Natal Mercury

Smashing action scenes...superb entertainment.

New York Times Book Review

Espionage in the le Carré class

The Observer

Brierley's style is first class, and his evocation of external bleakness...is superb.

The Jerusalem Post

One is definitely hooked from the first page

BBC French Service

Also by David Brierley

Novels

Cold War
Blood Group O
Big Bear, Little Bear
Shooting Star
Czechmate
Skorpion's Death
Snowline
One Lives, One Dies
On Leaving a Prague Window
The Horizontal Woman
The Cloak-and-Dagger Girl
Death & Co
Dead Man Telling Tales
Budapest Hand

Short Stories

To El and Back

Blue Chalk Red Blood White Lightning

David Brierley

SAFE HOUSE BOOKS

www.safehousebooks.co.uk

Safe House Books Ltd
London, England
www.safehousebooks.co.uk

Published by Safe House Books, 2025

BLUE CHALK
RED BLOOD
WHITE LIGHTNING

Cover design by Emily Dinsmore

A catalogue record for this book is
available from the British Library

9781739754044 *(paperback)*

This is for Mike
Master of Ripley Hall

The collapse of the Soviet Union is the greatest geopolitical catastrophe of the 20th century.

Vladimir Putin

Closer, come closer.

No, closer than that. What are you scared of? All right.

Now stare at the screen and what do you see? No mistaking it, is there?

I have opened my laptop to check emails. Hold it. There's one from someone I don't recognise. No text. Just a photograph with every detail sharp. You can see the cobbles; swear you can feel the smoothness of the old stones. On the cobbles is an outline drawn in paint or blue chalk. A man. It's a traffic accident and this is how the police have marked the position of the body. That's your first thought. Stay a minute - and you pull back a bit at the possibility – is it a corpse? A murder victim? On the wall behind the man is a street sign: Rue Tourbet. So, France. Or at least French speaking.

Who has sent it to me? Why? There is no message. I'm left staring at this photo of the outline of a man on the ground with an arm raised above his head.

What does it mean? Why have I been sent it? What the hell am I supposed to do? What would you do? Well?

ENGLAND 2018

CHAPTER 1

That's a bad start to the day. It doesn't get better.

Still dark when the telephone rings. The phone is on Mary's side of the bed. She doesn't answer. Why not? It takes me a bit before I remember she stomped off yesterday. No, that's not right. She wasn't angry, not seriously, she just said she needed a bit of breathing space. Motherhood brings these mood swings. I think. *Come on, idiot, what does a man know? She's taken the twins and gone to stay with a friend in Wales. Or maybe that crazy woman in Bath. She didn't say. This is why she's not answering the phone.* Yes, I'm more awake now.

I roll over the bed to pick up the phone.

'Hello.'

'Mr 'az? Mr 'az 'az?'

What? Maybe I'm not fully awake. There is this thing they do in bad movies: taking the phone away from your head and staring at it. I do that.

'Hello Mr 'az. Are you there?'

Away from my ear the voice sounds tinny. It's a woman's voice but not Mary's, not even Mary teasing. My brain stirs and I realise a number of things. The woman is asking for Baz Faz. She doesn't want to say the whole name out loud. Why not? Is she scared some computer program will snap to life with the full name? Does she think the spies are tapping my phone? Seriously? I'll cut the connection except… there is determination in that voice. She'll ring back.

Listen, I'm a reporter on a provincial paper in Oxford. Nothing more. My name is Bazil Potter and spies don't give a damn about me. No, hang about. I also write a weekly column called *Under the Carpet* with the byline Baz Faz. It's about the bad things that happen; the bad things that politicians, public servants, crooks and powerful people try to hide. Have I made an enemy?

'Mr 'az? Speak to me.'

So does she have something to tell me? And is she afraid?

'Who are you? What do you want?'

'Are you 'az 'az?'

'I don't spell it like that. But I know who you mean.'

'I must speak to you.'

'You are speaking to me. Go ahead.'

'Not on the telephone.'

'What's it about? Give me a hint.'

'Earlier I sent you an email.'

'The outline of a man…'

'Stop,' she cuts in. 'It is somebody you have written about. He may be dead. Murdered. I must meet you.'

That brings my brain fully awake.

'All right. Where are you?'

'Brussels.'

'Brussels? Bloody hell. You want me…'

'I am taking the train. Eurostar. I shall be in London before ten o'clock. We will meet at the station, St Pancras. What is the name of a café there?'

'There must be a Costa Coffee, but I can't be certain.'

'All right. We shall meet where the passengers come out from the Eurostar platform.'

There's probably more than one exit. This seems a rendezvous disaster. I'm being bulldozed into this. Hold on. I don't even remember agreeing to meet her. 'Not so fast. You said he *may* be dead. You've got to tell me…'

Again she cuts me short. 'I must run to catch the train now.'

'How will we recognise each other?'

'You mean I carry a bunch of red roses and you carry a copy of, I don't know, maybe *Pride and Prejudice*? I think not. I will recognise you. It will be easy.'

'Wait a minute,' I say but the phone is dead. What has she talked me into? Unknown woman expects me to throw clothes on and race to London. Me. Why me? Because someone I have written about may be dead. Or not. She is doolally.

I pull the duvet up to my chin and close my eyes.

It's no good. With my eyes closed I see the outline of that body done in blue chalk on cobbles.

It's somebody you have written about. He may be dead. Murdered.

Is it my fault? Like it or not I am involved.

Bloody hell. The reporter in me kicks to life. There's a story here. I throw the duvet back.

I will recognise you. How? I'm not some famous celebrity. I'm a hack on a newspaper.

The Eurostar from Brussels arrived at 9.57. I am sitting on a bench where I can be seen. I inspect the arriving passengers: first the ones in a rush, then the crowd, finally the stragglers. She has not recognised me. She is doolally. I was right.

On the train from Oxford I picked up a magazine. Maybe she missed that Eurostar. Or maybe there's another exit and she'll make her way round here. I read a few lines of the discarded magazine then lift my eyes to look at people passing. Some scurry as if they are running away from life. Some trudge as if their home has no one they're eager to see. After these profound thoughts it's back to the discarded magazine. The Minister of Tourism of Somalia is outlining the attractions of his country. I'd say he's got an easy job. There have been no recorded tourists for fourteen years. War is the reason. I look up. No one is recognising me. Back to the magazine. In Mogadishu the entrance to the cathedral is daubed with graffiti warning of mines. There is a hotel that offers lobster but advises you to bring ten armed guards to dinner. I look up again. Ah, at last.

A woman is coming towards me trailing a small black suitcase on wheels. Curly auburn hair like a helmet over her head. She has deep red lips. A sudden smile lights up her face. Her coat is open on a generous figure. I get to my feet and then she is past me and into the arms of a bearded giant of a man.

'So Mr Faz,' says a voice at my shoulder. 'I see you have an eye for a pretty girl.'

We have shown each other passports and I know her name is Lucija.

'I told you I would recognise you,' she says. 'It was easy.'

Side by side we stroll through the concourse. She looks round to see if anyone is strolling with us. At a rough guess I'd say about thirty people.

'Tell me.'

'I caught the first Eurostar of the day so I could be here early and look out for bad men. Then I waited for you to come and give yourself away. You would be looking for a woman you didn't know. Three or four single men came but left after a bit. Then a man came and sat on the bench. He was reading a magazine but looked up when a woman came near. Finally you thought you saw me coming and got to your feet like a true gentleman, except she ignored you completely. Your face was downcast because she looked, shall I say, voluptuous. Alas, I am built more modestly.'

I open my mouth but she stops me.

'No. Don't be a gentleman again. I'm not in the mood for compliments. We have a cup of coffee here and get to know a bit about each other. You will look over my shoulder and I will look over your shoulder so we know who is passing by. It is necessary.'

I think about this, about looking over each other's shoulders. So she expects trouble. Why don't I realise this? Why don't I just run away? I mean really run? She wouldn't run after me. We make mistakes in life. It's only later we realise this.

Lucija has cappuccino and I have espresso. She looks over my shoulder so I look over her shoulder. This seems too much like a child's game so I say, 'Tell me about Matthew. I know nothing about him except that three years ago – I remember writing about it – his wine shop was blown up.'

'First thing,' she says, 'is that he is Matt. To use his full name Matthew is a signal that there is some reason to be cautious or there is some danger. If he answers the telephone saying he is Matthew Clough then you understand he is not alone.'

'Sounds like a spy.'

'Yes.'

She is not looking over my shoulder, she is looking over her coffee cup right in my eyes. We hold it for a few seconds.

'Do I understand what you are trying to tell me?'

'Yes.'

'Right.' I draw a breath. What am I letting myself in for?

'But that was long ago,' she says.' He resigned. In fact he resigned twice. The first time for moral reasons. The second time… he agreed to do occasional little jobs for your spy outfit and it turned out to be dangerous. The Hungarian army tried to kill him so he resigned again.'

'So his wine shop being blown up was nothing to do with his being a spy in the past?'

Lucija shakes her head. 'In life the past is never past. So I have learnt.'

I say nothing. What can I? We seem to have lived entirely different lives.

Lucija's eyes drop to the table. Her hand is lying there, palm up, as if she was begging for something. I am the one who should be begging. I have come racing up to London to meet this stranger and I know just three things: that in normal times he is Matt Clough not Matthew, he used to be a spy and his wine shop was blown up. Well, I knew the last thing because I saw the smoking ruin.

'Please,' I say, 'explain about Matt and why he is dead, but you say he may not be dead. I am confused.'

'Confusion is normal,' she says. 'If you were not confused I would be disappointed. I will explain certain things. Naturally you will have questions but we do not have time to fill in Matt's whole life. So listen. Matt's mother died in childbirth. He never knew who his father was until he was told he had been a Soviet citizen but was now dead. Except he wasn't.'

'Excuse me.' I take a deep breath. I'm sure my face gapes like an idiot. 'Matt's father was dead, except he wasn't. Now Matt is dead, except you say he isn't.'

'It is time to bring Marx into the twenty-first century,' Lucija says. 'History repeats itself, first as tragedy, then as farce, finally as a TV series.'

We both look away. A policeman and policewoman are striding across the concourse. They're making straight for us. The female cop is on her phone, speaking and frowning. Then they change course and are past us. Lucija looks back at me.

'Matt's father – KK for short – was a Latvian so Matt went to Riga[1] . There he found out his father had been a bad man. I mean truly bad. He'd worked in a Nazi concentration camp, then in a Nazi munitions factory, then he had been a Soviet spy and then a British spy, working as a double agent for both sides. Now please pay even closer attention. KK had acquired a couple of dozen paintings by modern masters which had belonged to a German Jewish businessman called Rothstein. The Rothstein family were all exterminated by the Nazis. KK built a sort of art gallery for the paintings. All right. Enough family history. KK was an old man but now part of an international gang. Tell me what you think international gangs do.'

'Me? What I think?' Lucija is involving me. She wants me to be part of it. I know this but she is waiting. 'Drugs?'

'Correct. Go on.'

'Arms?'

---

1 See *Dead Man Telling Tales* by David Brierley

'Yes.'

'Foreign prostitutes?'

'Go on.'

'People smuggling.'

'Yes.'

She wants more. I decide to give it my wildest shot.

'Buying politicians. And senior policemen.' She wants more. 'Buying spies?' I say. She is staring in my face then she raises her eyes. 'Top floor spies?'

She nods. 'I told you KK was one of the bad men of our times. He fell out with his gang. They said he cheated them out of money. KK was killed. Matt was his son. So Matt owes them money. But it's more than that, much more. Matt knows their secrets. He knows names. He is a threat to the gang. Matt cannot be allowed to live. But suppose he is dead. I sent you that body outline on the cobbles. Also I got this. I don't speak the language but Google Translate is my friend.'

She produces another email, a print-out of a newspaper cutting. The email comes from tuninf@gnet.tn. The piece is in French. It says the body of an Englishman Matthew Clough was found on Wednesday night in the medina in Tunis. Monsieur Clough had a wine shop in a town near Oxford and he had come to Tunisia in search of wine to buy. It appeared the deceased was drunk after sampling too many wines and had tripped and fallen. This accounted for the bad bruising on his skull. Death was from a cerebral haemorrhage. His wallet and passport had not been taken so no foul play was suspected by the police. It was just a paragraph, but the reporter got a byline: Rym Dakhli.

'This newspaper report,' I begin but she butts in.

'Lies. Nothing but lies. Matt is no longer a wine dealer, not since they blew up his shop. Also he doesn't get falling over drunk. But if the newspaper report says he is dead then the bad men will stop trying to kill him. So if Matt is dead then he can go on living. Make sense to you?'

'Is it too early for a drink?' I reply.

* * *

We have left St Pancras station and done a crazy walk. Look at us. Arguing, you'd think. We walk and stop and gesture and just naturally peek to check no one is playing grandma's footsteps with us. Walk again and repeat. All right, nobody is following. We find a pub with an outside table.

'This way we can see anyone who has an unhealthy interest in us,' she says. I have brought out gin and tonics and she lifts her glass. '*Prieka.*' She holds a mouthful for a few seconds and then swallows. 'Now I have the taste of London in my mouth.'

The reporter in me has urgent questions but they'll wait. 'Lucija, I think I have the basics. Listen, there's one thing I don't understand. Matt discovers his father KK was a bad man.'

'A very bad man.' Again she butts in. I feel I am failing some exam.

'Right, a very bad man. He had become part of an international gang who were after him for money he owed. KK had a lot of very valuable paintings. Why didn't he sell one and buy off the gang? Problem solved.'

'KK tried to auction one but this alerted the authorities to looted art from the last war. There was a shoot out. It was like a Hollywood movie except with real blood. I saw the bodies.' She restores herself with another mouthful of gin. 'Now comes something that you may not consider moral. Matt took one of the canvases. It was a Gauguin from his Tahiti days. Palm trees, beach, bare breasted woman. It was beautiful. Rothstein and all his relatives had been murdered by the Nazis. There was no one to inherit the paintings. So…'

Lucija breaks off. She can see I am thinking about this. Has Matt stolen the painting? But if the family was all dead, who would own it? Some third cousin in Argentina if he could be found? Someone who had never heard of Rothstein? Maybe Rothstein had intended KK to have the paintings? And Matt was KK's biological son.

Lucija decides I have had enough time to puzzle over the ethics. 'Matt had inherited the gang that was after his blood so he decided he would inherit one painting as well. He hoped it would allow him to live. I don't know what the law says but the gang doesn't follow any laws. One painting would buy him a life.'

I nod. 'Yes.'

'He sold it eventually to a Hong Kong billionaire for thirty million dollars. US dollars not Hong Kong dollars. He opened a Swiss bank account. This was not as straight forward as he believed. He had to get in touch with the Hong Kong billionaire to help.'

'Everybody needs a Hong Kong billionaire from time to time.'

'Put your British sense of humour aside.' Lucija frowns at me. 'It is Matt's life we are talking about. All went well for us. We had an income to live on. We had a house to live in – don't ask where, it is not relevant. Until an email arrived from the bank saying new Swiss regulations required an urgent personal meeting. We don't know how the gang found out about the bank but it turned out the email address was different in one tiny detail. We didn't spot it. Matt arranged a time for an interview. They asked what hotel in Zurich he would be using in case of any last-minute change. Matt shouldn't have given the name of the hotel, but for once his brain seemed to have gone on holiday.'

She wants to refresh herself but finds her glass empty.

'You want another?'

'No,' Lucija says. 'We must keep our wits about us. Matt flew to Zurich. I flew to Riga. I still own an apartment there. Matt finally woke his brain up. He was checking in at his hotel and asked if there were any messages. No sir. Was that a slight hesitation? Matt said he was expecting people from his bank and was there any news? Oh yes sir, they had arrived and had gone up to his room to wait. Send a message up that I'll meet them in the Zwei Bären bar opposite. He went back out and ran to the entrance of the hotel's underground carpark. He didn't have long to wait. Two men came out of the hotel, went into the bar and came straight out. They looked each way down the street. Then one went left and the other right and ran. When it was safe, Matt also ran.'

I nod. I would have run too. Buggered if I know where.

'He telephoned the bank and they were indignant in a Swiss banker's way. It was a reflection on their professional competence that they would have sent an email demanding he fly from abroad to a meeting. That was the first thing. Then they were indignant again… But Matt cut the connection. He did more than that. He put his phone in a trash bin. Bad men could track where he was from his mobile.'

'You've spoken to him, obviously.'

'He used a public telephone at the central post office. He called my apartment in Riga. He asked if it was snowing.'

'Snowing? Why?'

'Safety signal. From when we first got together. Snow means he is all right. For four days I had phone calls. Once I was out but he left a message. Snow.'

'What's he going to do?'

'Good question. But first we need to find him.'

We. Notice how I am involved.

'Three days ago there was no message, no snow. Yesterday no message. Instead, I got the image of the body drawn on cobbles. Then the newspaper cutting. Matt had said you were someone I could trust so I sent the image to you. Still no message from Matt. No snow. And that is why we are here now.'

'We?' She has been bending over the table. Now she leans back and stares at me. I stare back. Matt has told her I am someone she can rely on. She doesn't see any need to say more.

'To do what?'

'Save him,' she says.

'How?'

'You're full of good questions. That is the journalist in you.'

Lucija has the names of two people Matt trusts in the Fortress: his name for the spies' building on the Thames. She has contacted one and arranged a meeting in an hour's time. I am not going. It is woman-to-woman. Maybe she'll speak more freely without me.

I speak to my editor, a no-nonsense old school veteran. I want time off, I tell him.

'Work?' he asks.

'Follow up to that blowing up of the wine shop.'

'I don't remember that.'

'It was three years ago.'

'Some follow up. Before my time.'

'The wine shop owner's life is threatened.' Silence at the other end of the telephone. I raise the big bold headline potential. 'It's an international biggie.'

'You're planning a foreign trip?'

'Probably.'

'Only probably?' He chews this over. 'Where to?'

'Not certain yet. The lead seems to be Tunisia.'

'Tunisia?' I don't like the way he keeps repeating what I say. 'I hear the wine is OK and the beaches are fine and you can go for a ride on a camel. Bazil, I am not subbing some jaunt. Go in your own time. No expenses. I'll buy anything good.'

The phone goes dead.

I must tell my wife who has decamped to Wales. No, not Wales. Mary's in Bath. She is not impressed either.

'I remember that wine shop blowing up. Got a fancy name: *In Vino Veritas*. Why are you involved now?'

'I got an email. It showed the outline of a body painted on cobbles. And there was a newspaper cutting giving Matt Clough's name.'

'Who sent you the email?'

'Matt's partner. The cutting and the photo are from Tunisia. But Matt couldn't send an email about his own death so he can't be dead.'

'So you're following this up in Tunisia?'

'Yes. At least I think so.'

'Alone?'

'With Matt's partner.'

'His business partner?'

'No.'
'Name?'
'Lucija.'
'Lucija?'
The phone goes dead.

CHAPTER 2

There's a Starbucks near Marble Arch and that's where Lucija and I meet. She makes a fuss about sitting on a stool which just naturally gives her a chance to check no one has followed her. She keeps her voice low.

'Her name is Heather and she didn't want to speak to me. I said it was about Matt and she said she didn't know any Matt. Then I said that at one time Matt had worked for her organisation and his controller had been Martin. She almost screamed *stop. Meet me at Speaker's Corner, in Hyde Park* she said. I went and there were no speakers and no Heather. I was told to come alone and carry a copy of *Woman's Own* magazine. I did a little walk round. There was no Heather. She's got cold feet. So I found a rubbish bin and threw the magazine away. When I turned round, there she was. Where had she come from?'

Is Lucija is asking me? I don't know. I wasn't there. I go back to earlier today and how she recognised me. Think. Lucija was on the look-out for a woman on her own. So…

'Maybe she attached herself to a group and broke away when she got close to you.'

'Quick learner, aren't you.' Lucija smiles for the first time. To be honest it's more of a beginner's smile. 'I'm going to recall everything as well as I can. Heather said, "You are not Lucija and I am not Heather and this meeting has never taken place. Understood?" I told her I had lived in a communist country so I knew all about clandestine meetings. We walked in Hyde Park. Whenever anyone got near us she stopped talking. She asked what I wanted to know. I said there was a Latvian called Krisjanis Kulbergs. "I know about KK. Total baddie. Worked for the Nazis then the Sovs. Martin had me find out about him."'

We had both ordered sandwiches and first Lucija and then I take a few bites. Possibly they are chicken sandwiches. I can't be sure.

'"Martin," Heather said. She looked over my shoulder and saw something or somebody she didn't like and beckoned me to walk with her. "I don't know you," she said. "I don't know Matt Clough. I knew Martin and they killed him. Bastards, whoever they were." We were walking down a tarred path but suddenly she looped her arm through mine and steered away to walk on the grass.'

'So you'd pass fewer people,' I said.

Lucija nodded. 'We looked like pals having a gossip,' she said: "Open spaces are good: no walls that listen, no parked cars, no dark doorways." We walked in silence and I didn't ask questions. I let her come to me. She said: "When Martin was murdered I didn't go to the office for a week. He was already retired so the bastards would reason he must have had someone slipping him information. Like me. I didn't know who the bastards were but I was sure they'd pick me out. My face was in mourning. I hid in my flat, not answering the phone, cooking little eggy things I didn't want to eat. After a week in purdah I went back."

'And did people give you suspicious looks? I asked.

'"Hard to tell. I said I'd had a bout of 'flu. I work in the sub-basement, no windows, neon tubes, so I looked grim anyway. Strange that while I'd been away the computer security system had been changed. Overnight, no warning. Was that paranoia? A specific threat? Trying to exclude someone or catch someone? Bedlam on the first morning apparently. I was sorry I'd missed all the fun."

'She gave a brief smile. It just flashed across her face and then she frowned.

'"Rumours started. War on the top floor. Factions. Power struggle. Hamas and Iran and Syria were hot. Usual requests for print-outs and background cross-checks. You'd expect that. But why a sudden interest in Latvia? And what happened in 1968 in Prague? That's ancient history, for goodness' sake. Name Krisjanis Kulbergs came up. His personal file was embargoed – only God could look at it. Then suddenly everything went quiet. Stopped actually. There had been two Deputy Directors. Now there was one. The one who lost wasn't sacked but took leave on medical grounds. Stress. Pressure of overwork was the official line. There is only one cure for overwork." Heather paused a bit. "Apart from being a hit and run victim."

'We'd crossed a grass patch and were back on a tarred path. Two men were walking towards us. Even before we could pick up the words we could tell they were American. Heather did this strange thing of moving behind me then edging round to my other side until the Americans passed. She hid herself completely.'

Lucija did a bit of theatrical business, moving her hand round her coffee mug.

'Heather was quiet a bit then put a hand on her chest. "I feel it here. Did I love Martin? Yes, no, sometimes, didn't give it a chance, a puzzle. But I cared. I still care. Martin's murder and the civil war inside the Fortress. They're connected. I know it. Do I have hard courtroom evidence? No. Who can I tell?" She looked straight in my face. "You. Nobody else. Who could do anything about it?" She is still looking me in the face. Maybe I can, I told her.'

Lucija looks down at her plate. Most of the sandwich has been eaten. Most of her coffee has been drunk. She doesn't want to finish the rest. She wants to get moving. She has told me about the meeting with Heather as if she had total recall. I've known reporters who claim total recall. When they are challenged they protest that what they say they remember is right in essence. I give Lucija this let-out.

'I told Heather that my Matt was her Martin except I didn't know if he'd been murdered. But I had to find him. And the only names I had were hers and the Deputy Director who had sent Matt to Latvia. Turn round, she said. She used my back as a desk and she wrote something on a pad. She tore off the sheet and stuffed it in my coat pocket.

'"Name of the Deputy Director who got the chop. You said you knew it but in this world names can change. No telephone number. Phones are not safe. Her address. She lives in Pimlico, Vincent Square. I wish you..."

'I don't know what. She broke off. Luck? Success? God's protection? She said, "I'll carry on to Hyde Park Corner. You head back to Marble Arch. Don't turn round to look at me. Go now."

'At the end her voice had changed, gone husky. Perhaps after all it was love she felt for Martin. There was a push in my back. Get going, woman. Don't look back.'

We are walking from Pimlico tube station to the address that Heather has given.

'What name does this ex-Deputy Director have?' I ask.

'Beatrice.'

'Is her surname a secret?'

'If you're a spy you can have any name you like. Oh lord.'

We have turned into Vincent Square. Heather wrote down the number but we don't need it. Parked with two wheels up on the pavement is a dirty white van. Two ladders are strapped on its roof. Close up we see the name on the side panel: *The Utter Gutter Company*. There is no telephone number to contact them. Two stubby aerials poke up through the ladders. In the front seat a couple of workmen are taking their ease. One hides his face with the *Daily Telegraph*. The other's eyes stare over the top of *Private Eye*.

Lucija ducks her head towards them. 'Beatrice has company.'

There are three steps up to the front door. An entryphone has four names, none saying Beatrice. I point my finger at one. 'Bet you a tenner it's this one.' It reads: *B.F. Off.* I press the bell and turn to look at the gutter men. They stare back. Nobody answers the bell. I press it a second time. Nothing. Is Beatrice out? Third time I press the bell in Morse – three shorts, three longs, three shorts.

A squawky female voice comes from the panel. 'If you're Jehovah's Witnesses you can bloody piss off.'

Lucija and Matt have their safety word *snow*. What can I offer Beatrice?

'Those men parked in the van look as if their ladders are tall enough to scale the Fortress.'

She considers this. Saying Fortress seems to work. 'What do you want?'

'A quiet talk,' Lucija says. 'To find out a little recent history.'

'Look at me.'

We take a step back and crane our necks to peer at the top windows.

'Cretins. The video camera. Look at that.'

It is directly above the door.

'What recent history?'

'About Tunisia and Matt who came to see you.'

'And?'

This is ridiculous. Time to put a stop to it. 'Those two geezers in the van,' I say, 'I bet they're listening to every word we say.'

'All right.' The entry lock buzzes. 'Twist the knob to the right and give the door a good kick. It only understands brute force. Climb the stairs. When you're out of breath you've arrived.'

'You are Beatrice, this is Lucija and I am Baz.' This is in my firmest voice, me trying to be in command. It doesn't last.

Beatrice looks at me, at Lucija and back to me. 'Really? Baz? Nobody who is anybody uses his own name. Where are you from?'

From the Foreign Office? Is that what she hopes? Maybe Scotland Yard? 'I'm from Oxford. Lucija is…'

'Academic?' she interrupts. 'Which college?'

'A writer.' I don't say I'm a journalist as that can put people's defences up.

'What do you write?'

'The truth, if I can find it.'

'You?' She turns to Lucija.

'I'm from Riga in Latvia. Have you heard of Krisjanis…'

'Stop.'

It's the second time today Lucija has been ordered to stop talking. Beatrice puts a finger to her lips and then points at the walls and up at the ceiling. She raises her eyebrows. Do we understand? She beckons. We follow. We go down a short passage to a bathroom. There is a shower over the bath and she turns it on. The splash isn't enough. She turns on the basin tap. She switches on a radio on a shelf. She finds a station that plays thumping music. She turns the volume up.

'Industrial metal. German Hardcore is good.'

'No wonder you were kicked out.'

She nods. Joking over.

'I had a security firm come in and do a sweep. They found bugs in the sitting room and my bedroom. Checking my bedroom I took as a compliment. The man showed me three little bugs in the palm of his hand. Are they live? The man nodded. So I screamed as loud as I could: *go fuck your mothers*.' Her eyes switch from my face to Lucija's. 'You don't approve?'

'Beatrice…. may I call you that? Fucking I approve of. Fucking your mother…' Lucija is not to be rushed. 'This should not be encouraged because it can have unfortunate consequences. I am thinking of Oedipus.'

They gaze at each other, the two women, while the water rushes and the music makes the window panes rattle. Beatrice's cheeks twitch. Could be a smile, not often used.

'I think we'll get along,' Beatrice says. She points to the edge of the bath. 'Sit down. So, first things first. Provenance. Who pushed you in my direction?'

'Heather,' I say.

Beatrice gestures with her hand – more.

Lucija takes over. 'Heather King. Dark hair. Cut short. She's not tall. Comes up to here. Works in Records. Says there was a power struggle and you were sent on sick leave. Overwork. Stress. So here you are.'

'With the Utter Gutter men keeping an eye on you,' I say. 'And I don't think you're stressed. You look angry, seriously angry.'

'Angry enough to kill, you mean?' Again that twitch of a smile – *only kidding*. The smile fades - *but don't tempt me*. 'All right. Heather works in the salt mines. She pointed you in my direction. What does she think I can do for you?'

'Does the name Matt Clough mean anything to you?'

'Go on.'

'And his former mentor and friend Martin?'

'Go on.'

'Uncovering a link between a Russian gang and corrupt officials in London including your own outfit?'

'Former outfit,' she says.

'Martin was murdered. And now Matt Clough…' Lucija brings out the email of the outline of a body on the cobbles. 'I received this.'

She hands the email to Beatrice who frowns at it. She doesn't mumble the usual soothing phrases.

'Oh fuck.'

'Plus a clipping from a Tunis newspaper about Matt falling down drunk and killing himself.'

'Convenient. Just a minute. Who sent the email?'

'That's the point. Matt knows this email address. Other people don't.'

'So a not-so-dead man sent it. Why?'

'A distress signal.'

'Meaning come and help?'

'Look at the photo of the body outlined on the cobbles,' I say. 'Now look at the top. There's a street sign: Rue Tourbet. The cutting is from a Tunis newspaper. Matt has made it plain. The search starts right there.'

Beatrice looks at Lucija. 'Do you speak Arabic?'

'No.'

'French?'

'I speak Latvian, Russian and English.'

Beatrice shakes her head.

'I speak French,' I say.

'So you're going too. Mr Valiant-for-Truth. I seem to remember the last river Mr Valiant crossed was the river of death. Just saying.'

She raises an eyebrow.

'Right, this is what I know,' Beatrice says. 'End of last week Matt Clough rang my doorbell just as you did. Was he a plant? A trick? He talked about his father. Nasty piece of work, right, and we employed him. He talked about Martin and his murder. He talked about the thugs trying to kill him and blowing up his wine shop. He was genuine. I could tell.'

Beatrice gets up to fiddle with the radio, retuning a station that doesn't need it. It's just punctuation. Now we move onto the next stage.

'Matt's father Krisjanis Kulbergs left a tape where he talked about a Soviet agent – young but headed up – right here in the Firm. A mole, Mr le Carré would call him. Years pass and the young man rises and rises. This is my adversary. I lost the battle, which is why I am here. But I haven't lost the war. I have allies in the Fortress. I'm the Queen across the Water - that's what they call me. I give the Utter Gutter men the slip – no problem, they're not official, just the two of them. And at night they're not here at all. I meet my chums. I keep up to date. My adversary we call Bardo because he used that workname at one time. That's Bardo without a "t", not Brigitte. Bardo doesn't want to be Director because the level of scrutiny of the top man is too high. The Director has to wear a watch with a tracker device in case of kidnapping. Bardo doesn't want that. With me gone he is the sole Dep D as we say. Nobody would know if he had a meeting in a pub. Except I have not gone. I have relocated.'

She pauses. We listen to the rush of water and the radio.

'Got carried away there.' She shakes her head then looks at Lucija. 'You and Matt are lovers?'

'Yes.'

'I'll tell you what I told him. One of my little whisperers in the Lubyanka-on-Thames passed me this snippet of information. Last Wednesday Bardo was booked on a flight to Valletta. End of winter break, he said, catch some early spring sun.'

'Why Valletta?' Lucija says. 'What's significant about that?'

'Come,' Beatrice says. 'Don't talk.' She points at the listening walls and ceiling.

The sitting room is light and airy. Old leather chairs are worn smooth. Walls are covered with bookshelves. Beatrice pulls us close so our heads are touching. Her voice is a whisper.

'Before I became a spy I was an academic, a historian. Why the hell is the Firm hiring an academic? Good question even if you didn't ask it. Eighteenth and nineteenth century Europe was my special interest. I could give the long view, not focus on day-to-day problems. Look at that map. It was a farewell gift from colleagues at Somerville. It's old and genuine so it must have cost a pretty penny.'

In a gap between bookshelves there is a framed map on the wall. It has a strapline at the top: *Europe in the time of Napoleon Bonaparte.*

'All right, *here.*' She points at a dot on the map. 'Valletta, capital of Malta. If Bardo was a philologist it could be interesting because Maltese is the only Semitic language written in western script. But he's not. He's a spy. So what's he doing there for a fortnight? He flew British Airways – confirmed from their computer – then maybe does a hop to…where? Sicily is close. He could take a ferry and tour round the Baroque towns. But how about this?' Her finger slides to the north African coast which is hazily outlined. 'Yes, Tunisia.'

Geography lesson over. We are back in the bathroom. She has brought us mugs of coffee.

'All right, Matt's father worked for us. Beavered away for the other side too. We knew that but thought we had the better deal. Suppose we got it wrong and the KGB was the final winner. Amazingly Matt had also worked for us, resigned, worked for us again until in

Hungary a clandestine meeting went badly wrong and he resigned again. That's when the conspiracy theorists rubbed their hands.'

'What do you mean?' Lucija asks.

'Suppose, the whisper is, he was the one who betrayed that meeting in Hungary. And Martin, Matt's controller, made all those trips to Iron Curtain countries which gave him ample chances to meet his real bosses from Moscow. Being dead, Martin can't defend himself. Everything that was black becomes white, and vice versa. Now it has happened to me. All those research trips I took when I was an academic – to Humboldt University in East Berlin, to Prague and Moscow – that was when I was recruited and groomed by the KGB.'

She remembers her mug of coffee.

'Shit,' she says to the coffee. 'Right. Enough of the troubles here. Bardo flies to Valletta. He needs a complete break. That was what he said. Said he needed some early spring sun. Said he rented one of those converted old farmhouses on Gozo. It's a small island and we have a retired field man living there. He couldn't find any trace of Bardo. Not a sausage, he said. That doesn't mean that Bardo isn't hunkered down there. I just believe he has gone to Tunisia. He has contacts because in the past he actually worked there for us. Even his workname Bardo he takes from the museum in Tunis.'

'Did he fly to Tunis from Valletta?'

'No record of him doing that. Means nothing. I have no idea what passports he is running. But it's an easy jaunt in a boat. Small harbour to small harbour, no passport checks. Bardo was working in Tunisia when Bourguiba was toppled. He worked hard and got a network of informants. He has contacts in the police. He has friends with influence. It's a society Bardo is at ease in.'

'You told Matt all this?' Lucija says.

'Yes.'

'In fact you encouraged him to go.'

'Careful. Matt came to me for information. I didn't force it on him. I simply told him what I know.'

Lucija is frowning. 'I come fron a country where you could die of someone else's talk.'

'Lucija, that is enough. If I hadn't told him – warned him if you like – then you could blame me. I told him how it is. Don't you badmouth me for that email you received. Listen. I'm telling you all this and maybe you think you have to go there. I'm not twisting your arm. Your choice. But don't bloody blame me for what happens if you do go.'

Lucija nods. It's not an apology but accepting what Beatrice says. 'I have to go to Tunisia. Matt has asked for help.'

'And I'm going.' I've said it already but this time with more conviction. Yes, Matt told Lucija I was someone she could trust and I speak French. Yes, the journalist in me is following the scent of a story. But it's more than that. 'It's personal. A few years ago the people Bardo works with tortured my wife. I'm not going into the details now. When I tried to rescue her she died.[2] Reason enough to want revenge. OK?

'Wait here a moment.' Beatrice leaves us.

'Tunisia,' Lucija says as if it is a headline. After a bit she adds, 'Why did he go to Tunisia?'

A scream from the sitting room brings us to our feet. We crowd the door and see Beatrice jabbing her finger towards the window.

'Do that once more and you'll get a fire extinguisher in your fucking face.' She turns round and sees us. 'Get back in the bathroom.'

It's an order. We are standing by the bath when she comes back. She's holding a page torn from a spiral notebook.

'Utter Gutter man up a ladder, outside the window, camera pointing in. It was you he wanted to snap. It's just the two of them so they're not from the Firm. If it was official there'd be a switch over of watchers.'

---

2 See *Budapest Hand* by David Brierley

'Not official?' Lucija says. 'So who?'

'Bardo. Look, if you're going to Tunisia you'd better wise up. Bardo is your enemy.'

'Enemy?' I latch onto that word.

'He'll try to kill you. One thing in your favour is he doesn't know what you look like. That's why the Utter Gutter man tried to get a mug shot.'

Beatrice remembers the scrap of paper in her hand. She's going to give it to Lucija but something makes her change her mind. Maybe it's the little spat they had. She hands it to me.

'Telephone number here in London, an answerphone service. You can leave a message. The bastards don't know about it. Don't telephone me here. Never use your mobile phone because they can pinpoint where you are. Got it? And I've put down the name of a man at the embassy in Tunis. You can trust him. He's on the side of the angels. Just say you're from the Queen across the Water.'

I glance at the paper. 'Is this his real name? A covername?'

Is this the third time I've seen her twitch of a smile? 'It's real. It just sounds made up.'

The contact at the embassy is called Hipkiss.

'I'll tell you about my last day at the Fortress,' Beatrice says. 'I'd just had my farewell chat with the Director. It was an exchange of views, full and frank and a lot of other words beginning with f, at least on my part. On my way out I came face to face with Bardo. He was dressed like an old-fashioned gentleman – pinstripe suit and shiny black shoes. I went right up to him and trod on his sparkling toecaps so he had to take a step back. "You've stolen my life," I said, "and one day I'm going to take yours." He flinched and said, "you're mad." I stuck my finger in his face and said, "what do the Yanks say? Don't get mad, get even." He stood there trying to think what to say so I gave him my knee in his balls and pushed past.'

She was an academic before she joined the Firm? Not like any Oxford don I've met.

'Which way was their van facing?'

'That way.' I point to the left.

'OK. I'll go out, shut the door and go the same way. You keep out of sight. They want your photos but I am their first priority. Wait a minute while they decide they have to go after me. Then you come out and turn right.' She looks from me to Lucija and back to me. 'When you get to Tunisia don't trust anybody. You don't know who is in Bardo's pocket. Have you got that?'

There's a final pause and a final word.

'God, I'd love to be coming with you.'

CHAPTER 3

I'm not prepared for this. I came to London to meet Lucija. I bought a day return ticket. You'd do just the same. There was no talk of going to Tunisia so now I have to buy a bag and clothes. I beg a bed for the night off my old chum Mike Simmons. We were hacks together on the *Mirror* with Mike doing the showbiz beat. He has taken unpaid leave to write a novel and is finding it hard going. He likes to have a glass or two of sauvignon blanc while we gossip.

'This novel writing lark,' he says. 'It's not like spilling the dirt on the latest celeb love affair. A novel is long. Know what I mean? It's not a six-hundred-word sprint, it's a three-hundred-page marathon. On and on, pounding the keyboard.'

'Come as a shock,' I say.

'Have you got any advice?'

'Keep at it,' I say.

'Keep at it. Good. Beezer advice, Baz. I'll remember that. Keep at it. Absolutely top-notch advice. Thanks.'

'Crackerjack,' I say.

'Wizard.'

'Even spiffing,' I say.

'More than spiffing. It's frabjous.'

'Truly the dog's bollocks,' I say.

'Dog's bollocks?' Mike peers at me over his glass. 'What's a dog got to do with it? Have you finished the bottle?'

One of those evenings, far from Bardo and Matt.

* * *

I don't know where Lucija is staying. We arrange to meet at Heathrow for the Tunisair flight. We check in together so we sit together. The Tunisair plane is 15 minutes late taking off but what's 15 minutes if you are dead. Or maybe not dead. Lucija has the window seat and stares out at grey clouds. I could say something banal about the gloomy weather but I don't. Odds on she's thinking about Matt. And me? I am trying to work out how the hell I've been talked into this madness. Finally the grey clouds give way to Mediterranean blue sky. She turns to me.

'Baz.'

'Lucija.'

'I think we both have some explaining to do.'

Lucija has the window seat. Looking beyond her I can see the blue of the Mediterranean.

'Our passports?' I say.

'Yes.'

I slip mine out of my pocket to show her. 'Hungarian,' I say. 'Name Bazil Fazekas. My parents were Hungarian. They got out in '56 when the Red Army crushed the uprising. They were refugees and settled in Oxford so that is where I was born. Three years ago I applied for a Hungarian passport. The embassy in London said no. I argued with them in Hungarian. No. My parents fled because of the Russian tanks. No. Then I told them about my uncle, a hero of the uprising. In Hungary all heroes are dead and this heroic death so impressed them I got the passport. I always carry it with me. And a new British passport too. Why? Because three years ago bad men sneaked into my house and stole my old British passport. So,' I tap my breast, 'both passports live here.'

She nods. And keeps nodding. I feel that in some way I have risen in her view.

'And the passport I am travelling on,' she says, 'is in the name of Chebrikova. Latvian passport but Russian name. In Riga I worked for the Citizenship Board. One of my jobs was to make sure bad men did not live in our country and get the vote and have influence. We found out that Chebrikov had been a Red Army colonel, so he was expelled, Chebrikova his wife was out too. I confiscated her passport. Look at her photo.' Lucija opens the passport. 'Not that much like me. But if I do this,' and Lucija tucks her chin in which makes her cheeks puff up and a scowl puts lines on her brow, 'now I can pass as Chebrikova.'

TUNISIA 2018

CHAPTER 4

The taxi driver at Tunis airport has a steel tooth that glints when he smiles. He has got it in his head that we must stay at the Hotel Africa. Probably he pockets a rake-off. The hotel is in Avenue Habib Bourguiba, bang in the centre of the city. It's a modest four or five floors but topped with a tower. Lucija opens her window to peer at it.

'No.' She shakes her head.

To me it looks a hotel for visiting American and German businessmen. Lucija has a more profound objection.

'No,' she says again as if I'd objected. 'In Riga the Hotel Latvija is a concrete tower like this. In Soviet times no Latvian was allowed in except maids and waiters. It was a place for party bosses and secret police and crooks from Moscow. Plus their bed companions. I look at this place and it brings back bad times.'

We want somewhere smaller, more Tunisian, I tell the taxi driver. His steel tooth flashes. We drive a couple of blocks up Avenue Habib Bourguiba – think Champs Elysées with palm trees - and take a left turn. We stop outside the Hotel Salammbo. The entrance is a doorway crammed between two shops. Tiled steps lead up out of sight to the reception. No doorman bows and scrapes, just an optimist selling sunglasses from a tray round his neck. Lucija nods approval.

Suddenly I am awake. Lucija and I had dinner at a restaurant round the corner and then decided sleep was the best thing. Tomorrow will be a long day. We know it.

Some noise has woken me. What? From Lucija's room, next to mine? I hear nothing. Maybe somebody has sneaked into my room. Bardo has tracked us here. The room is dark. I can see nobody. A black shape looms, but it's a wardrobe, grotesque, out of scale with the room. Most likely it was shipped from France and left behind when the French packed up and got out of the country. No figure lurks by it. I remember the security chain on the door. It's still in place. I'm alone in here.

I go to the window, part the curtains and peep out. The building opposite is dark. Offices, I guess.

The noise that cut into my sleep wasn't a scream, it was a bang. It wasn't a suitcase being dropped in the corridor, it was outside. My mind is fully awake now. There was a shockwave. Gas cylinder in a restaurant kitchen going up? Car bomb? An explosion, yes. My brain has been edging towards that.

The sounds of emergency vehicles start, far off, growing louder, stopping somewhere off to the right, out of sight. Fire engine, ambulance. Then more vehicles with two-tone sirens, copied from France. They switch to a rising whoop as if they've spotted their prey then die to silence. The cops have arrived.

Voices float up from the street. Three or four men are running to the right. Then in a comic double-take they stop, turn and run back. At least it is comic viewed from above. A couple of police are pounding down the road. Shouts. Whistle blown. They catch up with a straggler and trip him so he sprawls in the road. One cop hauls him to his feet while the other lands a fist in his stomach. He can't have had anything to do with the explosion. He was running towards it until the cops appeared. Lesson learnt. Always help Tunisian police with their enquiries before they start questioning you with a fist.

A cop turns his face up towards the Hotel Salammbo and I take a step back.

I wonder about Lucija. Did the commotion wake her? I could go and knock at her door and ask. Ask what? Did the explosion wake you? Yes, she says. Are you all right? The explosion wasn't in her room so of course she's all right. Man knocks at woman's bedroom door in the middle of the night and asks bogus question. Hey-ho.

So I think about knocking at Lucija's door and then I don't.

It is morning. Now here's a weird thing. I ask the man at the reception desk about the excitement in the night. 'It was an explosion, monsieur.' He gives me a distant smile. 'I would say that every day there are explosions in countries all round the world, in Africa, in the Middle East, even in France, all over. We Tunisians wish to be part of the modern world so naturally we must have an explosion of our own.'

'Was anybody hurt?'

'Ah well.' He tilts his head back to concentrate his thoughts. 'What was it the great Shakespeare wrote? "Macbeth doth murder sleep." I would say sleep was the only casualty.'

For a moment I am stunned. We have been speaking French but he had the quote in English. Is this a normal hotel worker? He raises his head, eyes staring over my shoulder. He seems to say this is something we should be wary of.

Lucija and I drink coffee and eat baguettes and fig jam and go out into the street. At Avenue Habib Bourguiba we pause. Looking right we see the police having fun. Their cars block the road, blue lights on the roofs revolving and flashing. Passers-by stop and gawp. The cops blow whistles and wave batons to keep them back. Do we join them? We have other business and turn left. The French embassy is just ahead of us. A tank is parked in its front garden.

'Like a war zone,' I say.

'It makes the French feel important,' Lucija says.

We pass through an imposing arch and enter a different world. The medina is a honeypot for tourists, but we are early. Shopkeepers are still arranging displays of coffee pots and tiles and necklaces and antique tables with the most authentic woodworm holes ever seen. 'Monsieur, madame,' we hear but their hearts aren't in it. We pause to consult a map and a man slips out of a doorway and says he will show us the Zitoune mosque.

'What is he saying?' Lucija is frustrated she has no French.

'He wants to show us a mosque. He says it is very old.'

'Old? That makes it special? Nothing here is new except the antiques.'

We are aiming for Rue Tourbet. Follow the map. We go down an alley selling T-shirts and jeans. We come to a fork. We take the left alley which is half blocked by heaps of builder's sand. It is as dark as dusk, the smell is musty, the sound is a woman singing. Her voice comes from the radio. Every radio plays the same station so she keeps pace with us, wailing. Her life sounds tragic. We pass bakers and greengrocers and a shop that sells used sewing machines, nothing else. No tourists come this way. No shop keeper implores us. We skirt round a high wall and enter a small open space with a stunted cypress tree. Everything here is in miniature. The medina was walled to keep out invaders and space was precious. This mini-square is cobbled. Have we arrived?

Against one wall are the sword leaves of irises. Clank-clank is a blacksmith doing his thing. Sparrows squabble over something. A teenager is kicking a football against a wall. He twists to gather up a rebound, sees us and stops. He hugs the ball to his chest and stares.

'There.' I point to the left. A sign says Rue Tourbet.

Lucija has the print-out of the email she sent me. It shows the outline of a body on the cobbles. With the street sign on the wall to guide us we work out where the outline must be. We walk forward and peer down. The blacksmith starts hammering again. Maybe he has been banging all the time, but I blocked out the noise.

We say nothing. We squat down to inspect the cobbles closely. Yes, on the sides of the smooth stones there are traces of blue chalk. Shoes have wiped the tops clean. I duck my head closer so the dots and dashes of blue chalk join together. A man's body. The body is not complete because something has washed away part of one side. But there is enough there: head, shoulders, half a chest, an arm, a leg. The leg is angled as if he was turning. The arm is raised high. Catching a ball? Wanting to ask a question, please sir? Revolutionary pointing the way?

Matt?

Here we are.

What are you trying to tell us?

We stand up and look at each other. The chalk marks are at our feet. What do they mean? The only sounds are the blacksmith's hammer and the pat-pat of the ball as the boy starts kicking it again, once reaching high – like Matt's outstretched arm – to catch the ball in mid-flight.

Lucija takes a couple of steps so she is standing by the shoulder. She peers down, frowning, then looks at me. Her face has an expression I can't read. Angry? Confused? Cheated? Determined?

'Is he lying on his back or his front?' she asks. 'What do you think?'

I turn this over in my mind. I decide the position of the head is the only clue. If he was lying face down his cheek would be resting on the cobbles – at least that is the most likely – and therefore the blue chalk would show an outline of his nose. It is difficult to be sure but so far as I can tell the chalk marks show no nose.

'I would say on his back.'

'So this is the right arm raised?'

'Yes.'

'Then it's not Matt.' She looks at me. 'I'm telling you it's not Matt.'

Not Matt? What does this mean? I ask, 'What makes you so certain?'

'A couple of months ago he was diagnosed with tendonitis in the right shoulder. He can raise his right arm to his shoulder but not right up like that. He physically cannot do it. So it's not Matt.'

We stand and stare at the hazy outline of the impossible man. Lucija holds the print-out of the photo she was sent. Matt must have sent it. Why? Because he wanted her physically to be here. It is an outline of someone else's body. Whose? We stand and stare. Neither of us has a thought worth sharing.

The blacksmith continues banging. He is down an alley a little further on. No help. There is a woman raising her voice in anger and then she is quiet. There is the pat-pat of the football and then that too stops.

'Monsieur? Monsieur?' The boy holds the ball against his chest. How old is he? Fifteen? Sixteen? But tall for his age. He is bashful with foreigners but eager at the same time. 'Monsieur, are you from the film company?'

'What's he saying?' Lucija asks.

I tell her while the boy's eyes flick from me to her and quickly away. He is bashful with women, I think. His eyes drop to the outline of not-Matt and come to rest on me again.

'I am a writer,' is my cautious reply. 'Why do you ask?'

'He said he was from the film company and it was all right and I wouldn't get in any trouble.'

'Then I'm sure you won't. Did he tell you his name? We're certain to know him.'

'He didn't say.' The boy is crestfallen. 'But he was English, I can tell you that. He had an accent like yours and he addressed me as *vous* not *tu*.' The boy smiles as his confidence comes back.

'What did he want?'

The boy points at the broken chalk figure on the cobbles. 'He wanted me to lie down here so he could draw round my body with chalk. It is what the police do. Then he took a photograph. He said it was publicity for the film. He gave me twenty dinars too.' He squeezes the ball against his chest.

'If it is for publicity he should have given you more.' I pull a note out of my pocket and hand it to him. 'It is lucky you were here when he wanted you. Are you here every day?'

'In the morning on my way to school. In the afternoon I play here with friends. There is nowhere else in the medina.'

'Has anyone else from the film company come to look at this?'

'I don't know. Not when I've been here.'

'You must be excited and want to see the film.'

'Yes. When is it going to open?'

'Making a film takes a long time. But you won't forget its name, will you?'

'*Death Points the Way*. He said it was about men who came to Tunisia in a boat to do something bad but they were tracked down by the hero and there was a lot of danger and chases and exciting scenes but the good man won in the end. It sounds really terrific.'

Super cool is what he actually says, a good French expression now. Lucija has had the wit to let him run on but catching this bit of English she looks at me. I give a nod.

'I must go now,' the boy says. 'I am already late. I won't forget. *Death Points the Way*.'

'So what does Matt expect us to do?' Lucija says.

'He's sending us a message,' I say.

'What?'

Matt has come to this backwater in the medina. No one has passed in the quarter hour we've been here. Matt must have waited until this boy came to play with his football and he made up a story about a film and drew the outline of the boy in blue chalk. Suppose the boy hadn't come? We don't know what Matt would have done. Thought of something. But the point is that the boy did come, lie down, Matt arranged his body in this precise way, traced the outline, photographed it and sent it to Lucija. So...

'Is the film's name significant?' I say.

'*Death Points the Way*,' Lucija says. 'We look at the outline on the cobbles...'

'...and see he is directing us to the wall...'

'...which looks just like an old wall...'

'...whitewashed at some stage but with no graffiti.'

The double act doesn't get us far. The whitewash covers plaster that could have been slapped on about the time talkies were invented. Nothing catches the eye. Whoa. Hold on. There are two blue chalk squiggles, carelessly drawn, next to a small window. No, not carelessly.

Matt will have put them there for a purpose. The window is deep set with a central metal bar to deter burglars. The windowsill has an earthenware pot with a geranium that has decided life is too much of a struggle. But look behind it. Hidden from passers-by giving it a casual glance, is a wine bottle. Did Matt put it there? It would have been hard. I struggle to get it out. Losing patience Lucija pushes me aside and slips in her smaller hand.

She holds it up. An ordinary bottle. It's empty. No dust or spider's web so it's recently put there. By Matt? Is he sending us a message? There is nothing scrawled on a scrap of paper and tucked inside. Nothing scribbled on the label. So the bottle itself must be the message.

Château Belvédère. Muscat sec. Millésime 2016. Mis en bouteille à la Propriété.

Matt, spy in the long distant past, is calling out to us. Spies use dead letter drops. Not Matt. The one-time wine merchant is using a dead bottle drop.

So why has he done this?

He has left clues but disguised them: the chalk outline on the cobbles, the raised arm, the bottle. They'd mean nothing to a passer-by. Even Lucija and I – and we are desperate - are baffled. All we have is the wine bottle.

Go on, Matt is saying, *you have to go further.*

CHAPTER 5

Lucija smiles at me. I find I am smiling back at her. We've done something. We are world beaters. All right, it is only an empty wine bottle we've found, but the blue chalk shows we are following Matt.

'Monsieur… Madame….'

Shopkeepers call out but we are hurrying now and they lose heart. We're not interested in leather bags and wooden camels and plates with quotes from the Koran. On, on. A sort of madness has taken hold. We hurry, even if it is only back to the Salammbo hotel. The maid is cleaning my room so we go next door to Lucija's. She runs a basin of hot water and dunks the wine bottle in it. I perch on the bed with copies of *Tunis Matin* and *La Presse*. These are the two French language daily papers. Neither carries a story about the explosion in the night – too late for today's edition. Lucija leans against me on the bed while we compare the two papers with the cutting that was emailed to her.

'It comes from *Tunis Matin*,' I say.

'How can you be certain?'

"Clough". I point at Matt's name in the cutting Lucija was sent. 'See how the descender is formed. Compare that with a "g" in *La Presse*. Different typeface.'

The old newspaper hand shows off a bit. Lucija goes to the basin to ease the label off the bottle. I look at the depression on the bed where she has been sitting. The coverlet has a design of triangles and circles in many colours. My parents had curtains like that. In the 60s and 70s it was called *Contemporary*. In Tunisia it still is.

Lucija dabs the label dry while I search *Tunis Matin* for its editorial office. I can find no address. Stupid.

We go to the reception desk and ask the man with the distant smile. He looks in the telephone directory for the address and points it out on our map. Over on the other side of Avenue Habib Bourguiba. We can take a tram which is confusingly called the Metro. Or walk. Or take a taxi but with half the avenue closed by the police this is difficult.

'The police came here while you were out,' he says

Something in the way he says it makes me look at his face. The hint of a smile is still there but his eyes look straight back at me.

'What did they want?'

'Police are the same in every country, always suspicious. Tunisian guests didn't interest them, only foreigners. We have two young Australian women and a French couple.'

The receptionist pauses and looks me in the eye. He didn't mention Lucija and me. I don't think he likes the police.

'There's you, of course. But you were in your rooms when the explosion took place so it was nothing to do with you. They asked if there were any British guests and I gestured at the register. You can see there are no British staying. I invited them to go and knock at the bedroom doors if they wanted to check. Of course most guests go out after breakfast. You, for example, were not here.' Again he pauses a beat. 'But they looked at the stairs going up and decided to leave.'

'Why did the police want to know who was staying?

'Monsieur, possibly it is different in your country but in Tunisia it is the police who ask the questions. We are the ones who must provide the answers. The wise man takes care how he answers.'

We walk. We round a corner and are out of sight of the hotel before Lucija breaks the silence.

'What was he saying?'

'The cops have been asking if any British people are staying.'

'So Mr Fazekas and Mrs Gerasimova are safe.'

'The receptionist has heard us speaking English. The police didn't ask about that. The wise man takes care to give the right answer.'

Crossing Avenue Habib Bourguiba we stop on the central strip. A block or two away is the Africa Hotel where the taxi driver wanted to take us last night. Windows on the fourth floor have been blown out. There is still a police blockade over half the road.

We carry on to Avenue de Paris. Bars and restaurants and fancy clothes shops could be in Paris. Rue de Marseille is different. Europe fades and turns into Africa. Now the café tables have men only. New clothes in shop windows have a tired look. Boys carrying trays with glasses of tea dodge between pedestrians. The buildings have no number so I stop at a kiosk to ask directions. I wait while a man buys a single cigarette. The kiosk keeper lights it for him. 'Just a little further, monsieur,' the kiosk man tells me. 'Two steps from here.'

Two steps and then some more and here it is: a building with the sign *Tunis Matin*. On one side is a shoe shop, on the other a cheap restaurant. A plate glass window has the current front page taped to it. *Tunisia-France: new dynamic is promised* is the lead story. *Israel raid in Gaza* is the second lead. Today's date is on the masthead but the stories could be any time.

Sharp elbow in my ribs. She nods her head towards the wall by the door. At shoulder height are two slashes made by a stick of blue chalk.

'Do you have an appointment?' the man at the reception desk asks.

'No, but it is very urgent.' I hold up my press card. He doesn't look impressed. I go on. 'I am sure Monsieur Dakhli will give a little of his valuable time on a matter of mutual interest.'

He looks even less impressed. 'It is Madame Dakhli.'

Rym Dakhli. Well, would you have known?

'Just tell her it's to do with the piece she wrote about Matt Clough's corpse in the medina. We have new information. She'll want to see us. Tell her Lucija and Baz are here.'

So it is that we are told to go through the reporters' bullpen where she will be waiting. One step inside the room brings a flood of memories. This is how newspaper offices should be: filing cabinets with drawers that won't close, cork pinboards, forgotten coffee cups, a calendar on the wall open at last month and some practical joker has adapted a fez to make a lampshade. It's a small room – I make it eight desks. Only three men working. Rym Dakhli is across the room, standing at an open doorway.

First impressions are important. She has a hand on the doorknob; no one passes without her say-so. Her head is up and her chin out: a fighter. Her hair is long and black with a faint auburn sheen as if it reflected a fire. Huge round spectacles dominate her face – nothing escapes those eyes. How old? Thirty-five? She wears a fawn jacket and skirt and a dark blue blouse with a white pattern that looks like overlapping fish scales. The blouse is tight so it emphasises her figure. My father would have taken an admiring look and called her a generous woman, one you'd never mistake for a man.

We walk towards her. I catch her eyes looking Lucija up and down. They switch to me. Those eyes watch me through the huge glasses, take me in, analyse me. Do I pass?

'Dakhli,' she announces, holding out her hand first to Lucija then to me. 'Rym Dakhli.' A woman offering a handshake first is unusual in France, and surely it is unknown in Tunisia. Her grip is firm. 'The receptionist says you have an English press card.' Her English is confident, the accent a little French, a little American. 'I would like to see it.'

I hand it over.

'This is last year's card.'

'Careless of me. This year's card must be somewhere on my desk.' I wave the detail away. 'An oversight. You know how it is.' Her look says she doesn't know how it is.

'An oversight?' She takes another look at the card. '*The Oxford Herald*. Are you the editor?'

'No. I…'

'Possibly the deputy editor?'

'A reporter.'

'I hope your reporting does not contain many oversights.' She turns her head towards Lucija. 'And you are Lucija obviously.'

Lucija hands her the Latvian passport.

Rym opens it. 'Lucija Trifona.' In a strange gesture she lifts up her outsize glasses. The two women inspect each other. Why am I reminded of dogs sniffing a rival? 'Come into my office, please.'

We follow her into the room and she gestures – close the door. Her office is just that: an office. I heard of a new editor who had a mini-grand piano installed. Some wit pinned a note on his door: *the ego has landed.* The piano disappeared. Rym Dakhli doesn't need that. There's a modest desk with computer, telephone, paper, diary, Anglepoise lamp and so on. The window has a view of a warehouse. On one wall is a clock and a large-scale map of Tunisia. Another wall has a photo of JFK.

'Before we go any further let me tell you certain things. I am the deputy editor. The assistant editor Chedly…' she gestures at the office on the right '…is away because his mother has chosen this time to die. The editor…' she gestures to the left '…is out consulting certain people in the Ministry of Information. Now I am going to tell you a secret.'

She eases back in her chair and talks to the ceiling.

'Tunisia does not have censorship. Definitely not. Please understand that. Instead – on very special occasions - we have guidance. Totally unofficial. Definitely. That is what Mondher is receiving this morning: guidance. He is being guided about our excellent relations with France, about the Israeli raid on the prison at Anha. And then, closer to home, that bomb at the Africa Hotel. This means he may be guided for hours and then more hours because it is lunch time.'

Is she serious? Then she lifts her outsize glasses again and I notice her eyebrows. They arch. In mockery?

'You know how a blind man will have a dog to guide him? Sometimes we are blind and cannot see what is in front of our nose. Fortunately we have these dogs in the ministry to guide us. Tread carefully, they say, do not put your foot in any shit. We don't want censorship in Tunisia. We don't need it. We have guidance.'

Her eyes drop to me. I am a fellow journalist. Don't make my job difficult – that is the unspoken message in her steady look. 'In the absence of these two *messieurs,'* her hands gesture to the offices on either side, 'it is my duty to make sure we have a newspaper for breakfast tomorrow morning. So our meeting must be short.'

'I have a question,' I say. 'How did you learn your remarkably good English?'

'Naturally I speak Arabic. When I was a child we had a Berber maid who made me a gift of her language. At the *lycée* we were taught in French. Sicily is two hundred kilometres away so I have a certain amount of the strange Italian they speak there. This is the twenty-first century so English is an essential tool. When I was younger I had – I'll call him a friend, a man from Boston – and that is the best way to learn a language. Enough of this talk.' She sighs. 'So you have come.'

Rym is cut short by a knock at the door. A boy who looks about twelve comes in with a brass tray and three cups of coffee. Lucija has held herself in long enough.

'You've seen him? Matt?'

'Ah Matthieu.' For some reason Rym turns his name into French. 'He came to this office four days ago. He sat in the same chair you are in. He had been sent here by someone from the British embassy.'

'Did he say who?' I ask. She shakes her head. I don't believe her. It was the hesitation while she wondered whether to reveal her source. Hipkiss, I decide.

'It was late afternoon. That is the very worst time when you have a morning paper to put together – except for all the other times. Can't talk now, I told him. The assistant editor was out on some business but luckily he'd be back in time to put the paper to bed. So we made a RDV for dinner at the Capri. Do you know it?'

She lifts her coffee cup up and looks over it, first at me, then at Lucija. It's just a bit of 'business' as actors call it.

'How many people live in Tunis? A million? Not even the government knows. But the people who matter, the decision makers, the power brokers – that is a very small village and they don't go to the Capri. Nobody will recognise me, wonder who Dakhli is sharing secrets with. I was the only woman in the room. Tunisian men when they get together with a drink are very loud. There was a TV showing football. All that noise meant no one could hear us. We are just a couple leaning close over a table because of the noise.'

What makes me glance from Rym to Lucija at that moment? No idea. What vibration has Lucija picked up? What woman-on-woman intuition? Her lips vanish as she clamps her mouth tight.

'Matthieu has heard something from the man at the embassy and I have heard something else and these things knit together like this.'

Rym meshes the fingers of her hands together. Why does her telephone choose this moment to ring and interrupt her?

'*Allo*.'

Then she switches to Arabic and listens and talks some more and jots notes on a pad.

'*Au revoir*,' she finishes in French. She turns back to us. 'The *commissariat* of police. About the explosion in the night. You heard it?'

'It woke me up,' I say.

'It wakes the police up too. They have been to many hotels checking what foreigners are staying. They believe a foreigner - an Englishman - is the perpetrator. Why don't they think a Tunisian could commit such an outrage? It is almost as if the police have received… guidance. They have been very busy but have made no arrest. However, they have come across a curious fact. The bomb in the Africa Hotel was placed under the bed of a room taken in the name of Matthieu Clough.'

Lucija draws in her breath, mutters something I don't understand. Then, hand over mouth, she stares at Rym.

'Don't worry. Matthieu was not in bed at that time. In fact the hotel says he paid a week in advance but has not stayed there at all. Curious, yes? There's more.' She consults the pad on which she jotted notes. 'Police enquiries this morning show he also took a room at the Hotel Maison Dorée and the Hotel Omrane. He hasn't slept in those hotels either.'

'So where has he been sleeping?' Lucija asks.

Rym spreads her hands and shrugs: who knows? There is another of those pauses while we can think what we like.

'He has been taking precautions,' Rym says. 'He flew on Tunisair so there is no secret about his coming here. That is why he tried to stage his own death.' She opens a desk drawer and brings out an old copy of *Tunis Matin* open at the page with the body outline drawn in blue chalk on the cobbles. 'If his death was reported nobody would come looking for him. That was his reasoning. That explosion in the hotel room…' again she spreads her hands. 'It seems that trick hasn't worked. That is very unfortunate. It means he is still in danger.'

'But he is alive,' Lucija says.

'I hope so,' Rym says.

We all hope so. But there is something about Rym's face, the twitching of the lips, the hint of a secret smile… the two women look at each other. I break the silence.

'He went to the medina, got a boy to take the photo and you published it.'

'Yes.'

'The editor didn't object to this made up story?'

'I would say the editor concerns himself with higher things, the world of politics, the celebrations for Independence Day next week, the guidance the French ambassador offers.'

'And Matt sent the photo to Lucija?'

'No, I did. Matthieu gave me the address and asked me to scan the photo and send it. By the time the newspaper was printed he had left Tunis.'

'Did he tell you where he was going?' Lucija asks.

'Listen,' Rym says. 'It was like this. Every week I speak on the phone with my father. My mother died two years ago and he is lonely. He is a wine grower on Cap Bon so we talk about how the vines are growing, how the last vintage is maturing, about his local news, whose wife has had twins. It is a different world from this. But there was a big excitement. This is where he lives.'

She gets up and points to a spot on the map along the Mediterranean coast east of Tunis.

'His house is on a cliff that looks down to the sea. A boat from Malta put in at the harbour. It was not a yacht but something like a large speedboat. It is not a big harbour, you understand, half a dozen fishing boats and no officials, no customs, no immigration. My father says it was a mystery because they weren't real sailors. They were seasick from a storm. They didn't speak Arabic and only one of them spoke French but not like we Tunisians speak French and not like the French speak French.'

'Did your father find out who they were?' Lucija asks.

'That is the same question Matthieu asked. Unfortunately I didn't know the answer. So he decided he had to go and speak to my father. He wouldn't use the telephone. He has developed a deep mistrust of the phone.'

Lucija opens her bag and takes out a tissue which is folded around the label of the wine bottle.

'Is this your father's vineyard?'

'Yes.'

'So where is Matt now?'

'I don't know.'

'Isn't he at Château Belvédère?'

'No.'

'How can you be certain? Is he with you?'

'No.'

They stare at each other until Rym decides she has had enough and stands up.

'It is better that you interview my father. I'll tell you how to get there. Now you must excuse me. No more questions. I have a newspaper to produce.'

If the situation had been different, if Matt hadn't been involved, I think those two women would have been friends.

CHAPTER 6

'I could kill her.' Lucija stares straight ahead. No need to ask who she means. 'Rym,' she says anyway in case I was in any doubt. 'Matthieu, Matthieu. I can hear her whispering it in his ear.'

On the pillow, right.

Matt paid for three hotel bedrooms. He has used none of them. He has to sleep somewhere. A hint of a smile flashed over Rym's face. I didn't miss it. Nor did Lucija.

'We're on our way.' I try to put a cheerful tone in my voice, something to change Lucija's mood. I score 0 out of 10.

'And kill him,' she says. 'Betrayer.'

What can I say? The great newspaper reporter who's been to accidents and disasters and tragedies and brought sympathy to the stories finds the words won't come. I wonder why and then give up. I peer out of the window at the Tunis suburbs and that doesn't cheer me either. Stacks of timber, graveyards of beaten-up cars, acres of clay pots, a café with tin tables and one old man staring at a glass of tea and waiting for something to happen. *Get a grip, Baz. What did you expect? The Taj Mahal?*

How much does Bardo know? No idea. When he was posted here he ran a network of agents. So Beatrice says. The network won't be complete any more but he still has informers and he still has influence. He knew that Matt had registered at the Africa Hotel but he didn't know that Matt hadn't slept there. Bardo had a high up contact in the police and got them to ask about British guests in hotels. Looking for Matt obviously.

Or perhaps me.

I stare through the window but what I am seeing is Lucija and me outside Beatrice's building in Vincent Square while I say we are interested in Tunisia and Matt. Two men in the Utter Gutter van staring. Did they have a directional microphone?

Hiring a car is impossible. Lucija hasn't brought her driving licence. Mine is British in the name Potter. So here we are in the back of a *louage*, a Toyota people-carrier that can take eight passengers. We are only seven. The driver beats a tattoo on his horn whenever we pass someone walking. Success. A woman on the wrong side of fifty waves him down. She is a bundle of clothes. She carries a basket with a duck poking its head out from a layer of sacking. The driver objects to the loud quacks. The woman has the solution. She unties the sacking, grabs the duck and wrings its neck.

We drive on in peace.

We pass a pocket of shanties, a factory or two, fields of broad beans, a furniture warehouse, then ploughed land and pasture. It is Rym who told us to take the *louage* to Soliman – quicker than a bus. 'At Soliman take a taxi to my father's house,' she said. She will telephone to say we are coming.

We arrive at Soliman and there are no taxis. The *louage* has emptied and the driver eyes us in the mirror. I hand him the fare for the trip from Tunis.

'Do you know Château Belvédère?'

'The château for wine?' It's not a difficult question so why is he staring at me? 'Yes.'

'Is it far?'

'It's before Korbous. Not far.'

I hold up a five dinar note. 'Will you take us?'

He is still staring at me in the mirror.

'You have business there?'

Why does he want to know? It's nothing to do with him. I don't answer.

'I am only licensed to drive to and from Tunis.'

I put the five dinars away and get out a ten dinar note.

'We are not hiring you. This is for friendship.'

'Friendship?' he echoes. His eyes switch from me to Lucija and down to the money. He nods. This is Tunisia. Everything arranges itself.

We start on a tarred road signposted to El Haouaria. After five minutes we swing off onto a dirt road. Our vehicle lurches and bounces. I have hold of the grab handle above the door. Lucija in the centre seat grips my arm. We pass a paddock with three horses that lift their heads to stare then canter off and turn to stare again. Fields show green shoots of wheat. The vineyards begin with the hills. We drop into a ravine, climb again and come to an abrupt halt by twin gateposts that lack a gate. A drive has been gravelled but not in this century. It is lined with eucalyptus trees and dips out of sight.

'Château Belvédère.' the driver says. 'It is not far to the house. You can walk.'

'And if the police ask if you have brought us here…' I am wondering how much friendship ten dinars buys.

'The police?' He stares at me in the mirror, thinking about what I have said. He shrugs. 'Maybe I have never seen you.'

We get out. The *louage* does a three-point turn and vanishes back the way we have come. The engine fades and we hear wind in the eucalyptus and crows arguing.

The gateposts are made of stone. One of them has a sign: *Château Belvédère. Prop: Mongi Dakhli. Dégustation sur rendezvous.* Lucija jabs me. I'm getting to know that elbow of hers. It wants to be my friend. On the stone under the sign are blue chalk marks. There are three this time, arranged to form an arrow.

The winery reveals itself piece by piece. Rows of vines, winter pruned. A drive sloping up but then gently down. The promise of the Mediterranean ahead. There is a line of conifers and the drive divides. A track goes off left to a warehouse with men loading a truck with cartons. Beyond the warehouse are two bungalows joined by a line of washing flying in the wind. We follow the main drive to the right. There's a big old cherry tree with a ladder lost in its branches. No blue chalk. The main house comes into view. It is a French colonial villa showing its age. One shutter is cockeyed and the paint is peeling off the window frames. Beyond the villa is a stupendous view of the sea. A man erupts out of the house and bustles towards us, arms wide in greeting. He is talking in French as he comes, his greeting cut to shreds by the wind.

'Good day, welcome…friends that Rym told…your car? Have you walked…again, welcome. I am Mongi Dakhla.'

He shakes my hand.

'I am…' I hesitate a moment. Think. Who am I? '…Bazil Fazekas.'

Mongi transfers his attention to Lucija, shaking her hand but not letting go. 'And you are Lucija. I have heard about you from Rym. But she didn't tell me how blue your eyes are, like the sky, a gift from heaven. I am enchanted to meet you.'

'What does he say?'

'He is pleased to meet you.'

'I think he said more than that.'

I look at Lucija, at her face. And yes, her eyes are blue. I just never noticed.

Mongi goes on. 'It is sad for a man to live here on his own. A house without a woman is like a meal without wine. It lacks a soul. You can open my heart but you will find I speak nothing but the truth.'

'Baz, now what?' Frustration at not knowing French tightens her forehead.

'More of the same. He has gone into poetic mode.'

'Is he going to give my hand back?'

'Possibly.'

'Certain wines go with certain dishes,' Mongi says. 'In exactly the same way each house deserves the right woman.'

'Baz?'

'I think he is keeping your hand. Possibly he is proposing marriage or maybe something less. Rym said he was a lonely man.'

This strange welcome is brought to an end by the arrival of an old woman with a tray of glasses, a bottle of wine, dishes of cheese, olives and dates. We sit on wicker chairs on the terrace with that wonderful sea view framed by bougainvillea.

'The cheese is Numidia.' Mongi is off again. 'It is a blue cheese made from sheep's milk like Roquefort. It needs a luscious wine to accompany it. I drink to your very good health. And to your happiness. Today I am happy because you have come.'

'Baz, why is he looking at me over his glass? Ask him about the boat. Ask what he told Matt.'

'Monsieur,' I begin.

'We are friends already,' he says. 'You must call me Mongi.'

'Mongi, we have come to find out what you told Matt about the boat.'

'Ah yes.' His eyes turn away down to the sea. 'The boat.' He lifts an arm to point at the horizon. 'It came from the east, both the storm and the boat. Our storms usually come from the Atlantic but this was different. It was as if the storm was pursuing the boat, determined to catch it, to stop it, to punish it. People now give names to hurricanes. Perhaps this great storm was called Poseidon, the god the ancient Greeks believed lived on Olympus and it had come to destroy this evil boat.'

'Baz, what is he saying?'

'He is being poetic again. He isn't saying anything yet.'

'But the storm turned away north and left us and so the boat arrived.'

'Where?' I ask.

'At the fishing port down below.' He makes a vague gesture, pointing at something out of sight.

'That's where we want to go.'

I am getting out of my chair but Mongi puts his hand on my arm to stop me.

'I was right here on this terrace watching the boat. I have these old binoculars. Here: see how big they are?' He hoists them up from under the table with the wine and food. 'Heavy. Look: Zeiss. Colour of sand, but scratched. I think some officer in Rommel's army lost them seventy years ago. You know, when the British and the Australians and others fought the Germans here because they couldn't fight them in Europe. I think that German officer had no more use for them.'

'Baz?'

'He saw the boat through these binoculars.'

'That's it?'

'He's making a Hollywood production out of it.'

'Why? Why is he taking so long?'

'He's lonely?' I shrug. 'He likes to have someone to talk to?'

'A sailor came ashore and spoke very bad French or maybe it was English,' Mongi says. 'That is what I have been told. They had come a long way and the storm caught them and it had been very dangerous but now they were here and they were exhausted.'

'Baz, we can't spend all day here. Why doesn't he want us to go?'

In the distance, very faint, there is the sound of a siren.

'Mongi, when our friend Matt was here, did he take a path down to the fishing port?'

'There is a path,' he says. 'I don't know how safe it is for you.' He is peering at Lucija's feet. 'Her shoes might slip.'

The siren is much louder. Abruptly it cuts out.

'Is that the police? Why have they come?' Lucija is on her feet. 'Did he call them? Is that why he has been talking so much?'

There is still gravel in patches on the drive. We can hear the car coming closer. Then it stops and there are raised voices. I think of the *louage* driver and how he stared at me in his mirror. A car door slams and we hear more voices.

'What are they saying?'

'The police ask if they have seen anybody. The workers say no, they were busy loading the wine. They saw nobody.'

'Are they coming here?'

There is a gunshot.

'Mongi, that's the police shooting, right?'

'We have a bird scarer. It makes a noise like a gun. It chases the birds from the cherry tree.'

There are no cherries. It is too early in the year.

'We're going.' I'm on my feet in front of him. What can I tell Mongi? 'The police want to arrest her. Don't tell them where we've gone.'

Will he? Won't he? Will it gain us five minutes?

'Arrest her? What for?'

Mongi's eyes are wide open. I can't read anything in his expression.

Then we are down off the terrace and running along a dirt path lined with oleanders towards the cliff edge. There is a voice behind us but the words are blown away by the wind. I hope it is Mongi. The police might shoot. Evading arrest, they'd call it. Lucija doesn't trust Mongi. Me, I have doubts about the *louage* driver. When he got back to Soliman he could have driven straight to the police station. *Trust nobody,* Beatrice had said, *you don't know who is in Bardo's pay.* The path veers to the left and now we are hidden by the oleanders. Ahead is the cliff edge. The path ends at a boulder. We come to an abrupt stop. On the boulder are two slashes made by blue chalk.

It is not a sheer cliff but it is steep. The path twists between rocks. The wind off the sea comes in gusts and we are blown to a standstill. We clutch onto each other, waiting for the wind to calm. Down below we can see the tip of a jetty and a breakwater built of boulders. And up above? I turn my head.

'Police?' she asks.

'Nobody,' I say.

'So why was Mongi trying to delay us?'

'You.'

'Me?'

Lucija looks in my eyes a moment and then away. 'So I am his fantasy? Really? So I should I pity him?' She shrugs. 'It is my experience that many men want to live in a fantasy world. I am an expert on this. Don't forget I lived in a communist country and that was a fantasy world on a heroic scale. Mongi's fantasy lacks ambition: just a woman in his empty house, a woman in his empty bed.' She takes a deep breath. 'We are wasting time.'

Lucija takes the lead, down, down, stones that turn under our shoes, run-offs where winter rains have created gullies, shrubs grab at us, gulls call out. We reach the bottom. Nobody has shot at us.

We enter the square of a village not big enough to have a name. Tamarisk trees give a little shade. Cats lift their heads to watch us. We walk out along a jetty where three fishing boats are tied up. Lucija bends low to inspect each hull. Are there blue chalk marks? No. We go back to the square. There are a dozen squat cottages built of breezeblocks. Nobody is about. One of the buildings has two metal tables with chairs outside. I stand in the doorway of this shop-cum-café. I see sacks of dried beans and chickpeas, a tray of eggs, a dish of dark red harissa, bottles of oil, candles, matches, ball pens, school notebooks, cotton reels, boxes of onions and tomatoes. Then I see a woman watching me and I order coffee.

When she brings the coffee outside I ask about the storm but she shakes her head. She fetches her daughter, a teenager. She wears pink trousers and a matching pink top. She pulls up a chair and sits down.

'My mother says you have questions. She is a stupid woman.'

Eyebrows have a will of their own and mine climb a little. The girl notices this.

'I mean my mother is not an educated woman. She knows no French so you must ask me.'

'I asked about that big storm you had.'

'You came down from the vineyard above. I watched from my window. You are like the Englishman who came down the other day. He came down the same way and asked about the storm and the boat that sheltered. We are on the tourist route now. We should build a hotel and then papa needn't go out fishing.'

'His boat is here?'

She lifts a foot to point at a fishing boat. Her toenails are painted pink to match her outfit.

'Did he go out when there was the gale?'

'He has more sense. He was checking the engine was all right when this big speedboat came in. He saw the name: *Calypso*. It was registered in Mgarr. Do you know where that is? No? It is the port on the island of Gozo next to Malta.'

Lucija wants to know what the girl is saying. She leans forward. I press my foot against hers. She glances at me and sits back.

'My father said they weren't real sailors. He could tell. They were in real trouble coming up to the jetty. He went to help tie up the speedboat. There were four men on board and he said they looked very tired. Before he became a fisherman my father was a sailor on a cruise ship and knows some English. Did you come through the storm, he asked. One of them – my father said he looked like a *milord* – nodded. All the way from Mgarr? Yes. But the storm was so bad they went first to Mahdia to shelter. My father thought about this. Mahdia is a big fishing port a long way from here. *So you sailed from Mgarr to Mahdia and now here – you are doing a real cruise.* The *milord* didn't say anything. But my father said he frowned as if he shouldn't have said that. His eyes were on the buildings here. You know...'

The girl slaps the metal table and then gestures at the other houses.

'The *milord* wanted to know if this shop sold vodka. My father said no but if they climbed up that cliff – you know, the one you came down – they could get wine. The *milord* said vodka was what the men drink and they had finished it all. What are they? Polish? Russians? The *milord* didn't answer. If vodka is so important, my father said, and you are heading west there is La Goulette, you know, the port for Tunis. The *milord* shook his head and said they were going to Bizerte. Your vodka cruise will be successful there, my father said. My father said he wasn't a real *milord* because he had no manners. He didn't thank my father for his help mooring the boat or the information he just nodded and turned away.'

'What happened?'

'The speedboat spent the night here. I couldn't sleep and I was staring out of the window. Perhaps something will happen. For a long time nothing happened except two cats arguing. Then a car came. It was dark and we have no street lights but there was a moon. It was a police car. The man who got out carried a small flashlight and walked along the jetty to the Calypso. He must have called out because someone came and put down a plank for him to go on board. Maybe he was half an hour in the cabin. Then he came back to his car and drove away. How did the police know to come? I suppose the speedboat has a radio. Why did he come?'

The girl shrugs at her own question and spreads her hands.

'I thought: this is as good as a spy film. Except Tunisia has no enemies so what is there to spy on? In the morning the speedboat was gone.'

'Where to? Bizerte?'

'Maybe. You want to speak to the *milord*?' She looks at her watch. 'The *louage* brings the schoolkids from Soliman in about ten minutes. You can take it back to Soliman, then go to Tunis, then to Bizerte. If you miss the *milord* there you must go to Tabarka. After that it is Algeria, then Morocco, then America.' She laughs.

'You see a lot,' I say.

'What else is there to do? I should be at college but I have been sick.' She pats her belly. 'The woman's curse. Your friend would understand.'

There is the noise of a car's engine.

'The *louage* is early. You are in luck. Quick. It doesn't wait long.'

'Tell me.' So I tell her. Lucija's eyes are on my face. Am I telling everything? Am I hiding something?

'And Matt?'

'I didn't have time to ask. The *louage* came.'

We are in the back seats. A man from the village is in the front talking to the driver. They're not listening to us.

'Did Matt spend the night there?'

She's thinking of the girl dressed in pink with pink toenails.

'He wouldn't waste time here. He'd be after Bardo. That's who the *milord* must be.'

Finally Lucija's eyes turn from my face and she stares out of the window. She doesn't see the passing country, she sees Matt with Rym. We do the trip to Soliman in silence. There is a bus to Tunis just about to leave so we hop on that.

There are kids with daypacks, women with shopping bags, men with nothing to do but looking important about it. The seats we are on had a discarded newspaper. The old newshound picks it up even if he can't read it. This is the moment our day takes a sudden lurch. The paper's masthead is in pink and yellow. The script is in Arabic. No interest to us until I see the photos just below the fold. I stare and stare. The caption is in Arabic but I know what it says: *wanted by the police*. The photos, reprinted from passports, are of Lucija and me.

CHAPTER 7

We are in Tunis, Place Barcelona. Evening rush hour. People are hurrying, people are shouting into mobile phones, people are staring at us. Men offer trays of chewing gum and plastic combs. Shoeshine men clack their brushes to catch our attention. On the far side of the square is the railway station. On another side is the metro station, metro as in tram. The trams go round three sides of the square before setting off for their destination. The fourth side is the nearest to Avenue Habib Bourguiba. The Hotel Salammbo is tucked into a street down there.

Lucija is standing in front of me, almost touching. It means our faces are half hidden. We could be friends saying goodbye not international criminals wanted by the police with our photos in the paper.

'Bardo said he was going to Bizerte,' Lujica says. 'Matt will have gone after him. Do we go straight there? Maybe pick up our bags first?'

'I'm making a phone call,' I say. 'Wait inside the station. I'll be back in a few minutes.'

'Who are you calling?'

But I am already on my way. There is a public phone by the ticket office for the tram. I ring *Tunis Matin* and ask for Rym.

'Oui,' she answers.

'We saw you this morning,' I reply in English. 'We have just come back from…'

'Wait. I give you another number. In three minutes you telephone me on that.'

It's her mobile number. Assumption: she's leaving the building. She was happy to speak in her office this morning but not now we are international criminals wanted by the police.

I stare at my watch. Three minutes drag when your eyes are fixed on the second hand. I ring the number she gave me and she answers at once. I can hear traffic noise in the background.

'You've seen my father? He's all right?'

'Your father is lonely.'

'I know. I thought perhaps your friend…'

'He thought so too.'

Why have we started like this? I'm not ringing a dating agency.

'Matt has been there and talked to your father. He went down to the port. But you know all this.'

'So what is new?'

'There was a boat that put in after a storm. Three Russians were on board and an Englishman. He is the man Matt is interested in. The boat left and headed west along the coast. So Matt must have followed.'

'Russians,' she says. 'We have too many Russians now. In the days of the Soviet Union the Russians were all spies. Now they are all crooks.'

'Or both,' I say.

'Indeed, or both. I hear rumours but we can't print rumours. "Guidance" frowns on it. Now, talking of "guidance" we have been given the photos of a man and woman and told to print them. The police want to question them. Possibly they are the international terrorists responsible for the bomb in the Africa Hotel. The photos only look distantly like anyone I have seen or it would be my patriotic duty to warn the authorities. Are the names Potter and Trifona known to you?'

'More important, they are not known to our hotel.'

'But you had to show passports, yes?'

'Yes.'

There is silence and then what I think is a grunt, perhaps amused, while she works this out.

'The photos have already appeared,' I say. 'We saw our faces in one of the Arabic language papers.'

'Enough,' Rym says. 'I must go back to my office. One last thing. Speak to the man at your embassy, the one with the funny name. It is important you talk to him.'

'Who were you telephoning?' Lucija asks.

Simple question. But she hates Rym. So if I say I have just been having a little chat…

'I have to speak to Hipkiss, the man at the embassy. Remember? Beatrice told us about him. But it's too late now.'

I'm not lying, just dodging the question. I should be a politician.

It was dusk when we arrived in Tunis. Suddenly it is night. No city is dark but the street lamps do not give enough light for anybody to recognise international terrorists. At the Salammbo the receptionist looks up from his newspaper. Has he been studying our photos? No. I catch a glimpse of Roger Federer jumping to smash a ball over the net.

'What a wind,' I say, the bright and cheerful tourist. 'We went to Cap Bon and were nearly blown in the sea.'

The receptionist takes his time considering this. Is he searching for another Shakespeare quote? No. 'It is the season. But in the south it is already hot.'

'We should go there. That's a good idea. We can take the train to Sfax, see if that is better.'

So the international terrorist lays a false trail. The receptionist slides my key across the counter without asking the number. He knows us. But he doesn't produce Lucija's key. Why? He looks at her and says nothing. I give her room number and he lays her key down on the counter and still says nothing.

We start up the spiral staircase and just as we climb out of sight I look down to the reception desk. The man's face is angled up towards us, his smile a distant memory.

It is two flights of stairs. The walls are covered with tiles, white with a blue motif. It is tiles all over the public areas right down to the street. At the street entrance the tiles are green and yellow. Tiles. Why are they a fixation? I'm not really thinking of them. I am seeing the receptionist's face. No smile. And the business with the keys.

'Lucija.' My voice is soft. She turns to me. 'Don't go in your room yet.'

She opens her mouth to say something and I shake my head. I put out a hand to stop her.

I slide the Yale key in the lock of my door, turn it, press down on the handle. Gently, gently I ease the door open a crack, peep in, then wider. What am I expecting? I have a memory-flash of the receptionist with his mournful face. I'm not expecting a bomb. The receptionist would never accept that. If he knew, that is. I take a step in, peer behind the door, give a sweeping look all round the room, in all the corners, under the bed. Nothing.

'It's okay,' I say.

She hesitates, her eyes holding mine. My uneasiness has infected her.

'What were you expecting?'

'The unexpected.'

Her eyes drop to the key in her hand. The unexpected. She frowns then slips the key in the lock of her room, turns it, eases the handle down. Another moment of hesitation while she lays her ear against the door. Nothing. She pushes the door half open.

'Argh.'

She slams the door, twists the key, holds on to it.

'Policija.' Native language bursts out of her. Her eyes are wild. 'With a gun.'

A male voice in the room says something. The door handle shakes.

'My bag. Get the pen out of it.'

Two male voices now. First in Arabic, then in French. *'Ouvrez la porte.'*

Her shoulderbag is every man's nightmare of chaos but a pen sticks up from a side pocket. It's a sturdy metal job not a plastic

Bic. She grabs it and jabs it between the key and the handle. It stops the key turning.

Both men in the room are talking at once. Voices raised. *Open, open*, one keeps shouting in French. *I'll shoot through the door*. Lucija doesn't understand the words. She understands the fury in the voice.

'Hold the pen.' I'm urgent. 'For God's sake don't let it drop.'

I snatch the scarf from round her neck. It's cotton, thin, long. The staircase is right by us. I drape the scarf over the steps going up. Steps going down are logical but they're not visible from her door.

'In my room.'

She lets go of the pen squeezed between the key and the handle and we dart into my room and close the door. We hear muffled voices through the wall and stare at each other. Don't shoot, I send silent messages to the police, don't bring everyone clamouring to know what's happening.

'How many of them?'

'Two.'

'Two? You sure?'

'No,' she says.

Sound of metal on tiles. The pen has dropped. We hear the door open. Silence but not for long. The voices are harsh and urgent as they move into the corridor. They'll have their pistols in their hands. They want to shoot the international terrorists but where have they gone? *Look: the whore's scarf. They haven't tried to get away downstairs, they're hiding on the roof.*

We hear the police as they move out into the corridor. We hear their raised voices, then the sound of shoes on tiles and the voices move away. Do the voices follow the scarf up the spiral stairs? I open the door a crack. No one is pointing a pistol in my face. Men's voices are echoing and they are from above. How long before they come racing down the stairs? On the wall is a sign, green on white, a stick man running with flames licking at his back. An arrow points the way. We race to the end of the corridor and a door that gives out onto the fire escape. Below is a dark alley. Beyond and out of sight is the bustle of Place Barcelona.

The fire escape is metal with broad steps and a handrail, painted black around the time Reagan was president. Rust flakes off on our hands. Lucija goes first, I am a step above her head. We go down one storey, then another and stop. Below us is a gap to the ground. There is a metal ladder in brackets you are meant to slide out and down for the final escape. The ladder is normally pulled up so burglars can't climb up from the street. I squeeze beside Lucija and grip the ladder. It won't budge. Together we hammer with our palms to loosen it. No go. Rust has welded ladder to brackets.

In our scramble I left the emergency exit door open two floors above. We can hear a man's voice, excited. End of our grace time. The police know how we have escaped. Are they peering down, pistols raised for a shot? The treads of the steps shield us. I look down. Can we jump? The yard below is crammed with planks and builder's rubble and an oil drum.

We can't jump.

Go back. Quick. Up. The police are coming down, shoes scraping on the metal treads. Dirt and dried pigeon shit fall on our heads. I reach a platform with the emergency door to the second floor. The door opens with a screech. Have they heard? I'm through into the corridor, Lucija joins me. Door closed, locked. We pause a moment and hear two pairs of shoes clatter past and continue down the ladder. A shout then silence. They are wondering if we jumped into the builder's mess. Are they going to jump?

'Baz, come on.'

At the spiral staircase I stop Lucija while I race up one flight and along the corridor. The door to the fire escape stands open. I close and lock it. The police are trapped on the fire escape.

Now it is down the stairs, not running, no panic. The receptionist is behind the counter, head raised. What can he hear? Voices? Fists banging on a locked door? I bring out dinars and count out enough for both rooms for two nights. Then I add more in a separate pile. The receptionist's head is still raised but his eyes have found their way to the money.

'We've decided we'll go to Sfax tonight.' I've hardly got any breath. The words are barely a whisper and the receptionist frowns. I try a smile and thump my chest. 'Got a bit of catarrh.' I break off again. Is catarrh a French word? I've forgotten. I've forgotten everything except we need to get out. 'There'll be a train to Sfax at this time, won't there?'

He stares at me. I watch his hand, how it creeps across the counter towards the money.

'Your luggage?' he says.

'We'll be coming back so we'll leave it.'

His hand rests on the money. *Take it,* I urge. In my head. His eyes go inside my head and hear me. He drags the money across the counter and holds it against his chest. He keeps gazing at me. He doesn't look at Lucija, denying her existence.

'This morning they came and looked at the register and weren't interested. This afternoon, late, not long before you returned, they came back. This time they showed a photograph. Is she staying? I studied it. Is she staying? Now they are speaking louder. Women with blonde hair all look the same, I said. She could be staying. It could be her cousin. It could be someone else. Show us your register again. They have a different name from this morning and it matches the name in the register. So they went up to wait in her room.'

His eyes lift towards muffled voices coming down the stairwell. It can't be the police. They are trapped. Unless some hotel guest let them out.

'If they ask me I must tell them. They are police, you understand.' He pushes the money out of sight under the counter. '"Where has she gone?" they will shout in my face. They will be very angry because you made fools of them. They asked about a train to Sfax

I must say. I must tell them quickly before they lose their manners, you understand.'

He nods to himself. That is the way it is.

That nod he gave us before we left - how long does a nod last?

Place Barcelona again. The train station is on the far side of the square. When the receptionist tells the police we are going to Sfax they'll be racing down here. We lose ourselves in a bus queue. Lucija jerks her head up to speak to me.

'That pen has a history.'

Pen? Oh, the pen that stopped the door key turning. Men with guns are after us so let's worry about a lost pen. Stress does crazy things.

'A factory outside Riga on the road to Sigulda used to make rifle barrels. This was back in the Soviet days. The Soviet Union collapsed, Latvia was free, no contracts with the Red Army. So the factory switched to pens. Strong like a rifle barrel. The pen was a symbol of our freedom. I've lost it. Do you understand what it meant to me?'

'Lucija...' What do I say? 'That pen saved our lives. Without it we'd have had pistols in our faces and men with itchy trigger fingers, Think of that pen as a freedom fighter. That pen is a hero.'

Fairy tale. But we both feel calmer.

A bus comes and there is a scramble to get on. We are exposed so we move to stand in a doorway.

'Problem,' I say. 'Bardo knew the names Potter and Trifona. Now he knows Chebrikova. That's the name the police looked for in the register.'

'How does he know? It's not possible.'

'I can't say. But listen, he'll have contacts in Riga. Find out about Trifona, he says. What did she do? And someone, somehow, knew about you and Chebrikov and his wife. Did you tell anyone?'

'No.' She lets out a breath. 'Well, sometimes we gossip a bit. You know, just between friends.'

There are friends and then there are 'friends'. But I don't say it. What's the point?

'We started with four names,' I say. 'Now we're down to one.'

We make it to Monoprix before it closes for the night. A couple of shirts, underpants, socks, toothbrush, toothpaste, razor for me. Hold it. I should grow a beard as a disguise and put the razor back. Backtrack. I think of my passport photo and pick the razor up again. There are shelves of wine but we need something stronger. Vodka. There's no choice. The vodka is called Molotov. I blink. Imagine offering your friends a Molotov cocktail. My father was an expert at making Molotov cocktails. He learnt how when Red Army tanks rolled into Budapest in 1956. Molotov vodka it must be.

We walk away from the centre, past the train station. The street gets darker and less crowded. On the right a building has a sign saying simply Maghreb. Is it for the hotel or the café beside it? All we have had to eat since breakfast is some dates and cheese so we go into the café. There is a chicken on a spit so I order that and chips. There are two tables of men. They stop talking to look at us. Watch their faces. Do they frown? Do their eyebrows rise? Do they mutter about us? No. A television on the wall has a game show that no one gives a damn about. Not surprising. The game show seems to be in Italian. The food comes with salad and a dish of red harissa. I order Coca-Cola and under cover of the table I add slugs of vodka. We eat the meal in silence.

The hotel next door is like all hotels near railway stations. It is a place for people who have missed the last train in life. There is a bell on the reception counter and when I bang it a man appears from a back room. You don't see many fezzes in Tunisia but he wears one. The fez looks tired as if he wears it in bed.

'For the whole night?' is his response when I ask for a room. That tells you everything about the hotel.

'Provided it has two beds.'

He looks at Lucija and back to me and shrugs. 'Your passport.'

He produces the registration *fiche* and I write FAZEKAS in bold capitals so even the dimmest cop will know I'm not the wanted criminal Potter.

'Twenty dinars,' the man says.

The stairs are lit by a forty-watt bulb. Half-way up Lucija stops.

'He only gave us one key.'

What this means has only just struck her. I say, 'When we registered at the Salammbo you had a separate room and had to fill in a separate *fiche* It's the law. You were Chebrikova. But Bardo knows that name now. He probably won't check a hotel like this but it's a risk. The police aren't looking for a Hungarian called Fazekas so that's who we are. We have no choice.'

She stares at me.

'Lucija, it's got two beds.'

'Oh,' she says. She turns over in her mind what I have told her and starts climbing the stairs again.

We're in the bedroom now. While I lock the door Lucija gazes all round our home for the next ten or twelve hours. Yes, there are two beds though they are pushed together. On the wall is a framed photo of the Alps under snow. The curtains on the window are already closed as if no guests have ever wanted to look at the outside world. In a corner there is a basin with a mirror above it. A bidet has a well-used bar of pink soap and a towel that could double as a table napkin. There is one bedside table and one chair. There is a closet for people with not many clothes. That's it. And the two beds.

We both turn to stare at the wall with the closet. We can hear a man's voice from next door followed by a woman's laughter then the man again. No idea what he is saying.

'Have we come to a brothel?' Lucija asks.

Well, there's a question. Before I can answer she goes on.

'No. In a brothel you don't get two beds in the room.'

She lowers herself on the edge of a bed, frowning at her knees. It's a ridiculous situation. It's still early and there is no distraction, no television, not even a radio. We have no books. We just have ourselves and the beds.

Wrong. We have the vodka. There is a pink plastic mug on the shelf above the basin. I inspect it. The last user had deep red lipstick. I wash and dry the mug. I fill it two-thirds full with vodka.

'It's been a very long day.' I hand the mug to Lucija. 'We've had a bad scare. We need this.'

She sips. 'I don't like the taste of vodka.'

'That's why Russians knock it back in one go.'

'I know how Russians drink vodka. Half the people in my country are Russian. I know all about Russians and now they are here, three of them in a boat. Matt is hunting them and we are after Matt.'

That sums up the situation. She puts the mug to her lips, hesitates, and takes a bigger mouthful. She makes a sour face. 'Your turn.'

Without Coca-Cola it is fiery going down with a strange aftertaste. What's it made from? Beetroot? Figs? I think of Mary – before we were married – and drinking vodka in her bedroom after we had had a shock like Lucija and I have just had. But it's complicated to explain to Lucija and I'm weary.

'My turn,' Lucija says.

We shunt the mug back and forth until it's empty. We need more. I refill the mug.

'I had a colleague,' I say. True. Mary and I weren't married then. Why is Lucija staring at me? Oh, I didn't finish speaking. 'Used to put a bit of toothpaste in the vodka. Turned it into a sort of mint cocktail.'

She is still staring at me. 'Isn't it strange making a drink so terrible that it's better with toothpaste?'

'It's best really cold. You know, out of the freezer. Sort of numbs the taste buds.'

We seem to have run out of things to say about vodka. I tip the mug back and drain it.

'Do you want more?'

'We should try to get some sleep.' She considers me, sitting down on the hard chair. I moved it so I was facing her perched on the edge of the bed. 'You'll have to turn round while I get undressed.'

For a moment I say nothing. Through the wall is the sound of the woman. She gives a moan. Why do I think she is faking it?

'I have a better idea. I'll turn off the light. Then I won't see you.'

The room is darkened but the curtains are unlined. Light from the street seeps through. As my eyes adjust I see Lucija, but Lucija as a ghost. Her head is angled in my direction. I turn away but my ears catch the sounds of her undressing, cloth rubbing over skin. The room is small and she is close. There is an eddy of air – I feel it – as she eases out of her blouse. Tiny chink of metal as she undoes a belt buckle. Then a zip.

My neck muscles are tense. I roll my head round and round to relax them and end up gazing at the mirror. It's not Lucija I see but a phantom moving arms and shoulders. It could be a sequence from a dream. I don't intend to watch but there is a fascination to it. She ignores the wire coathangers in the closet but rolls her clothes into a ball and lays them on the floor. Her head turns. She is looking in the mirror. Can she see my eyes?

'Why are you just sitting there?'

'There's no room for us to undress at the same time.'

I turn back from the mirror. My eyes have adjusted to the dim light through the threadbare curtains. She is standing at the foot of the bed. So near. She's wearing bra and pants. There's enough light to see that. Then she disappears under the covers. Does she turn her back on me as I undress? I bundle my clothes up and put them on the chair.

We lie in our separate beds. Why was I exhausted before and alert now? Because she is there. We are not close friends. Then I think back over the past three days from that wake-up email of the body outlined on cobbles in blue chalk and everything that followed. You can't go through all that without forming a bond, trusting each other, sharing intimate thoughts. I'm not surprised when she speaks.

'Do you think he slept with her?'

Not surprised but it is difficult to frame an answer. Matt and Rym have been on her mind all day and in the conspiracy of darkness I am to share what is gnawing at her.

'He needed somewhere to sleep.'

It sounds false. Even as I say it I know that. I catch an impatient movement from Lucija.

'I said *with* her.'

Are there blue chalk marks on the headboard of Rym's bed? That's what has been nagging at her since she met Rym this morning. Still I try to wriggle out of it.

'How would I know?'

'Baz, you're a man. You've met the woman. From a man's perspective: have they slept together? Have they made love?'

'You have to think of the culture here,' I say. I'm edging closer to saying it. 'It's an Arab country but the French influence is strong.'

'What does that mean?'

'It's not just what the man wants.' Stop squirming. 'If Rym wanted to sleep with Matt, then yes.'

'Oh.'

That's all. Oh. I think of what she said on the stairs when she learnt we'd be sharing this room. It was the same: oh.

'In other words,' Lucija goes on, 'yes.'

I try to turn her mind in a different direction.

'I've never asked this until now but I think I need to know.'

'What?' she says.

'When Matt finds Bardo what does he intend to do?'

She knows what Matt intends. She must do. But there's no immediate reply. I hear her body shift under the cover. That's how close we are. She takes a breath.

'Kill him.'

CHAPTER 8

'Good morning. British embassy.'

Not in Arabic, not in French, in English.

'I want to speak to Mr Hipkiss.'

'One moment.'

The line goes to sleep, no Vivaldi's Four Seasons, no Greensleeves. I'm using the same telephone in Place Barcelona as yesterday. Lucija is getting money from an ATM. Above the trees I see blue sky and clouds moving fast.

'Hipkiss.'

This is the new slimline diplomatic service, no protective secretary.

'I am a friend of the Queen across the Water.'

That's all. I'm not prepared for the avalanche of words.

'Hmm, yes, *marvellous*. Hoping you'd ring. It's about that chap who designed our new embassy, inspired architect really when you consider the budget constraint with the Treasury breathing down our necks and the vital need for security in these troubled times, details like that which I know you're after so we must meet and I'll pass on my wisdom but please don't come here as I'm just about to leave to see a man about a dog so I suggest a wee trip to somewhere with an enchanting view and no telephone calls to disturb us.'

All in one breath leaving me no time to speak for the tape recorder.

'Fine. I was just...'

'Fine indeed. So I suggest you have the real Tunisian experience and take the little train out to Sidi Bou Said, charming place though it is a mite too pretty for its own good because it attracts the guided tour crowd who think they're being really daring leaving the hotel sunloungers, so what you do is leave Sidi Bou Said station and walk to the roundabout then go left up the hill to the old village and I'll be in the café on the steps and you can't mistake me because I wear a Panama hat, say in one and a half hours, does that suit you?'

'All right. So I'll be…' I drift to a stop. 'Are you there?'

I'm in Barcelona Square and nobody recognises my face. When I look round the only suspicious thing is four women sharing a mobile phone and all speaking at once. No worries.

I'm still holding the telephone. Its silence has a solid quality. It wants me to speak. It wants to send someone to comfort me. I've never thought of silence like this before.

I put the phone back on the hook.

She's changed. Lucija is not the same person who watched me make a fool of myself at St Pancras station. She was in command then as she went about unravelling the mystery of Matt's death and return to life. She knew there was danger in Latvia, danger in London and danger in Tunisia. But then she was hunting for Matt. Now she is the one being hunted.

We are walking from Sidi Bou Said station. We are two suspects, wanted by the police, with our photos in the papers. People walking past ignore us. A couple of tourists, that's us.

'Baz.'

'What?'

'Look ahead.'

There it is, the roundabout Hipkiss told us about. And there are two police astride motorbikes. They are looking our way.

'We can't turn around.' I say the obvious. 'They'll come after us.' We carry on. 'We're a couple of sightseers. We're on holiday. We're having fun.' One of the cops says something to his partner. 'Lucija, talk to me. Smile. Laugh. We're having a great time in lovely Tunisia.'

'I can't laugh.'

The cops are looking at us again.

'We mustn't look worried. Worried means guilty. Remember that sleazy flea pit we slept in last night. Remember swigging vodka and taking our clothes off in the dark and not watching in the mirror. That's one for the memoirs. Go on, talk to me.'

'My brain has frozen.'

The cops are about forty steps ahead. Then we have to get past them.

'We have to keep speaking. Tell me something important in your life. Or a joke. Just do it.'

'In 1991 when we were struggling to be free of the Soviet Union, Russian troops shot and killed my husband. This was in Riga. I was there. I saw it. Is that a joke? Are you going to laugh, Baz?'

'No. I am managing to smile but that's not how I feel. Look at me. See how happy I look. I know I should look shocked. Your husband was killed and my face has frozen with a smile. Oh God.'

'What?'

'One of the cops is staring at you. Yes, definitely.'

'Why me?'

'Because you're an attractive woman, that's why.'

'Oh.'

'Ten, nine, eight.' I'm counting the steps. 'Say something. Tell me more about your past.'

'I met Matt and we became lovers. Then I got a message that he was dead and I got one of those stupid thoughts that won't go away… I am not good for men, they always die.'

'That's not true. I'm not dead.'

'Baz, you're not my lover. Even last night… there we were… that cheap hotel… beds pushed together… I half expected you …'

Her voice trails off. We both stop talking. The police have seen something they don't like. It's not us. It's a car. The driver didn't indicate or he's on his mobile phone or he's not wearing his seatbelt. I don't know. But the car is past the police and they turn their bikes and are after him. We watch them out of sight and then she turns to me.

'We did it, didn't we?' she says.

'We did. Yes.'

We go up the hill from the roundabout and enter tourist land. There are toy camels, fezzes that no one wears, signs promising pizza, ceramics spilling out of shops, stands of postcards. I hesitate then pick up a postcard.

'What are you doing? Saying wish you were here to your editor?'

'Just checking.' I have half turned round. 'Could be someone following.'

She puts a hand on my shoulder and leans in to look at the postcard and just naturally back the way we have come. Nobody. I replace the postcard. We reach the old village. It could have been moved here from southern Spain, one of those *pueblos blancos*. Buildings are cubes of white set at angles with doors and window frames painted blue. The street has cobbles, palm trees sigh in the wind.

Lucija touches my shoulder again but I've already seen it. Ahead is a café spilling down steps. There are four or five little sitting areas, the smallest with room for a single table. A man in a Panama hat has a perfect view of anybody approaching. He's wearing a light grey suit and a tie with red and blue stripes. He's watching us. He leans a little to one side so he sees past us. He is checking we are coming alone. A pro.

No need to introduce ourselves. On the table is a copy of today's *Tunis Matin*. As we approach Hipkiss focuses on our faces, down to the paper, up to our faces again.

'I'm happy to say you do not photograph well.'

I look down again at the paper. Rym hasn't done any retouching; no fake hairstyle for Lucija, no Clark Gable moustache for me. Guidance would not approve. She has used a light grey tone over our passport photos so we stare at the world through a clammy fog. Hipkiss half rises from his chair to shake Lucija's hand, then mine. He turns to call out to the old waiter in something a lot better than phrasebook Arabic.

'Your Arabic is impressive,' I say.

He looks in my face and for a moment I think he's not going to respond. Finding nothing devious in my remark or my face he says, 'My first posting was in Lebanon which was *interesting*. Know what I mean? I'd done Arabic at university and there were times, nights particularly, when I wished I'd chosen, oh, say Italian, even Thai. Syrians seemed to have taken Beirut over. They were hiding behind every palm tree. My face got to be too well known. I had to leave. I was looking forward to a bit of home leavc before being posted out here. It's safe here. When you've had your car booby-trapped you appreciate safe. True? To be honest Tunis can be a bit dull. Until now. Thanks to you.'

He smiles at Lucija. Is that veiled hostility or a compliment? Lucija doesn't know how to take it.

'Is your Panama a veteran of Lebanon too?' I ask.

'No, alas.' Hipkis sighs. 'It's a successor. I was much attached to the original but it didn't leave with me. It was on the front seat of my car and I was just coming out of the apartment block when my driver turned the ignition key. The hat was reduced to fragments.'

Lucija looks at me. The silence is terrible. Never mind the bloody hat, how about the driver? Is it some kind of test? Hipkiss seems to be watching how we react. How should we react? I have no idea because at that moment the waiter arrives with a tray of coffee cups. He stands while Hipkiss removes the newspaper and brings out from his briefcase some printed sheets. *The new British embassy,* I read, *a breath of fresh air.*

'For your article,' Hipkiss says. 'Full of fascinating facts. Lotfi Rebai was the architect. Local chap, quite brilliant. He used three thousand cubic metres of reinforced concrete just for the foundations. Need more than a plastic bomb to make a dent in that.'

The waiter hobbles away.

'*Hal tatahadath alearby? La?'* Hipkiss looks at me and then at Lucija. 'So you don't speak Arabic butt you speak French? Anyone who is educated here speaks French.'

'I speak Latvian,' Lucija says. 'And English. Also Russian.'

'Well, Russian may come in handy.'

'I'm here as the French speaker,' I say.

'Also,' Hipkiss says, 'you are a man. That is important. Tunisia is a confused country. It is trying to marry its traditions with the twenty-first century and finding it uncomfortable. It is still a male-oriented society. Rym is very much an exception, bless her.'

Lucija leans forward to speak but something holds her back.

Hipkiss picks up the fact sheets about the new embassy. 'Concrete, concrete, concrete. Personally I hate the stuff. I loved the old embassy building. Seen it? Near the medina.'

'Seen the outside.'

'Wise man. The inside was stripped. I'll tell you a little story to show you the man you are up against. Bardo, I mean. I was moving out of my rickety old office to come to this new Alcatraz. Furniture gone. Carpet sold to some scoundrel in the medina. Computers and microfiches transferred under armed guard. Guess what was found behind the painting of Her Maj smiling her inscrutable smile? A tiny microphone. My office had been bugged. It was the office traditionally used by whoever had my responsibilities. Going back a few years that was you-know-who. My dirty mind says it was a leaving present from Bardo to his successors.'

'Don't you do an electronic sweep?' Lucija says. 'I worked for the Citizenship Board in Riga. Sound boring? Well, I had to track down former KGB spies, Red Army officers and Russian mafia because we didn't want them. So I was a target. The bad men wanted to know what I knew about them. My office was checked once a month for bugs. It should have been every week but…' she shrugs.

Hipkiss gazes at Lucija a moment. I think he is reassessing her. Until now he has seen her as a worried girlfriend. She has changed into a person he feels kinship with: someone worth spying on.

'The bug they found was prehistoric in its technology and its battery was long dead. Shame really. Rather spoils the story.'

'No bugs behind the pictures in the new embassy,' Lucija says. 'Did Matt come there to see you?'

'Ah.' He says it as if Lucija has asked an astute question. 'We are not having this get-together at the embassy for a very good reason. New listening devices – the most sophisticated ones – are undetectable. Or nearly. They're tiny. They can be slipped into a light fitting or buried in concrete and you'll never know. Hundreds of people worked on constructing the new embassy. It only takes one.'

'But you did have a meeting with Matt.'

He looks away down the steps and then back at her. 'The Queen across the Water contacted me. Our agreed signal. I went to a public telephone and called her at a number she uses, but not often. She told me your friend was coming to Tunis and she'd given him my number. Well thanks, I thought, nothing like spreading my name about. To do with Bardo, she said. She has this fixation with him, the cause of all her woes. I was to give your friend all the assistance I could. Her actual words – you're ready? *Give him a leg up so he can kick Bardo in the fucking arse.* That's the way she speaks, right?'

Hipkiss pecks at his coffee cup. He looks surprised to find it empty.

'Your friend telephoned.' Hipkiss pauses. Something makes him uneasy. I can see the frown in the shadow of his Panama. 'Late afternoon. That's when we spoke. I knew from the Queen across the Water that it was important. But there is a world of difference between being important and being urgent. We spoke,' he says again. There's another pause. I think he wants to get everything right in his mind. Now it is me he speaks to as if telling Lucija makes him uncomfortable. 'He gave me his name. You remember this morning I gave you no opening when you could use your name but he came straight out with it. "This is Matt Clough." Then he went on. "It's to do with Bardo." He came straight out with that too. Alarm bells started ringing in my head – shut him up, get him off the line. "Oh, the Bardo *museum*," I gushed. "Marvellous place, one of the wonders of the world, we must meet, I can tell you fascinating things." He used to be in our shadow world years ago and he picked up I wasn't happy with talking on the phone. He muttered something. "Got you. Good. We'll meet." Then I'm afraid I had to put a brake on it. Couldn't be that evening. I'm a commercial counsellor. That's my cover at the embassy. I have to live my cover however tedious it is. I had a meeting with people from the transport ministry and the airport authority because of development plans. Drumming up business for Britain, that's what diplomats do now. I made a rendezvous for the next morning.'

'Here?' I ask.

'Not here. This is not my office away from the office. Never develop a routine.'

'How did he sound?' Lucija asks.

'Impatient,' Hipkiss says.

'He wasn't pleased to be made to wait?'

'I didn't realise it was urgent. I wanted to help but he's not one of us and I had official business I couldn't cancel.'

'Couldn't you have seen him after your airport meeting?'

'Could have but didn't. If he'd told me it was urgent…'

'You didn't give him a chance,' Lucija cuts in. 'you shut him up.'

There is a moment's silence. They stare at each other. Lucija is not diplomatic in pointing out the fact. As Hipkiss continues her mouth opens in disbelief.

'Anyway I told him I'd meet him at nine-thirty next morning. Take the TGM – that's the suburban rattletrap you came on – out to La Marsa. End of the line. Walk out of the station and dawdle. There's a pastry shop there so buy a sticky bun and eat it on the street. If he remembered his training he'd be checking other dawdlers, though heaven knows in this country there are always a lot of them hanging about. The main road curves round to the left and has flash restaurants but carry on down to the road that backs onto the beach. Go along that road at half past nine and I'll approach from the other direction. Classic encounter procedure, lets us both check the other's back. Recognition signals: I'll wear my Panama hat, he is to carry a handkerchief as if he has a cold and blow his nose a lot. It's a crash meeting out in the field but everything is agreed, everything is fine.'

Lucija shakes her head. 'You told him all this on an open line from your office?'

'She's right, you know. You wouldn't let Matt talk and then you make arrangements to meet on an open line.'

'Those are two different things,' Hipkiss says. 'And I'm always arranging meetings on the phone. Shall I go on?' He looks at Lucija and then at me.

'What happened?' I ask.

'Windy morning. Spot of rain in the night but the clouds have broken and there's a good spring sun. I'm early. It's what I liked to do in Beirut when I was uneasy. You know, check who's sitting in a car, who's idling on a street corner reading a newspaper.'

He straightens in his chair.

'Your friend, he's come early too. Same reason, most likely. Check the scene. Perhaps he's had a bad experience in the past.'

'He had. He had to run for his life.'

Hipkiss glances at her and waits but she says no more.

'No one is swimming,' Hipkiss continues, 'not at this time of year. I am walking along the beach road, eyes left, eyes right. Everything normal, no shady idlers. Then oops. Gust of wind blows off my Panama. Helter skelter it goes with me in hot pursuit. Twenty metres, thirty metres until gotcha. I jam the hat on my head and keep a hand on it this time. Then, looking ahead, I see this man striding towards me. He digs a tissue out of his pocket and makes a big performance over blowing his nose and Bob's your uncle. We make the rendezvous only it is twenty-five minutes early.'

Why is Hipkiss taking so long? Laying the base for the big scene to come? Maybe, just maybe, he feels guilty about what he is going to tell us.

'Right off I notice the tension in his face, thin lips, white marks under his eyes. I know what it's like to be on the run, trusting nobody. Except he has to trust me.'

He thinks about this and nods.

'We talk. Not small talk, how are you today, none of that. He launches straight in as if he has no time to spare. He uses the name Beatrice – not the Queen across the Water – says she spoke well of me and what do I know of Bardo. Big question because I know a lot. I'm thinking what to say and your friend seemed angry. Why am I holding back. All right. I know someone in the Garde Nationale who is good for tittle-tattle. He told me about a boat from Malta that came in out of the storm. Something odd about it. Russians. None of them sailors.'

'Did they come here?' Lucija points down towards the sea.

'That I don't know.'

'But you were already taking an interest in Russians,' Lucija says.

'Taking an interest in Russians poking around in the Med - is Putin planning something? - that's part of my job description. I'm not the only one. There's Rym Dakhli who works on *Tunis Matin*. Her sources are almost as good as mine. Her heroes are Woodward and Bernstein. She's always on the look-out for a Tunisian Watergate. I've already seen Rym, your friend said.'

Lucija takes a breath and I think she is going to explode. Hipkiss notices this too.

'Wait,' Hipkiss says. 'We are strolling slowly. We're old chums chatting. More than idle chat; your friend was so intense.' Hipkiss has slipped into the present tense because he is reliving this. 'I have been concentrating on him. Now I turn my head – I don't know why - and see a man on the beach where there hasn't been anybody before. Who is he? Why is he there? He's not a swimmer, not exercising a dog. He's jogging or pretend jogging because it's not easy with sand. He sees me watching him and he pulls up abruptly and tugs at a mobile phone in his pocket. It's a struggle because he's wearing a tight lycra tracksuit. He gets it out and punches in a number and he is gazing fixedly in our direction. Red alert. I swivel to warn your friend but he's gone. He's across the road and streaking over an empty stretch of land. Building site, I guess. He's jumping from one stone to another, skipping across patches of creeper.'

'He runs every day,' Lucija says.

Hipkiss shakes his head as if he can't believe how fast Matt was running.

'That jogger on the beach scrambled up and set off after him until he realised it was hopeless and came back to me. By now a police car had come into view, no siren which they normally love, but going fast until it reached me. Three men bundle out, plain clothes. "Stop, you stop," one shouts. In English, mark you. They knew your friend was English. One is holding a pistol and is pointing after your friend. It's hopeless because he is already too far. He lets off a shot anyway until a colleague grabs his wrist. A foreigner shot by the police is so troublesome to explain. Bad for the tourist trade.'

Hipkiss tries a little joke but gets no smile from Lucija.

'What happened to Matt?'

'He's got to the esplanade road and…' Hipkiss shakes his head. 'He disappeared. Simple as that. There are always taxis. Or he could have gone into an apartment block and exited through a service door. There's a bit of a market. Maybe he lost himself there. Or the toilet of a café. This wasn't a grand slam police sweep. This was just Bardo using a few contacts.'

Like last night at the Salammbo, I think, just a pair of them.

'Then the police were onto me, shouting all at once, Arabic, French, bit of English. I was polite. I told them the man approached and asked about a decent restaurant and we got chatting. They got a bit heavy and the chap with the pistol waved it under my nose. "Stop!" I shouted at the top of my voice. That took them back as no one shouts at the police here. I got out my passport and pressed it against the muzzle of the pistol. "Are you going to shoot me through my diplomatic passport? Try explaining that to your president." That was in French. I switched to Arabic. *"Sayeb zebi."* That was the end. You don't swear at the police in Tunisia unless you are someone with a lot of clout. They didn't say another word.'

'And that's why you wouldn't let me get a word in on the telephone,' I say.

'You never know who's listening. Never.'

Hipkiss has closed his eyes. For a moment he seems drained. Lucija is not satisfied.

'But the police were onto Matt because of your phone call.'

'Matt's phone call,' he corrects. 'And they were Bardo's contacts not the whole Tunisian police force.'

'Matt had to run for his life. Where is he now?'

'No idea. I guess he wouldn't dare contact me again. No one has mentioned his name to me.'

Lucija pushes back in her chair. On her face is a look of bafflement because she is no further forward. There is underlying anger too – at Hipkiss and Bardo, at Matt for his betrayal of her, and Rym of course. I am the only one who escapes.

I break the silence.

'Your friend in the Garde National who mentioned the boat from Malta that came in from the storm…'

'Yes?'

'Russians on board you said. There was also an Englishman.'

'It was the Russians he mentioned.'

'The Englishman was Bardo. We're certain of it. The boat is called the Calypso. It was seen at Cap Bon. It was headed this way. But where is it now? Has Matt caught up with it?'

'Bloody hell. Bardo with Russians. Of course.' Hipkiss has been thinking. 'Why have I been so obtuse?'

'That strikes a bell?'

'Oh yes. What is your friend up against? What was the boat's name again?'

'Calypso.'

'Right. You've got to see Lannouz.'

'Who?'

Hipkiss doesn't answer. He is already going down the café steps.

CHAPTER 9

Ten seconds ago Hipkiss was in a rush. Now he stops.

'My car's there.' He nods to the left at a car with diplomatic plates.

When Lucija starts to move he touches her arm to restrain her.

'Check first,' he says. 'Always check. The CD plate makes the car stand out. Or I could have been followed here. Maybe the waiter made a phone call.'

The first tourist coach of the day has arrived. A guide holds up a green, white and red flag on a pole.

'Italian,' Hipkiss says. 'Cruise ship.'

He watches as the tour guide leads his party off. He stares past the coach. Then he leads us to the car. He tells Lucija to sit in the front passenger seat next to him.

'You're a tourist,' he says, 'eager to see the sights.'

He checks the mirror before he starts the engine, checks again. He takes off his Panama and hands it to Lucija.

'Take good care of this. I don't want to lose a second one.'

'Why? What do you mean?'

I'm in the back so I saw his eyes rise to the mirror. They rise again.

'We've got company,' he says. 'Joker in the Peugeot wearing dark glasses. We were coming down the steps and he saw us. He started the engine and his riding lights came on. Who told him we were at the café? Waiter told Bardo, I suppose. Bugger, bugger, bugger. I liked that café.'

'What does he want?' Lucija says.

'You,' Hipkiss says.

'Me?'

'You are trying to catch up with your lover so they only have to follow you.'

'So if we just stay here and don't go anywhere...'

'Won't work. Bardo will use his Plan B.'

'What's that?'

'I don't know, do I? But how about this. Kidnap you and tell you his merry men will rape you until you tell him where Matt is.'

'But I can't tell him because I don't know.'

'True. You would be in for a very nasty time.'

'Oh.'

'Right,' says Hipkiss, 'now we'll do it my way. Let's see if that joker can drive.'

We pull out. Hipkiss is driving sedately.

'I'm giving him a chance. Yes, definitely following us. He could have overtaken but he didn't even try. All right. Lucija, you may want to put the Panama in front of your face so you don't see.'

'Why?'

'This could be a mite hairy?'

'Hairy?'

It's a bit of slang she doesn't know.

In the back I see Hipkiss's eyes flick up to the mirror, back ahead, then to the right. Great view of the sea. Sidi Bou Said is built on a cliff but after a minute the cliff gives way to something that Is only steep. A turn-off leads to a road going down to the marina. A truck is coming towards us. Without warning Hipkiss hauls the wheel over and we take the side road down. We have cut right in front of the truck. Long blare of horn.

'You OK?' Hipkiss says to Lucija.

She doesn't answer.

'Right,' Hipkiss says. 'This is how the Americans have it: pedal to the metal. Second thoughts, don't put the hat in front of your face. I need you.'

'Why?'

'I'm driving. You look in the wing mirror. Keep your eyes on our tail.'

How could I have got Hipkiss so wrong? It's the Panama hat. Makes him look a Foreign Office gent. He's not.

'Before I went to Beirut and got my Panama blown up…' Pause while Hipkiss changes gear… 'I had survival training. Driving was a big part. Bugger its official name. We called it *Run for your Life*.'

I can see his face in the mirror. Lips parted, teeth clenched. Then his face changes. A quick smile. I look ahead. The road is going down, down, down. Houses on either side, big gardens, an old colonial villa with bougainvilla over the terrace. Like Mongi's. Yesterday. That was a long time ago.

'He's still there?'

'Yes,' Lucija says.

'Ha,' Hipkiss says.

What does that mean?

The road curves. Out the other side there's a truck half blocking the way. Hipkiss slams on the brake. Squeal of tyres. A man is unloading crates of water. He turns towards us. He's shouting something. Hipkiss is fighting with the steering wheel. He hits the kerb and the right wheels lift up. The car is going to flip over. No it doesn't. We are past the truck and back on the road.

'Our friend?'

'He's doing what you did,' Lucija says.

'Is he gaining on us?'

'No.'

'Are we pulling ahead?'

'No.'

'Damn.'

Houses look more modern. Gardener holding a hose jerks round and splashes Lucija's window.

'Lucky that wasn't a gun,' Hipkiss mutters.

Around a bend and Hipkiss hits the brake pedal. Speedboat on a trailer is parked at the side of the road. We squeeze past.

'OK?' Hipkiss asks.

'Me or the tail?'

Hipkiss doesn't answer. We are aiming straight towards a small bay. Yachts and pleasure boats tied up at a quay. Blue sea beyond. An esplanade runs beside the sea and then bends away. We're going to join it. There's a crossing ahead. A hundred metres. Traffic lights are green for us. There are two motorbike cops at the side of the road. Same pair we saw earlier? Surely not. Fifty metres, forty metres, thirty metres. Traffic lights go amber. A car is waiting to cross. The lights go red. Hipkiss is not going to stop. Nor is the other car. Hipkiss just makes it and we hear the other car's horn as we flash past. Doppler effect. A wail. At the last minute Hipkiss hauled over the wheel and now he corrects.

'Chummy make it?'

'Can't see him in the mirror,' Lucija says.

I squirm round to look back. 'He's swerving round the back of the other car.'

Then we hear the siren wail of the motorbike cops.

'The cavalry's coming,' Hipkiss says. 'They won't bother us. They'll see the CD plate. Diplomats aren't worth the hassle. But chummy…'

The sirens grow louder. Nobody speaks. Then the sirens begin to fade. I think it's the first time Hipkiss has taken his eyes off the road to look in his mirror. He lifts his foot off the accelerator. 'One cop at the side, the other in front. Slowing him down.' His eyes shift in the mirror to look at me. 'Damn, but he was good.'

'Welcome to Carthage,' Hipkiss says. 'The Romans had a party here and left it in a mess but it's been tidied up.'

We are passing a triangle of public garden with a headless torso. A gang of boys is kicking a football. I touch Lucija's shoulder.

'Remember the boy with the football in the medina? Death points the way?'

'Baz, that was yesterday.'

Right. A lifetime ago.

A station has a sign Carthage Amilcar. We swing left. The villas are set back from the road in gardens shaded by catalpas. Rich people live here. Very rich people have gate houses with guards. Their heads swivel to keep us in sight. Just past the Greek embassy Hipkiss turns into a side road and parks.

'The CD plate explains why we are here. We are just popping in to say hello to the Greek ambassador.'

'But we're not,' I say.

'No, we're not. I don't much care for ouzo.'

We walk back to the main road and go right. The next building is another grand villa, two storeys high, a garden filled with hibiscus and roses. When we get to the gate a man in uniform steps out of a sentry box. Hipkiss speaks to him in Arabic, holding out his diplomatic passport and moving it from side to side like a stage magician. The sentry frowns at the passport while he has a telephone conversation. The frown stays on his face but he nods. The gate is rolled back.

'Bravo,' Hipkiss mutters.

A sign announces the building in Arabic and underneath in French: *Centre Tunisien des Etudes Stratégiques*. Hipkiss slows to a stroll as we walk down the drive. Tall palm trees could be a guard of honour. 'We are coming to see Lannouz,' Hipkiss says.'The sentry said he was "in conference". That can mean anything from seeing the president to being on the potty. Then there was a correction – conference over - and here we are.'

'But why are we here?' Lucija asks. 'Why are we seeing this man?'

There are two steps up to the front door. As we climb them the door opens and we go in. A slim young man with a clipped moustache is waiting. Hipkiss greets him in a barrage of Arabic as if they were old chums. A nod is the only response. Chairs line the walls but not for us. We are shown into a meeting room. The young man murmurs something and leaves.

'He says to have the goodness to wait two minutes. This is not so severe as Lannouz being in conference but there is no telling if this means two minutes or a Tunisian two minutes.'

Hipkiss shrugs. He doesn't sit down. He believes we won't wait long.

'All right. The Centre for Strategic Studies is the meeting point of political, military, academic and security pundits. What is strategic about a little country, a blip on the top of Africa, you object? Perhaps you didn't actually object, Lucija, but I saw you frown.'

'We're wasting time.'

'No. It'll be worth it. It is because little Tunisia is not a big player that the Centre works. When there is a difficult situation everybody contributes, everybody sees the problem from a different point of view, everybody benefits.'

'So it is a sort of Spies'R'Us.'

Hipkiss ignores this. He gazes through the French windows at the manicured garden. Distant sounds of pans and crockery and women's voices reach us.

'So what is Lannouz? Some ten star General? Professor of Trigonometry?'

Hipkiss turns back. 'He was a career diplomat.'

Lucija shakes her head. 'Has this great career diplomat seen Matt?'

Now Hipkiss shakes his head. 'You don't understand. We are approaching this from a different angle.'

'I think we should leave. This is a waste of time. Baz, you're very quiet. Baz?'

I am looking at the door we came through. Hipkiss turns and smiles. Finally Lucija turns.

The man standing in the doorway must be Lannouz. How long has he been listening to us squabbling?

There's a small smile on his face. It stays there as he walks forward, speaking to Hipkiss. I think the smile is part of him. Look, it says, I am your friend and whatever you need I can help you. Lannouz has come up to Hipkiss and is shaking his hand while he speaks rapid Arabic. He asks questions and Hipkiss manages to squeeze in answers and then Lannouz holds up his hand.

'Please do not think I was being discourteous speaking to my friend. I was establishing which language was best for us to speak. So. One of us speaks Hungarian, one speaks Latvian and also Russian, two of us speak Arabic, three of us speak French, but all four of us speak English, so that is settled.'

Lannouz is in his fifties, trim and fit. His hair is neat, black but shot through with grey. Hipkiss wears a diplomat's suit but Lannouz has tan slacks and an open-necked blue shirt with a button-down collar. He is the picture of a banker or an international attorney or indeed a diplomat relaxing,

He takes a couple of steps so he is in front of Lucija. 'I was at the United Nations in the dying days of the Soviet Union. So far as I was aware no Latvians were in their delegation. I suspect it was felt that free New York air would give them unhealthy thoughts.'

'If there were any Latvians they would have been spies.'

'Madame, I beg you, do not be too harsh about spies. If spies did not tell their masters what their enemies were thinking there would be many more wars.'

'So,' Lucija says, 'are you hinting you are spies here?'

'We are searchers after truth. Tunisia does not wish to have enemies but sometimes others wish to impose themselves on us. We need to know about that.'

He was going to say more but he stops. The same young man with a moustache comes into the room with a tray of orange juice and we sit at an oval table. The silence is too much for Lucija.

'You don't have far to look for an enemy because…'

Hipkiss cuts her short. Does the young man understand English? He is taking no risks.

'Lucija, have you tasted the orange juice? It's really special.'

Lucija frowns and then gives a slight nod. Got you. Close mouth.

Lannouz chips in. 'Our cook has an admirer in the Greek embassy. Not the ambassador but one of the gardeners. They have planted orange trees from Corfu – very special – and the gardener gives our cook a basket of oranges over the wall. I don't know what she gives him in return.' There is the hint of a smile on his face.

We watch the young man leave with his tray.

'Back to business,' Lannouz begins. 'Gerald rang me earlier.'

Who's Gerald? It turns out it is Hipkiss.

'I said that two good friends of mine are on the run from certain corrupt police and need help and it is urgent.'

'Urgent,' Lannouz says. 'All right. In two sentences tell me who you are and how I can advise you. Anything longer might incriminate you. And possibly me.'

'Better,' Lucija says, 'I'll tell you in one sentence. I have come to Tunisia to find Matt Clough whose life is in danger.'

'Matt Clough?' Lannouz thinks about this and shakes his head. 'Is he one of the intelligence fraternity?'

'He is my lover.'

'An excellent reason for finding him. Of course, if you find him your life is in danger too. Who is the danger man?'

'Bardo.'

'Bardo?' He looks at Hipkiss. 'This is true?'

'He took a flight from London to Malta and then hired a speedboat. It was caught in that storm and put in at a small harbour – no name that I know of – and next day continued sailing west. That's all I can tell you. We are almost certain it was him on the boat plus three Russians.'

'Bardo with Russians?'

Hipkiss nods.

Lannouz looks at Lucija, holding her eyes. I would say he was judging her and making a decision. 'If this is the situation – and I'm not saying you might be lying but there may be other facts - I would say that the search for your lover has become strategic.'

'Strategic,' she says. She frowns a little as if the word troubles her. Whole areas of her life are a blank but I do know in her job she questioned people and listened carefully to what they said. Is this man to be trusted? Is he hiding something? Where do we go from here?

The journalist in me has been quiet but now I say: 'We are after Bardo because we know that is where Matt is going. But for you it is strategic because Russians and Bardo have business together? Why? What business? What sort of Russians?'

Lannouz nods. 'We are used to Russians.The St Petersburg Symphony Orchestra or the Bolshoi Ballet. Soft power, the Americans call it. But with Putin the Russians have changed. I see men in tight suits, a certain swagger when they walk and expect you to stand aside, always with a phone in hand, stony faces, eyes searching the room. Are they doing business? What kind of business? In Russia when they use the word *biznezman* it means a crook. Tell me: what is the name of the boat Bardo and the Russians were on?'

'Calypso.' Lucija and I answer together. You'd think we had practised.

'Good. First I'll find out if she has docked at La Goulette. He may be meetng someone in Tunis from the Russian embassy. Or maybe less conspicuous is Bizerte. Bardo worked at the British embassy here so we have photos of him if we do a police search. Bardo may have some friends in the police but I have more.' Briefly he smiles. 'Then he may have sailed further west. There are small fishing ports and then we come to Tabarka. Tabarka maybe. Yes. Tabarka is interesting because it is right up against the Algerian border. I have a friend in Tabarka, a good friend. Now if you will excuse me I'll start the search.'

Lannouz has slipped away. We are on our own, Baz, Lucija and Hipkiss whom I cannot think of as Gerald.

The President who wants to be friends with the world gazes down at us from his portrait on the wall.

I think of Mary. I must phone her. When is there time? And my editor. Is this growing into something big enough to interest him?

On an impulse I take Lucija's hand. She looks at me. I squeeze her hand and smile. We're on our way. She keeps hold of my hand but there is no smile in return.

I know what she is thinking. Rym with that knowing look on her face. Matt has some explaining to do.

He does it again. How long have we been alone? Ten minutes? None of us heard it but the door is open and Lannouz is standing there. This is a different Lannouz. The change in his face is a warning.

He checks the door is closed then takes a step into the room, then another step. His smile has vanished. There are frown lines between his eyes. He looks at Hipkiss and holds a finger to his lips. Hipkiss is not quick enough and Lannouz raises his eyebrows. Understand? Hipkiss nods. Lannouz looks at Lucija, puts his finger to his lips and raises his eyebrows. She nods. Finally, my turn. I nod.

Are we going to play charades?

Yes.

Lannouz stabs an urgent finger at the four walls and the ceiling then cups an ear.

Microphones. We nod.

Lannouz runs a finger above his mouth. Moustache? We nod.

He holds both hands in front of him. We don't understand. So he lifts something and offers it to each in turn then holds something to his mouth. Got it. Slim young man with moustache who brought in glasses of orange juice. We nod.

With a finger Lannouz punches half a dozen times on something, holds a hand in front of his face and mouths.

Telephone. We get that.

Lannouz points outside then imitates someone at the steering wheel of a car.

Got that.

Lannouz puts a hand above his eyes. Is he peering at something? None of us understand. Shake of head. Now Lannouz indicates each shoulder. Of course. Uniform.

He puts his hands together. Then his left hand clamps round his right wrist. Then the right hand clamps round the left wrist.

Lucija and I look at each other. What does he mean? Then I get it. I whisper in Lucija's ear. 'Handcuffs.'

I nod at Lannouz. Got it. And he points a finger first at me then at Lucija. We are going to be arrested.

Lannouz lifts both hands to hide his face. He is ashamed. He has brought this on us.

He beckons us to the French windows. Rattle of the handle. Locked. The key has been removed. We search, all of us. Panic is edging in. No key on the floor, no key on the table. Nothing on the window ledges or under the plant pot or the mat. Table drawers are empty. The windows are double glazed with security bars. Lannouz pushes the curtain aside and the key is hanging on a hook screwed to the frame. The door opens and we step outside.

Lannouz's voice is a whisper. 'My humblest apologies. *Je suis désolé.*' This doesn't seem enough and he whispers something in Arabic to Hipkiss. 'Who could have known that Bardo could have penetrated even here. Just now I overheard that young man on the telephone....' He doesn't complete his humiliation. 'You hear that?'

Sound of a far-off siren.

'But where is...'

Lannouz doesn't let her finish. 'Do you have paper?'

Hipkiss is a diplomat. Of course he has. He hands over a pen and small pad. Lannouz scribbles something and tears off the sheet. 'My best guess. You must go. Certain police... I will tell them you went to stroll in the garden while I went to the toilet. When I came back you had gone. Now follow that path past the kitchen. You will come to the service gate. It is kept closed but the key is always in the lock. Hurry.'

'But how...'

'Go now,' Lannouz interrupts. The siren is closer. 'Now.'

We've reached the side street where Hipkiss has parked his car. He has the keys in his hand. The siren is much louder. Then it stops.

'This is what we do,' Hipkiss says. 'Amilcar station is just across the main road. We passed it coming. Go there now. Take the train back to Tunis. Run. I'll go to the main road and stand with my hands on my hips. The police will stop and ask me – of course they will. I'll tell them you ran off at the sound of the siren. I went after you but you caught a cab. I heard you tell the driver La Marsa. That's the opposite direction from Tunis. All clear?'

'But…'

'Go.'

'Where's Bardo gone?'

Hipkiss remembers the sheet of paper Lannouz gave him and hands it to Lucija. She glances at it.

'Tabarka?'

'That's his best guess. Go go go.'

We hear voices. We run.

CHAPTER 10

We sit side by side. We're not runaway terrorists. Not us. We're tourists, again. See how we stare out of the window. No worries.

The little train rattles over the causeway, lake on the right, harbour on the left. La Goulette I suppose. We're not talking. That's not natural. Tunisians are not silent.

'Lucija?'

'What?'

'Can you see the Calypso?'

'I don't know what it looks like.'

'It looks like a speedboat with Calypso written on the stern. It's not that difficult.'

She stares out of the window then looks at me.

She says, 'I can see a big bird.'

'That's a cormorant.'

She is not interested in the cormorant. She stays silent.

'That man down the carriage keeps looking at us. Are we international terrorists?' I say. 'Maybe we have just had a lovers' tiff.'

'We haven't had a tiff,' she says.'

'And we aren't lovers.'

'No,' she says.

We run out of things to say. The train slows for signals, then turns into the terminal station in Tunis.

We hold back on the platform. Passengers brush past. Straight ahead is the exit. Follow them? The police are on the look-out for us. The exit is where they'll be. It's not just the regular police. Does

Bardo have the resources to cover here? Why would he? Hipkiss has said we are going in the opposite direction. Bardo is smart. He may decide that is a bluff. No telling. My brain hops about, confused. Just a minute. Some passengers peel off to go down steps to a side exit. Today is a day for using side exits. It leads to the metro stop.

Why has life become so confusing?

'Baz?' Lucija says. Just one word. It's in her tone of voice. *What's got into the man?*

'This way.'

We are in a *louage*, side by side, heading out of Tunis. In our hands we have baguettes stuffed with tuna, salad, fried potatoes and a hero's helping of harissa. I get a prod in the ribs from Lucija's elbow. She doesn't speak, just nods to the right. An arrow points to the Musée Bardo. No getting away from the man. We carry straight on. There's a pay station and then the *louage* starts accelerating. A sign gives destinations. Beja, I read, and Nefza and Tabarka. Tabarka could be a hundred and sixty something kilometres. I think. Could be be another figure altogether. We pass it in a blur.

Forget the figure. It's a long journey. Staring through the dust-flecked window loses its appeal. Thoughts come. Not thoughts. Nothing so connected. Memory flashes. Trapping the police on a fire escape. Tyre squeal drive with Hipkiss. I'm an action hero. Blue chalk mark to blue chalk mark. After Matt. What is Matt planning? Does he even have plans? What did Lannouz find out? If he found anything out. Russians appearing. One of Putin's long games? Lucija is brooding. Do I think Matt has slept with Rym? Yes.

Oh.

The *louage* takes the exit road to Beja. It's a nothing place, single story concrete block houses, Independence Day banners across the road, mosque, police station, café, municipal building. We are slowing, slowing, stop. Lucija turns in her seat.

'What are you looking at?'

'You,' I say.

'Me? Why?'

'Simple.' I smile at her. 'Because it's better than that.'

I nod at the window. The *louage* has halted by a butcher's shop. The carcass of a sheep hangs from a hook by the open door. As we look a drop of blood oozes from its slit throat.

'Oh.'

Back on the toll road. It winds through hills and back down to the plain. We pass a field with a flock of sheep. It's a big flock. Try to count them and you'd fall asleep. The crazy thing is that every single one is black. I should point out this fascinating fact to Lucija because her face is drawn together in a frown. It would take her mind off Matt and Rym. We pass a sign that says Tabarka 15 kms.

Then it happens.

There is a bang and the *louage* veers off the tarmac. Bloody hell. Bardo is shooting at us. There is a shout from the man behind us and a woman screams. The *louage* comes to a halt. Nobody moves. Then the driver says something in Arabic. The man at my shoulder translates into French. I was wrong. Bardo wasn't shooting at us.

Lucija has grabbed my arm. 'What did he say?'

'One of the tyres has blown out.'

We all get out. The driver gets busy with the spare wheel and a jack. Lucija wanders back along the road and after a moment I follow her. Out of hearing of the other passengers she pulls up in front of me.

'I must have a pee,' she says. 'It was getting urgent. The barbed wire fence stops me getting into the field. Baz, stand just there. You will hide me from other people.'

I don't move. I look at her. Why me? Why not one of the women? Because Lucija doesn't speak French or Arabic. She raises an eyebrow. Well?

I turn my back on her. I no longer see her but I hear her. My imagination brings us closer together. I hear her feet crunch dry grass. She hasn't moved far away because I can hear the rustle of cloth on skin. There is the crack of a knee as she squats. For a moment there is silence. Then I hear a spatter on dead leaves. There are men who are aroused by a woman urinating. Don't ask me why. I am not one of them. And yet. Something has changed.

'Thank you, Baz.' I feel her hand on my shoulder. 'You can turn round now.'

She is smiling.

'I should have been a sociologist because they always come up with crazy ideas,' she says. 'Me, I have invented the pee test: can a man resist sneaking a look?'

'And I passed?' I say.

She raises an eyebrow. What does that mean?

Between us we have one small bag. We grabbed it from Hipkiss's car while the police siren swelled. We show one passport, mine, the only safe one left to us. I ask for one room while Lucija tours the reception lobby of Les Mimosas, studying old sepia photos of the hotel on the walls.

The receptionist is a sweet girl who responds well to a smile. A name tag on her blouse says she is called Shamsi. 'I give you the best room in the hotel. It is the one Habib Bourguiba had. You know, the man who led us to freedom.'

'He stayed here?'

'The French government didn't want to make him a martyr so they didn't put him in prison. This was internal exile.'

You'd think we were prospective tenants inspecting our new home. Bathroom: check. Wardrobe: check. TV: check. French windows out to private terrace: check. We step outside to check the view, down to the garden and swimming pool, away to the sweep of the bay, blue water mirroring blue sky. The town is a patchwork of white walls and red tiled roofs. To the left is a promontory which boasts a fairytale castle with a billowing flag.

'So this is exile.' Lucija closes her eyes and enjoys the feel of late afternoon sun on her face. 'In Riga I knew an old man – neighbour in my apartment block – who was exiled to Siberia. This was in the Soviet days. His crime was he played the radio too loudly.'

There is more to this. I know there is. 'Too loudly?'

'He opened his windows and turned the volume up full. People stopped in the street to listen. Then the police came. His crime was he was tuned to Radio Free Europe.' She holds up her hand. 'When he came back from Siberia he had lost the fingers on his right hand.'

There is still more. The look in her eyes tells me. 'Frostbite?'

'Accident with a chainsaw. He had been cutting down pine trees. Without fingers he couldn't work in the camp any more so he was released. He'd been in the camp for five years. Five years! Yet I saw him saluting the Hammer & Sickle at a May Day rally, that same right hand raised. Why? I asked him. "Because nobody can see I am sticking up my middle finger at them."'

Lucija nods at me – crazy life in those days. Then we both turn to the noise from the bay. A plane is coming in on final approach, wheels down. It's the size of an executive jet, too far away to make out its markings. It could be Tunisian or French or British. It could be Russian.

There's an airport here. We hadn't known that.

We are quiet watching the plane until it sinks out of sight. We turn and go back into the bedroom. We never finished inspecting our temporary home. Now we do. There is no evading it. The bed. Just the one.

Lucija says nothing. Nor do I.

We have reached Tabarka. Where is Bardo? Where is Matt? Our hotel is on a rise at the east end of town and we walk down and head into the centre. Maybe we'll spot Matt taking a stroll. Daylight is fading, street lights coming on. People cluster on corners, all male, all Tunisian. No European faces, no Russians. We make a right turn and head down to the harbour. There are cafés and restaurants set well back from the water. Closed. The holiday season is some way off.

This is the fishing port. Men stack empty crates on boats. We step round tangles of nets. This is a waste of time. The feeling grows in me. We come to a squat building marked Garde Nationale with a couple of motorbikes parked. This marks a change. We leave the fishing boats behind. Now it is pleasure boats. No pleasure for us. We are out of luck. Then it happens.

Lucija squeezes my arm and ducks her head towards the edge of the quay: three blue chalk marks. Take it easy, I tell myself, you're not far past that police station. A casual glance. No one watching us. Now we are both staring out into the harbour. There, maybe twenty-five metres out, is a speedboat. A big one. It is bigger than anything you'd want for waterskiing. It is anchored with its stern towards the jetty and a dinghy tied to it. In the fading light we can just make out the name: Calypso. Underneath in smaller letters are two words. The dusk makes it hard to be sure but I think they are *Mgarr Gozo*.

There is a soft glow in one of the portholes. No sound of voices. Just one Russian left on board as a guard? He rowed the other Russians and Bardo ashore then came back to the boat. My best guess.

'Is he on board?' Lucija whispers.

She means Matt.

'No.'

'How can you be sure? He could be a prisoner.'

'If he was a prisoner he couldn't make the chalk marks.'

'So where is he now?'

Stupid question but I don't say it. Instead I say, 'Finding a safe room for the night.'

Lucija is close to me and I can see the frown on her head. Something in what I said has reminded her of Rym.

'Come on,' I say, 'the captain's not going to invite us on board for drinks.'

We return to the centre of town. The main street is naturally named after Habib Bourguiba. Café tables are full, men with glasses of mint tea. It's not the tourist season but some restaurants are doing early business. Half a dozen European faces. No Matt, no Russians, no Bardo who might be mistaken for an English gentleman.

Now it is fully dark. A cold breeze from the sea nips at our faces. Enough. Back at Les Mimosas Hotel there is a log fire burning in the lounge. There is also a waiter touting cocktails. Even the names are a turn-off. Fancy a Jackson Pollock? It's Cointreau, pineapple and fig liqueur. An El Greco is ouzo and orange. A Salvador Dali is… but Lucija jerks my arm. We go downstairs to the restaurant. The fish is fresh, the wine is good, we talk about tomorrow. We'll split. Lucija will go to the airport to see if anybody knows about Russians flying in. I'll stay in town and do the same.

'How?' she asks.

'I'll think of something.'

I already have but I'm not telling her.

And so to bed.

Last night in Tunis we shared a room – no choice, we had to - but it had twin beds. Here in Tabarka we didn't even try.

The switch by the door turns on one light. It is on the wall close to the bed. The bed is king size. Obviously we could put pillows down the centre but we don't discuss it. I move to the window. I'm hoping for a view of the castle walls. No. What I see is the reflection in the glass of Lucija. She stands stock still at the foot of the bed. She's staring at my back. No, that's not right. Her body is square on to me but her head is angled towards the bed. She wiggles her head. What does that mean?

'Hm. Maybe I'll take a shower.' There is silence. Then I see her nod to herself. 'Yes, that's what I'll do.'

'Good thinking,' I say.

It's a big room, A chunk was taken out for a bathroom. This creates what might be an alcove except it is much bigger. The bathroom door doesn't lead into the bedroom proper but into this large alcove. I come back from the French windows and perch on the chair in front of the dressing table. Shower. Lucija has the right idea. I'll have one when she's finished.

From where I am sitting I can see part of the alcove. I stare at that. Why do I do that? It's not interesting. It has a cream painted built-in wardrobe, nothing else. Bourguiba would have had plenty of room for his suits. There is a strip of light on the wardrobe. I fix on this strip of light, fix on it with stubbornness until my brain makes a lurch. Why can I see this strip of light? Lucija has not closed the bathroom door. That is why.

I hear water running. She's switched on the shower. I hear splashing. She's soaping her body. Rinsing. The sounds stop. Silence. Not quite silence. A succession of noises so tiny I find myself straining to identify them. Rough towelling on her skin. My mind slips back to this afternoon. It was the same when the *louage* tyre blew out. She didn't call over one of the female passengers when she needed a pee. She used me to shield her and my ears isolated every creak and zip and tinkle when she crouched.

Together Lucija and I have gone through so much. Intimacy has grown between us. I have been part of her shower, soaping her body, rinsing it, drying it. Silence again. I listen to the silence. What is she doing now? The answer is nothing.

When she comes back into the room she is naked.

Oh.

Oh is Lucija's word. Climbing the stairs at that cheap hotel last night, realising we would share a room. *Oh*. We didn't make love. Not even with vodka as a nightcap. I could hear her breathing in the bed beside me. And she asked if I thought Matt had slept with Rym. *Oh*. But we didn't make love. It wasn't inevitable then. It was the drive from Tunis to Tabarka that was the tipping point. For hours I was close to her while her insides churned. Matt the betrayer. Rym the predator. Then the tyre blew out. She had shot Rym. In her imagination. I had shared that gunshot with her. She went to have a pee and she wanted me to protect her.

I'm mad. None of that. People want to kill us but we are alive.

I get to my feet and we both stare.

'Baz...'

We are on the trail of her lover, her partner, but it is my name she calls.

She is beautiful. A girl can be pretty. Lucija is lovely like a woman.

'I'm going to have a shower,' I say.

'Shower? For God's sake.'

I am frozen. It's the Hungarian blood in me. It holds me back while her body says come closer. A Hungarian sees complexity even when everything is simple. Stupid thoughts flickering through my brain.

'Oh God,' she breathes. 'Am I going to be humiliated?'

'Lucija.' She is very close so I reach out to touch her skin and then everything is simple. I undress and she watches me and then we tumble into bed. She scrambles off – what is this? – but it's to tug back the sheet and blanket so we are both naked. She stretches out beside me. Her arms are crooked on the pillow, hands up by her head. *Look, look, look,* her arms insist, *I have surrendered.*

'Hold me,' she says, 'just hold me.'

I hold her. Just holding her is not going to be enough. We know it isn't.

Already yesterday evening seems a long time ago. We came back from town and had dinner and we came upstairs and then she had a shower. Early to bed means a long night. Who's complaining?

I don't know what the time is when her voice cuts into my half-sleep. 'Baz.'

'I'm here. This is my hand.'

'Nobody else exists,' she says.

What has been turning round and round in her head. 'If you say so.'

'We're not betraying anyone. We're not punishing anyone. We're not hurting anyone. You must understand that. I have been in a revolution. You haven't. You haven't had men in uniform shooting at you. When the world moves on what you need… it is desperate… is contact, touching another person. You are a good man and I am a good woman. We do this for each other. There is love in it. No room for negative feelings.'

This is what has been in her head.

'Baz, hold me again. You must.'

It's dawn and we can hear the first muezzin. It is quite far off.

CHAPTER 11

Last night was last night. Stop dreaming. Get on with today.

The sweet girl in reception smiles at me. I have a favour to ask so a little chat will help. I smile back and pretend I haven't already seen her name tag.

'I'm sorry but I don't know your name.'

'Shamsi,' she says.

'Shamsi. You were born here?'

'Yes, but my father came from Lebanon.'

'What does Shamsi mean?'

'It means *Of the Sun*.'

'So you are Sunny. Lovely name and so is your smile.' Enough. You're not chatting her up. 'Shamsi, I want to make a telephone call.'

She says to use the telephone in our bedroom. I don't want to wake madame I say. Shamsi smiles because I am so considerate and lets me into an inner office. Sitting at the desk I notice yesterday's guest registration forms in a neat pile. I pick up the phone, punch in the international code and then Mary's mobile. I am dialling my wife while I still have the smell of Lucija's body in my nose. Don't think like that. The phone rings. While I listen I pick up the *fiches* for the hotel guests. There are five. On top is the one I filled in for Monsieur Fazekas. The phone rings. It's an hour earlier in England so Mary won't have gone out. Anyway she'd have taken her mobile. Maybe she's busy with the twins. The phone rings. Is it significant the Fazekas form is on top of the file? Someone studying it? Odds are four-to-one against. Stop being bloody paranoid. But paranoia is necessary because Bardo is after us. Maybe Putin has sent goons after us. The phone rings. I listen to it, concentrate on it. Is it sending me a message? What message does an unanswered phone send? The phone rings. Then I cut it off. I'll ring Mary later. I thank Shamsi and say I got no answer.

Lucija and I eat breakfast in a room flooded by morning light while we discuss the day ahead. It's agreed we'll separate.

'You'll take a taxi to the airport,' I say.

'Yes.'

'And me… I have to find someone who can tell me where the Russians have gone and what they are doing. I'll ring Hipkiss and see if he has any bright ideas.'

It's not Hipkiss I'm going to ring.

'*Allo*,' She answers on the fourth ring. Unlike Mary.

'I don't think even our mothers would have recognised us from the photo you printed yesterday.'

I'm a spy, keeping my name secret from listeners.

'One moment.'

I've left the hotel. I'm using a public telephone so I am secure at this end. I don't know about Rym.

'Good morning, Mr Terrorist.' Rym is on the line again. There is no background noise of traffic or street voices. She's locked herself in the ladies' toilet, I assume.

'As a journalist I deplore you doctoring our photo. As a friend I say thank you.'

'Have I got the expression right?' she wants to know. 'Dog don't eat dog.'

End of courtesies. Time to move on.

'We are now in Tabarka. Everybody has got here before us, including your good friend. We haven't seen him but he is definitely here.'

'I know.'

She knows. I think about this.

'He telephoned you?'

'Yes.'

Can one short word show smugness? I disappoint her. I'm not going to pry into their night together.

'Were you able to give him any useful information? Anything you could share with me?'

'Matthieu knows I have a wide network of contacts. He wanted to know what the Ivans were up to. That was the word he used. Ivans.'

'More secure if anybody is listening.'

'Nothing is secure. You're not using your mobile?'

'No.'

'Or phoning from your hotel. Which is it, if I need to get in touch?'

'Les Mimosas.'

'I couldn't help him but I've been thinking. You're a fellow journalist so I'll give you a contact. His name is Abdelkader. Tabarka is his town and he hears a lot. Abdel's phone number…'

'Just a minute.'

This public telephone is in a shop that sells stationery. The sign outside says *Taxiphone*. A normal taxi is a car that is metered so this is a phone that is metered. Logical? The shopkeeper has been watching, enchanted to hear English. I ask for a pen and paper. I just want to borrow a pen but he sees a business opportunity. He takes a Bic pen from his stock and blows the dust off a small notebook.

'OK.'

She spells Abdelkader's name and gives me his phone number. It is dark in the shop and I hold the notebook to the open door.

'Now I must go.'

There's a crashing in my ear. I was right she had locked herself in the loo. In case any nosey parker is hanging about she has just flushed it.

'Oui?' Tunisians answer the phone in French even when they switch to Arabic. But has Rym given me the right number? Background noises sound as if it's coming from outer space.

'Rym Dakhli gave your number.'

No response. A great silence greets this. No, not silence. Faint voices, distant and distorted, pings, squawks. My brain does a skip. Nothing is secure. Rym says that while she squats in the toilet. The Queen across the Water says it. And Hipkiss. My brain goes back to last night. Lucija says *Am I going to be humiliated*? The image of her naked body is powerful. I frown and drag myself to the present. Listen. Work it out. Sounds from an alien world. Is that it? No, don't be stupid.

'It's Abdelkader I want to speak to.'

The squawks are faint. It could be an American cartoon, Bugs Bunny, Donald Duck. Hold it. *Star Wars* was shot in Tunisia. Maybe the noises come from a film set?

'Maybe I have the wrong number. Does the name Rym Dakhli mean anything to you?'

'Yes, certainly.'

I am startled. The voice in my ear is male and deep.

'I need to meet you.'

'Why?'

'I need information. Rym says you can help.'

'What information?'

'I'm using a public telephone. I'm not talking about it here.'

Silence except for half heard squawks.

'So. Are you in danger?'

'Yes.'

'Where are you?'

'Avenue Habib Bourguiba.'

'All right, this is what you do. Walk along the avenue to the end. Keep walking to the souvenir stalls by the old harbour. Wait there.'

'How will I recognise you?'

Abdelkader doesn't answer questions. The phone is dead. I take the phone away from my head and stare at it as if I could see his face. A long, long time ago I did exactly the same thing, staring at the phone. That was when Lucija first rang. Look where that has got me.

* * *

The same men are at the same tables. There are no western faces, no blue chalk marks. Could be Abdelkader sitting there, glass of tea half masking his face, checking me out? No telling. He sounded like someone used to authority, giving orders. Go there, do this, walk down this street while I size you up. So I'm strolling along, innocent tourist, getting memory flashes. This one is of Hungary, walking a certain route with Jozsef – cousin, cop, killer - while a frightened little informer checked us out. We were tracking down my missing wife Eve. We found her. Cue a wild west shoot out. Eve died. My fault. Jesus, why has this sprung out from my memory box?

Souvenir stalls stretch along the side of the old harbour. I get offers of coral, birdcages, carved wooden wild boar. A breakwater has been built. Beyond it are rock formations, rusty red. I gaze at them, daggers rising from the water. God, I'm in a mood this morning. Lack of sleep. Whose fault is that? Turning and coming back gives the stallholders renewed hope.

'Monsieur, monsieur, pas cher.'

On I go, sun gaining strength, sound of a car's tyres on loose grit. The souvenir sellers' eyes slip beyond me and hope dies in their faces. At the sound of footsteps I turn and see a man in uniform coming towards me. He is like my cousin Jozsef but bigger. The car he's coming from is marked *Police*. A frown is tightening his forehead. He barks something in Arabic and the stallholders fall back. He stops and turns his frown on me. When he talks it is the deep voice of the man I spoke to on the phone.

'Are you staying in Tabarka?'

'Yes.'

'Which hotel?'

'Les Mimosas.'

'Passport.'

His eyes follow my hand as I dip it in my pocket. There are terrorists about. Maybe I have a gun. I give him my passport. He flicks through to my photo and checks it against my face.

'Stay here.'

Where would I run to? Now he is sitting behind the wheel of his car, speaking on the radio. I can just pick up the squawks of the reply. This was the background noise I heard on the phone. The car is angled so I see him perfectly. He has a thick neck which always disturbs me. He holds the passport so it catches the sun. I watch as he flicks through the pages. He is not talking. Then I see the abrupt clenching of his eyebrows. His head tilts as he stares at me. He says something short then gets out of the car. He strides with a lot more purpose than when he came. My passport is in his left hand. His right hand is unsnapping handcuffs from his belt.

'You will come with me to headquarters. There are questions you must answer, serious questions.'

'What's wrong?'

'The hotel *fiches* have been delivered. No Potter was registered as staying last night. I have looked through your passport and there is no immigration stamp. You have entered Tunisia illegally. Do not try to run away or I will shoot you. Do you understand? Hold out your hands with the wrists together.'

I blink. Potter not Fazekas? Both passports are in my jacket. Always. But I dipped my hand in the wrong pocket. I feel cold steel on my skin. How could I be so bloody stupid?

He makes me sit in the passenger seat next to him. His pistol he balances on top of the dashboard.

'Don't try to escape. Don't try to grab the gun. Don't even think about it.' His thick hand makes a karate chop towards my throat.

He makes a three-point turn. The stallholders have formed a group to watch. He heads back to town as far as the roundabout and turns left to cross the causeway. The old harbour on the left has no boats at all, just a bit of beach big enough for a couple of sunloungers. On the right the new harbour is busy. There's the Calypso, nobody on deck. The storm that passed through piled sand on the road. We get past that. The radio squawks but he ignores it. I don't ask where we are going. No point. The road curves, we are off the causeway, climbing until we reach a parking lot under the castle wall. He swings the car round so we have a view right down to the souvenir stalls. There is a ticket office but it is closed. No other cars are parked. We are alone. No witnesses. He still hasn't spoken. He digs a handful of coins out of his pocket and searches for a key. I watch as he unlocks my handcuffs.

'They are simple fellows down there.' He nods towards the stalls. 'A bit of theatre impresses them that the police know their job. Which of course we do. Sometimes. You are Rym's friend, correct?'

I rub my wrists where the cuffs have been. There is the slightest curl to his lips; *that's nothing, my friend.* Careful how I answer him. Careful how I deal with him. First impression is that he is a bastard. And he has power. Life shows it is better to have a bastard with power on your side.

'You are Abdelkader? She didn't tell me you were a policeman.'

'Life is full of surprises.' He holds up my British passport. 'No immigration stamp. How did you enter the country? You swam?'

He shifts a bit in his seat to get a clearer view of me. I am registering his wrestler's build and thick neck. His hair is clipped close to his skull.

'I don't like waiting,' he says.

'I have two passports.'

'British and French?'

'Hungarian. My parents were Hungarian.'

'Hungarian? That's new to me.'

He holds out his hand and I give him my Hungarian passport.

'Fazekas?'

'Fazekas translates into English as Potter.'

'You speak Hungarian?'

He asks the question the way a sceptical cop does: go on, prove it.

'Bassza meg – hagyjon békén.'

'Let me have a guess,' he says. 'You told me to fuck off.'

I smile my mystery smile.

'Hungarian is not an easy language,' I say. 'It has prefixes and suffixes so the meaning of a word often hides in the middle.'

'We have politicians like that.' He looks at the immigration stamp. 'OK, it's all in order. You can go now.'

Is that his idea of a joke? I'd be happier if he was smiling.

'Rym thinks you could help me with a little information.'

'Does she? Women.' He scratches his chin. 'You know her well? She's your girlfriend?'

Petite amie is the French expression he uses.

'I've met her. We share a profession.'

'The profession of whoredom and the profession of journalism – do you know the difference?'

I could make a snappy comeback about cops and criminals but after two seconds thought I give my mystery smile another outing.

Abdel goes on. 'She came here, showed a little…' He cups his hands under imaginary breasts. '…and I'm to open my horde of secrets to any man who has caught her eye. What do you want to know?'

Tabarka is Abdel's town. Rym said that.

'I'm told a lot of Russians have come to Tabarka. I haven't seen any. Where are they? Why are they here?'

Abdel stares at me.

'You fly to Tunisia. Then you make your way to Tabarka. Why? Because you have heard there are Russians here. You look round and can see no Russians. And you don't know why they should come in the first place. Do you expect me to believe that?'

'There's more. I am starting with the Russians.'

He is still staring at me while he makes up his mind.

'OK. Follow me.'

He doesn't bother to lock the car; you don't steal a police car in Tunisia, especially not Abdelkader's car. We go up the path that hugs the castle wall. We arrive at a gatehouse with an immense wooden gate. The knocker makes a thunderous noise. Nobody comes. He picks up a huge stone and hammers at the gate. The gate doesn't budge. Nobody comes. He gets out his pistol and lays the muzzle against the lock. He pauses then puts the gun back in its holster. He wouldn't be able to lock the gate when we leave. He looks at the top of the wall but nobody is peering down at us.

'This is not a place to climb in when you lose your key.'

Is this his little joke? No, he doesn't do little jokes. He is pointing out the objective truth.

'Follow me,' he says again.

We are back again above the carpark.

'Genoese fort, very old,' Abdelkader says. 'It was the Genoese army that built it centuries ago so our army naturally considers it is theirs. They have inherited it. Never mind it was a different army. Military logic, right. The fort was good against bows and arrows. Cannonballs weren't much good either. Those large metal balls bounced off. The military mind moves slowly. Now the danger might come from the air. So what use is it to the army?'

He looks at me so I shrug.

'It takes time but the army agrees the fort is no longer useful so this will be the town museum. Also there will be plays and concerts. You've seen the ticket office. This is very cultural so there'll also be toilets. Then…' a stubby finger jabs my chest. 'A new order comes from Tunis, from the Ministry of Defence. Cancel the last order. Close the museum. Forget culture. The proper procedures have not been followed. Signed by the Deputy Defence Minister. Do you know why?'

Of course I don't so I say 'No.'

'A better offer has been tabled. Or passed under the table. That is more likely. Forget broken pots and old Roman coins and a rusty anchor. There'll be a casino. Certain Russians have made promises to certain influential men in Tunis. Maybe certain bank accounts in Switzerland prosper. I don't know. I don't try to find out. Such knowledge can be dangerous.'

He goes quiet but he hasn't finished. He stares out across the old harbour to the stalls of tourist tat. There are no tourists.

'Tunisia already has casinos – Jerba, Hammamet, Tunis – but not Tabarka, And the casino the Russians propose is very special, I would say unique, unbelievable. Literally unbelievable. It is a Super Casino with original features. Amazing. So far there are only whispers but it is my job to listen to whispers. It is to be an off-shore casino. Off-shore? But we have just driven here.'

In case I have forgotten he points down to the road.

'It will *become* off-shore,' he explains. 'There will be a fence and a gate. Right there, at the end of the causeway. Show a foreign passport and you can come in. A Tunisian identity card will not do unless you are a maid or a cook. See, the Russians say, it will provide jobs for local people. Well, a few. And no Tunisians will be corrupted by gambling. But there is more.'

His arm moves to the bay which is the old harbour and has no boats in it.

'I said it was unbelievable. Just listen to this. Pay close attention. Cruise ships will anchor in the old harbour. They'll come from Spain and Italy and Cyprus and Istanbul and maybe even Odesa. You know those airbridges they have at airports, take you straight out to the plane? Here there will be a seabridge so the passengers stroll ashore then up an elevator enclosed in tinted glass built against this castle wall. The passengers with their euros and dollars and pounds are delivered right to the Super Casino. You see the beauty of it? These rich foreigners eager to lose their money do not have to enter Tunisia at all because this is all off-shore. It will be a foreign country. That is how I see it. Our laws will not apply. I will not be allowed in to investigate any suspicious events. Me, Abdelkader, keep out. Those cruise passangers can bring in drugs or arms and I must stand with those stallholders down there and watch. But certain high powered men in Tunis have been persuaded this is an excellent idea. Maybe you ask yourself why.'

His arm drops. When I glance down I see his thumb and forefinger rubbing together. When I look at his face again I see darkness in his eyes.

'Who will pay for all this?'

'Excellent question, Mr Journalist. Certain Russians will pay. Oh, there is a company witth an address in Belize and they want to build and run the Super Casino but the money is Russian. The important people do not say this but it is not just important people who work at the Central Bank in Tunis. Little people do. Little people whisper. And they ask themselves questions such as what kind of Russians have the hundreds of millions this will cost? Kindly old babushkas? I think not. Do you?'

I shake my head.

'Cruise ships will anchor down in the old harbour,' he says. 'And supply ships. In fact any ship. Nobody will know what it is carrying.'

He nods to himself.

'If the little whisperers in the Central Bank say the money has arrived,' I say, 'why is nothing happening to build the Super Casino?'

'Maybe,' Abdel says, 'it is not a Super Casino at all. What do you think?'

What do I think? I think a lot of things. Perhaps *think* is stretching it. My mind flits from one thing to another. Rym started me off, giving me Abdelkader. Abdel arrested me, brought me up here and took the handcuffs off me. But he had made his point: see how easily I could arrest you if you don't cooperate. He gives me far more information than I expect. Why? Because he expects something in return while the feel of the handcuffs is still fresh. I don't have a razor sharp brain but I do have a journalist's suspicion. I have a nose for when something is not right.

'There is no Super Casino,' I say. 'It is a smokescreen.'

'For what?'

'I don't know,' I say, 'and you don't know. Two negatives create a positive. We make up a team?'

'Team?' Abdel frowns. He doesn't like the idea. 'In a team everybody contributes. I'm waiting.'

'You haven't mentioned Bardo.'

He stares at me. More.

'Bardo used to work at the British embasy.'

'I have heard of him. He left Tunisia years ago.'

'He has come back. He was on the Calypso which is anchored in the port.'

The Calypso is out of sight but I gesture.

'Why is Bardo important? What is he doing?'

'That is what we have to find out. Bardo is a Russian agent. And he is high up in British Intelligence. He is Deputy Director.'

'I don't believe you,' Abdel says.

I have surprised Abdel and his frown shows he doesn't like being surprised.

'You have to because it is true. He is very good at his work for British Intelligence. That is perect cover for his other job. He works for the Kremlin too.'

'Does Bardo have a name you can give me?'

I dig out the pad and pen I had to buy earlier and write Bardo's real name. Abdel watches me write.

'You are scared of Bardo. You won't murmur his name even out here where the wind blows away our words.'

'In Tunisia I am learning the value of silence.' Darkness comes back in Abdel's stare so I soften what I said. 'In the United States there was a famous political family. No, not the Kennedys, the Longs. Huey Long was a crooked governor of Lousiana. His brother Earl was just plain crooked. "Don't write anything you can phone," he advised. "Don't phone anything you can talk. Don't talk anything you can whisper. Don't whisper anything you can smile. Don't smile anything you can wink."'

For the first time I see something that could be a smile on his face. 'And don't wink anything when you can use a bullet,' Abdel says.

He raises an eyebrow and then he nods.

CHAPTER 12

'I am not responsible for your safety.' Abdelkader has stuck his head out of his car window. That's his parting shot. I don't want you as my security guard. That's my parting shot. I never get to say it. His car drives off with a growl. I need to be away from him. He is too much in my face, too close, too tough. I want to be away from that frown of his. And his handcuffs. Once was enough.

He has volunteered the information that he is going to find out more about Russians coming to Tabarka. Will they have snow on their boots, I asked? His frown added an extra wrinkle. Somewhere along the dark alleys of his life he has lost his sense of humour.

I watch the back of his car until it disappears. Good.

Now think about it. Be realistic. A casino up here? A Super Casino with its own Berlin Wall. That'll keep out the riff-raff. Cruise ships anchored just down there. Think big: add a helicopter pad. Cut off from Tunisia, beyond its jurisdiction. Abdelkader keep out. Is this possible? I look again: at the town, at the bay, at the fort, and beyond it the sweep of the coast. Algeria is over there, just out of sight. The doubts collect in my mind. Physically being here and seeing it I ask myself: is this what has convinced Bardo to make a clandestine visit? It's not even a building site. Why would Bardo risk coming here? There is something else. There has to be.

There's a café just ahead, biggish one, half a dozen tables outside with men talking. Or not talking, just looking. Not much traffic on Avenue Habib Bourguiba so why stick a roundabout in the middle of it? Answer: because they needed somewhere to put a statue of the father of the country. Don't think of him like Ghandhi. Bourguiba looks as if he has just enjoyed a good lunch. Past the statue is a scruffy bit of park with unhappy trees that wouldn't give shade in summer. Lucija and I agreed to meet here at lunchtime. And here's a little miracle. She arrives at the same time as I do. What are the odds against that? I stand and watch as she strolls into this little square. I take in the hints of the body under her clothes. She is scowling but her face softens when she sees me.

'So how is Hipkiss?'

We have chosen a bench away on its own. She is laying out the picnic she has bought.

'Hipkiss is Hipkiss.' I had told her I was phoning him. I pick up a baguette with hardboiled egg and take a bite. When I next speak it is natural to change the subject. 'I rang a man called Abdelkader and arranged to meet him over there.' Wave of baguette. 'Turns out he is a cop of some special kind.'

'Didn't Hipkiss warn you?'

'I found out the hard way. He put handcuffs on me and drove up there where no one could hear me scream. He didn't beat me up. He did it to impress the souvenir sellers. That was what he said. And to send me a message; don't mess with me. Then he came out with a fantastic story.'

I tell her about the super casino and Russian money and crooked men in Tunis and nothing at all happening to build the super casino and she asks the inevitable question.

'Matt? Did he mention him?'

'No mention of Matt. Nor of Bardo.'

'Blue chalk marks?'

'No.'

'My turn. I'll tell you about the airport and the men. It's not nice.'

She's an actress showing her range. Disdain, anger, sneaky trick, triumph, sexy – she can do the lot. I'd hire her.

'The airport is real but small. There are maybe charter flights in the high season but not now. So why are there these four men sitting in a line and switching their eyes to me as soon as I enter. No, I am wrong. The arrivals board had one flight coming in from Stockholm later in the afternoon so why are these four men waiting? I walked past them to the information counter and ask about incoming flights and then I turn round and walk back. Slowly, you understand, so they have time to talk among themselves. They were speaking Russian which they did not expect me to understand. Would you like to know what these great Russian philosophers said about me?'

'I can guess.'

'Yes, they suffer from a lack of imagination. Their eyes follow me, measure me. One of them says I am too old. The next says that old means experienced. The third says that old means desperate for it. The fourth says a fuck is always a fuck. They speak one after the other so I feel my body is being passed from one to the next. My breasts have been squeezed, my bum has been prodded by these ugly Russians with thick necks and scarred faces.'

She goes silent. I say: 'The cop who arrested me this morning also had a thick neck.'

'Baz, don't be stupid. You didn't have to listen to him wondering if your tits were too small.' She needs a sip of water. 'I spoke to them in English. One of them understood. I asked if they were waiting for the flight from Sweden. No. They didn't say why they were waiting. Instead these great thinkers wondered if I was still moist down there.'

She doesn't make a gesture but her eyes lower and lift.

'I asked if they knew whether the charter flight was usually on time and of course they didn't. Then – listen Baz – then I become a bad woman. I ask what hotel they are staying in because maybe I could have a drink with them tonight. This is translated into Russian and they stop looking at me and look at themselves, thinking about the possibilities. But the English speaking one says: "We don't stay in a hotel. We are waiting for Mr Big and Mr Big likes to be private."

So there's no chance of a drink? "No, is private. I tell you, is not in town." He frowns and I think I see the first shadow of suspicion on his face. I decide that is all I can get so I start to leave and say I hope they don't have to wait too long. The English speaker translates and the one who said old meant desperate for it says in Russian, "Mr Big from Gazprom is always late unlike one of his bills which never is." So the bad woman gives them a regretful smile and says "Ciao" and walks away. The bad woman knows from the silence that the boys are watching her so she gives her bum a wiggle. Oh, bad *bad* woman.'

She shakes her head and is silent. No, there is one more thing.

'Now I want to go to that castle.' She waves her hand in the general direction.

'Lucija, there is nothing to see. Nothing is being built. Nobody is there.'

'Baz, I want to go to that castle. I need to do something – anything – to get those men out of my head. Don't you understand?'

I'm getting to know this route. *Hello Habib, my old friend, hello tea drinkers, remember me*? Skirt the roundabout. Cross the causeway where men are clearing drifts of sand from the winter storm. Now there is a choice: the road I drove up with Abdel or a path. For me the road has bad karma. We take the path which is rough so we are watching our step and not talking. The path rejoins the road at the parking area which I recognize from this morning. Two things have changed: there is a parked car and a man with a tray of souvenirs held by a strap around his neck.

'Madame, monsieur, pas cher.'

The tray holds bracelets, necklaces and brooches of pink coral stolen from the reefs. We shake our heads.

'Quelque chose spécial…'

He puts on a great performance of peering over each shoulder for spies lurking in the bushes. From an inside pocket he draws out a piece of thick paper, grubby and creased. More glances left and right to increase the value of his treasure. He unfolds the paper and there it is. A coin. Heavy, looks silver, smoothed by time or the clever men in back rooms of the Tunis medina. Fifteen hundred years old? Last week's vintage? Take your pick.

Again we shake our heads. He seems resigned to our lack of interest. I watch as he limps away to the shade of a tree. I turn to Lucija and find she is looking down past the abandonded ticket office to the bay. I give her the highlights. Cruise ships anchor there. Elevator goes up the castle wall behind. Passengers whipped up to lose their money at the casino. Then down again and cruise ship sails away. Oh, and Algeria is just round the corner there.

When I stop she stares at me.

'Truly? You're not kidding me?'

'These are the rumours. And certain big men have been paid off. Maybe the super casino will offer something very special.'

'You mean,' Lucija says, 'like Russian roulette?'

Does Lucija mean this as a joke? I think so. But her face is deadly serious.

'Does your friend the cop believe this super casino rubbish?'

'Just because he put handcuffs on me that doesn't make him my friend. And no, he doesn't believe it. He has gone off to find out about certain Russians.'

'So Bardo is meeting these Russians who are flying in. And Matt is after Bardo. So we find where the Russians go and we find Matt.'

'We don't know how Matt will do this, but he is resourceful.'

'Sure. He'll find some woman and sleep with her and she'll tell him.'

The Rym/Matt night together is still festering.

'Before we do anything I must have a pee.' She is shifting from foot to foot like a little girl desperate to go. 'What is it about Tabarka? I get this sudden urgent need. Like on the *louage*.'

'They built the toilets here for the museum which didn't open. The toilets are locked.'

She checks in case I am wrong. Dry leaves have been blown into piles beside the basins.

'The souvenir seller is out of sight. Pee here. No one can see you.'

I am wrong. God, how wrong.

She is facing the bay below and muttering. 'Cruise ship down below and the passengers don't even get to see the town. I have never heard…'

She stops.

'Baz!'

She is pointing, just with a finger. There at the top of the castle wall are two figures, head and chest visible above the parapet. They are staring down at us. Something about the way they hold themselves - square shoulders, short haircut – I don't like. They wear identical shirts. Uniform. Security. Police. Army. No telling.

One of the men shouts at us in Arabic.

'Let's move,' I urge but Lucija is ahead of me.

There's another shout from the castle wall: *'Arrêtez-vous.'*

We are already hopping over low sage bushes, kicking empty drink cans, eyes looking out for broken glass. Stop? What kind of idiot does he think we are? We go faster. Lucija half stumbles in a hole. A thorny bush almost gets my eyes.

Then it happens.

Crack of a pistol shot behind us, thud of a bullet hitting something solid. We're at the end of the toilet block. We slam round the side of the building so the maniacs can't shoot at us. But when I risk a peep round the building the men have vanished from the top of the wall.

'They've gone,' I say.

'No, they haven't,' Lucija says. 'They'll be coming after us. They're police looking for international terrorists or they're Bardo's men.'

She points at the parked car. It is not marked *Police* but that means nothing. Certainly it is not the souvenir seller's. He has heard the pistol shot. He knows trouble. He is limping with surprising speed towards the bushes. We start down the road. It curves round to the left so now we are hidden. We are jogging more than running. Thank Lucija's shoes for that. All we must do is keep on the road and we'll reach the causeway and safety. Is anywhere safe in Tabarka? We haven't gone far, maybe only fifty metres, when there is the sound of a car door slamming behind us, a second car door, the firing of an engine. How have they been so quick?

We don't say a word. We scramble off the road, push between bushes, trip over trailing vines. Water oozes from a tiny spring. There's a clump of rushes, stems as thick as fishing rods. We make our way behind them. We are screened from the road. We catch a glimpse of the car, a flash, no more. We hear the car going down the hill until a curve in the road. Silence. It's gone. There is just the sigh of the breeze and our own breathing.

'Police?' Lucija asks.

'Bardo's chums whoever they were. But Bardo seems to have good connections in the police.'

'They recognised us?'

'They know a western man and woman are wanted for questioning and we didn't stop when ordered to. Suspected terrorists shot while trying to escape. I can imagine big headlines. But now's our chance to…'

I don't get to finish the sentence. I turn and take a foot forward. Lucija snatches my hand to pull me back.

'Wait.'

For what? Lucija is right. She is still gripping my hand as the seconds pass and then I hear it. Scrape of shoe on loose gravel on the road. We crouch down. The rushes are good cover. They are fed by that little spring. I think: *jungle*. There's no sound from our pursuer but he hasn't gone away. He is stalking us. My eyes find the tiniest of gaps between the rushes. He walks into sight, one policeman, coming back from the direction the car went. His head swings round to search the other side of the road. I lose sight of him. We don't move. Another tiny gap in the rushes. Now it's the pistol

I see. It swings left and right, searching for a target. His finger is inside the trigger guard. He's trigger-happy. They're the worst, the very worst. Shoot first, ask questions later. He's level with us. He stops and stares at the reeds. Lucija is still holding my hand. Her grip tightens. Don't worry. I'm not moving. Something catches the cop's attention and he's gone. Her grip squeezes again.

'Wait,' she breathes in my ear. 'It's a cop trick. It's what they do in Riga.' I can just hear her whisper. Why is she telling me this? Nerves? No. She wants me to know she is up to their tricks. 'Police called out because of some trouble. They drive past and nobody's there. The police car parks round the corner and the cops come back on foot. Still no trouble so the cops go back to their car. Sound of two doors slamming and the car driving off. The trouble-makers come out of hiding, arms waving, we fooled the cops. Not so fast. Two car doors slamming was a trick. One cop strolls back round the corner. In one hand he holds handcuffs, in the other hand he holds his pistol. *Your choice*, he is telling the boys.'

There he is again, the cop with the gun, thirty paces beyond us. He's moving on cat's paws. Another few steps. Now we are hardly hidden at all if he turns back. But something has his attention. He steps off the road and vanishes into the bushes. We can hear him moving, a branch snapping. His prey is somewhere not far away. We catch the sound of more footsteps. We see him again in a small clearing. Abruptly he stops. He's spotted us. No. He swivels part way to his right and shoots into the bushes near him and there is a cry. The policeman disappears from sight but we hear crashing through a thicket. A second time we hear the policeman shoot. We hear a voice, just one. It's the cop shouting an order. There is silence. No reply. Then we hear a crashing of bushes and we catch sight of the cop bursting onto the road. He is going downhill towards the car where his colleague is waiting somewhere just round a curve. The cop is shouting. No idea what but he sounds urgent. *Come quick. I've shot the bastard.* Something like that.

Suddenly he stops in the middle of the road. He swings back to look towards us but the rushes are our disguise. His pistol moves to the other side of the road. Back to our side. He hears nothing. He sees nothing. I think he has just remembered there are two terrorists. Then he decides he needs back-up and continues on to where the car is waiting.

Lucija looks at me. 'We have to check.'

I nod. 'We have to be quick.'

We step round the damp patch that has nourished our reeds and head uphill. It's not far, not far at all. The undergrowth has been trampled, a silver ring and a leather bracelet dropped. Then it starts: the blood. We follow the trail of red on green leaves. Some of the red drops have been smeared. The cop's uniform will be smeared. He'll get rid of the evidence fast. Or maybe nobody will care. Beyond a tree trunk a leg is twisted on the ground. Bit by bit the body is revealed: a second leg, hips, the waist, shirt with a patch of blood, an arm flung out. The second arm is trapped underneath him because he was shot in the back as he tried to run away. No, not run away, limp away. It is the souvenir seller. No need to see his face. The strap of his tray broke as he hit the ground. Coral like a pink wave, necklaces, shells, ear rings, postcards are scattered. It is Lucija who kneels to feel for a pulse. She needn't bother. If two bullets hadn't killed him there would have been a third.

'Bastard,' I say.

That's not strong enough for Lucija. 'Fucking bastard.'

I look at Lucija and see how her lips are clamped shut. I nod. Spoken like a trooper. Now get out.

We approach the road cautiously. A few steps. Stop and listen. No sound of a car bringing the cops back. Take it very slowly now. The road goes down and then there is a curve. When we get to the curve a gap in some eucalyptus trees lets us see down to the beginning of the causeway. That rough track we walked up joins this road right at the bottom. There it is, the police car, angled across this road. The super casino – at least in the fiction – was going to have a gate there. The car is as good as a gate, with a policeman to guard it. Even while we stare at it the second policeman runs into sight and stops in front of his colleague. He is making his report, hands gesticulating. An arm is raised. It's pointing up towards us. They both turn to stare. Do they see us through the eucalyptus trees? No telling. They both have pistols in their hands. We have to get past them.

They are not radioing for an ambulance. They don't want to explain how the souvenir seller got shot. They're not acting officially.

We stand, staring down at them.

'So?' Lucija says.

'So,' I echo.

CHAPTER 13

I could be dead. It suddenly strikes me. That hitman got the souvenir seller but he was after me. And Lucija. I look in her face and see it has struck her too. We know Matt so we are in the firing line.

We are standing and trying to drum up a useful thought when we hear it. A plane is coming in from the east. It is banking as it flies over the town and the bay and then straightens. It is sinking on final approach to the airport.

'The Russians have come,' Lucija says.

'The man from Gazprom. Putin's mouthpiece.'

So where will they be going? That is where we'll find Matt.

The way out of the trap we're in is down there. I don't know that we discuss it but we start moving. We get off the road as the cops could come back. We move down the slope towards the sea. There is no path but there are scrubby bushes that hide us. We are heading towards a cliff. The slope gets steeper. The shrubs die out. We follow the edge of the cliff, down, down. The cliff dwindles as it gets nearer the police blockade and we bend double. Then Lucija stops.

'My ankle,' she says. 'Stupid city shoes.'

We squat on the ground so I can massage her ankle.

'OK,' she says.

A mess of stones and rubble is at the end of the cliff. Plus one big boulder very nearly the size of a bus. How it ended up here is a mystery. The boulder gives us wonderful shelter but when we peep round the end we see the car. One of the cops sits in the front seat speaking on his radio. Who is he calling? What for? Whatever it is it will not be good news for us.

All right. This is like Checkpoint Charlie. There is no way to reach the causeway. On our left there is another rock, big, but not so forbidding.

'Foot OK?'

Lucija nods.

'God does not favour people who sit down and wait for their fate,' I say.

'Meaning…' She points at the rock.

We're cautious as we creep round it in case the cops have put a guard there but why would they? It's the start of the breakwater: sea one side, harbour the other. We set out along this breakwater. Maybe a dinghy will have been blown here by the great wind. This is no promenade. It is a scramble over rocks. Sometimes on all fours. Check behind. We're still hidden from the police car.

'Wait,' Lucija says.

It's not her foot hurting. She's forgotten about that. She's staring at the harbour. On the far side we can see the flag which marks the Garde Nationale office. On the right is where leisure boats are anchored. Calypso is somewhere in that cluster. Towards us are the fishing boats. No need for Lucija to point. I've seen the movement too. It's a skiff. A man is standing up, facing forward. In his hands is a pair of oars, stubby ones, which he stabs at the water. He can see exactly where he is going and makes his way round boats and anchor chains. He clears the crowd of fishing boats.

Now he is rowing across clear water. He is the only human visible and we watch in silence. Is he our rescue boat? No.

He tucks the skiff into a recess half-way along the breakwater and slips over the side. He is holding an anchor which he drops. Then he collects a trident. We're still watching. Sometimes he is thigh deep in water. Sometimes he balances on a rock. He moves slowly. He stops. He plunges the trident into the water. He lifts it out with a small octopus writhing on the barbs. He pulls it free and its legs wrap round his forearm, almost to the elbow. He drops the trident and tears the octopus free. We hear the suction pads ripping free of his skin. He hurls the octopus at a rock three or four times. He peers at it. Is it dead? He takes no chances and hurls it at the rock some more. Enough. The octopus is tossed in the boat.

I'm a journalist. If I write flights of fancy the subs cut them out. But there is something about this ritual – man hauling octopus from sea and savaging it to death on the rocks - that is primeval. The fisherman hasn't been sent by some ancient deity but he just appeared when we needed him.

No need for words. We continue along the breakwater. The rocks are torture to cross. We slip, we stumble. Glance back – still out of view of the cops. Lucija does a bit on all fours. I graze a hand. We wade so our shoes squelch. By the end the man has noticed us and stopped his hunt to stare. We stand facing him. Lucija supports herself with a hand on my shoulder. She's a bold foreign hussy.

'Bonjour, monsieur,' I say.

His eyes flick from me to Lucija and back to me. He doesn't reply. Shit, I think, he's only an octopus hunter. He's had no schooling. He doesn't understand French. We can offer English, Latvian, Hungarian and Russian but that will be no better.

'We have a problem,' I continue in French. 'We are here and we want to be over there.' I wave my hand. I make sure I indicate somewhere the other side of the Garde National station. 'You have a boat and we would like you to take us. We pay you, naturally. No problem.'

Fishermen have faces like no other. With the wrinkles, the sun and wind burn, the scars, the week's beard, there is no telling his age. His eyes are puzzled. He doesn't understand, I decide. But it's not that.

'There is a road,' he says. 'There it is.' He gestures at the causeway in case we might have overlooked it. 'Why have you come out here to ask me?'

Good question. His voice is rough. I strain to make it out. Subtitles would help. I am pondering my answer so he asks his question in a different way.

'Why don't you walk on the road?'

'Ah, there is the problem.' I draw a breath. Sometimes in life you have to risk everything. I point back along the breakwater. A scrap of car shows beyond the big boulder. 'Her husband is waiting for us. See his car?'

Silence. He is considering this.

'Where are you from?'

'England,' I say though I can see no point to this question. Oh yes, perhaps I can. 'We thought we had escaped but her husband followed us, first to Tunis, now to Tabarka. He is English too.' No Tunisian manhood has been tainted. That's what I am saying.

The octopus fisher moves his head so he is staring out to the deep sea beyond the breakwater for guidance. Then it is back to us.

'Why are you afraid of him?'

'He is a brute, jealous, violent. He has a gun. He has already shot at us up near the fort. Twice he shot. He killed someone else. But he is still after us. He has sworn to kill the lady.'

'He's already killed someone? Up there?'

'Yes.'

He is frowning at the trident in his hands. I notice the middle finger on his left hand is missing the tip. Should I say more? The scum's drinking? Chasing after other women? The fisherman is twisting the trident while he makes up his mind.

'Come on,' he says.

The bottom of the boat is not meant for escaping lovers. It is tiny. He prods the octopus aside and out of a locker he produces a plastic sheet for us to crouch on. Rummaging in the same locker he produces a stubby umbrella and opens it. He hands it to Lucija.

'Hold it to that side and hide behind it.'

He stands upright and with his stubby oars he turns the boat until it is facing the quayside. The umbrella shields us from evil eyes. He starts off across the harbour, not hurrying, normal progress. A bit of the giant boulder is visible round the edge of the umbrella.

Each stab of the oars shows a bit more boulder. Now the nose of the cops' car. If we can see them they can see us.

'Pull the umbrella down a bit.' I murmur.

Our course will take us past the anchored fishing boats. Then it's the pleasure craft. I catch a glimpse of the Calypso, nobody on deck. Our fisherman pauses and the skiff drifts.

'It will be twenty dinars,' he says, 'to take you across the harbour.'

Lucija wants to know why we are not moving.

'He's telling us the price.'

'Which is?'

'In pounds about a fiver.'

'Five pounds? To save our lives?'

'You think I should haggle?'

She gives me a look.

I tell the octopus fisherman that is fine. He thinks a moment – should he have asked more? – then starts rowing again. A ramp leads up to the quayside and that's where he drops us. Lucija and I scramble up and wait a moment. What do you say to a man who has saved your lives? Nothing is safest. We watch him. He stands up in his boat, prodding the water with stubby oars, heading back towards the breakwater.

A block away from the quayside is the Publinet office. We need to do some research. A dozen terminals are ranged along the wall. The woman in charge points to a computer at the end where there are two chairs. The keyboard isn't in Arabic but in French so it is not QWERTY but AZERTY. *Vive la différence.*

We start with Abdelkader.

Abdel is an Algerian nationalist in the 19th century, a hydraulic engineer, an ice hockey player, a doctor in Maine and more. No go for us.

We move on to Gazprom. It is a Russian company that focuses on exploration, production, blah-blah. Majority shareholder is the Russian government. So Putin tells Gazprom what to do. No arguing. Stand up to Putin and you get your orders to leave. See that open window over there? Use it.

Trouble is that Google has 22 million entries for Gazprom. We scan page after page, looking for the give-away detail. Gazprom uses the Nord Stream pipeline that supplies Germany. If Putin decides to blow that up it will teach those Nazis a lesson. It would punish the Poles and the rest of the Nazis in the north of Europe. But how about southern Europe?

And next is a story that has Lucija and me staring at each other. Gazprom is going to set up its own private militia. It may be like the Wagner group that fights wherever Putin wants. Putin denies it is anything to do with him. Of course he does. Maybe we have it wrong. Maybe the super casino is a façade for Putin's new Gazprom militia. Boats anchor down below. Who knows what supplies are stored in the castle itself. Or who gets in through that big wooden gate when darkness falls. Noseyparkers keep your distance. There'll be no second warning.

But there's still something missing. Think. Algeria is just round the corner from Tabarka, Google tells us. Algeria sells gas to Italy and southern Europe. The pipeline supplies thirty per cent of Europe's gas. It actually runs from the Algerian gas field across Tunisia to Cap Bon, then along the seabed to Sicily. Mainland Europe next stop.

So now the Tunisian minister, Mr Big from Gazprom and (best guess) some top man from Algeria are meeting here because it is conveniently close to the border. On the *Oxford Herald* I write *Under the Carpet*. But that's about Oxford baddies. This is way bigger. I write this story for the *OH* but the national press will jump on it. It's worth killing Matt for. And us.

How far ahead of us is Matt?

I am at the Taxiphone office. I am going to ring Rym. Lucija wants no part of that and has gone back to the hotel. The Taxiphone owner treats me as an old friend or at least a good customer. I have Rym's mobile number and she answers on the first ring.

'Allo.'

No need for my name if I speak English so I say: 'And *allo* to you too. I hope it is convenient to speak to me.'

'It is not. One moment please.'

I know the routine. She is locking herself away in the toilet. Speaking to me makes her want to have a piss.

'It is not convenient.' Rym again. 'You must be brief.'

The subs are screaming: *Where's the bloody copy?* You're still writing it. Deadline is on top of you. I know those days.

'Have you heard from Matt?'

'Matt? You think I spend my nights dreaming about that man?'

'I'm sure you have more interesting thoughts.' She is thinking of a repartee and I move on. 'Have you any updates on the big meeting here?'

'Big meeting?'

'Bardo has come here. The Deputy Defence Minister from Tunis is joining the party. Mr Big from Gazprom flew in this morning. If Gazprom is involved it is on Putin's orders. But I think there must be someone from Algeria.'

'Your reasoning?'

'Reasoning is a bit strong. A feeling in my guts. Algeria provides gas to southern Europe. Putin would like to get a stranglehold on that. So some big cheese from Algeria has to slip over the border. If I stepped outside now I could almost spit into Algeria.'

I stop. Over to you, Rym. But her reply is oblique.

'We have a spy in the office. He was here when I arrived this morning. Man in his late twenties, I would say. Short hair and polished shoes. Who's this new man, I wanted to know. *Stagiaire*, I was told.' Slight pause. 'Trainee. Trainee? First I've heard of it. Where is he from? University, someone said. No, he's too old. Refugee from the *Gazette du Sud*? That's down south in Sfax. You see nobody likes to ask him because he is a spy.'

'Keep an eye on his shoes,' I say.

'Why?'

'If he keeps shining them, he is not a trainee.'

'Why do you Brits make a joke out of everything?' She pauses. 'Maybe you're right. Maybe Mr Shiny Shoes is from the Ministry of Defence and the Deputy Minister wants to know what we have found out.'

I hear the toilet flush. Sign this conversation is ending.

'What's your phone number?'

'I'm not using my mobile in case Bardo can trace me.'

'Then where are you staying in Tabarka. Remind me.'

I've told her already. Maybe she's forgotten.

'Les Mimosas.'

The phone goes dead. That's her way of saying goodbye.

The driveway to Les Mimosas climbs up through a bit of garden with oleanders and statues. How do our minds work, fizzing, making leaps? I am transported back to Budapest five years ago. Statue Park is in its outskirts. Unwanted communist statues were abandoned here. My parents were Hungarians who escaped in 1956. So I have family in Hungary, aunts and cousins including my cousin Jozsef. Jozsef is special[3] .A policeman of a secret kind. Also a killer when it's necessary. Statues played a role when I was trying to find my wife Eve who had drowned (except she hadn't). Jozsef took me at a gallop past the statues of the toppled leaders of the old regime. A lot of toppling. We came to a halt in front of the statue of Ferenc Munnich who played a significant part in crushing the 1956 uprising. That was when my uncle – Jozsef's father – was killed. Jozsef smoked and coughed while he explained just what I was up against. Ferrenc Munnich's bastard son was now boss of a gang that smuggled drugs, people and arms. This was not just in Hungary. It had tentacles across Europe. Politicians and top secret police were in their pockets. Bardo is one of them. And Bardo is connected with Putin.

---

3 See: *Budapest Hand* by David Brierley

That is a lot to be thinking about. I slowed almost to a halt as I climbed up the slope to our hotel.

I go in our bedroom and find Lucija with a scowl on her face. She has been brooding

'What have you found out?'

'From Rym?'

'That woman. Yes.'

'The defence ministry has posted a spy in the newspaper office to check on what they find out. They are typically cackhanded about it. About Matt? She's had no contact. She knows nothing.'

Is no news good or bad? Lucija is thinking about this then brightens.

'Let's go into the town for dinner. Then we come back here and go to bed.'

So that is the plan. I've no complaints.

CHAPTER 14

'What was the fish?'

'Marbré.'

'Which is?'

'*Marbré* is *marbré*.'

I get a look from Lucija, the same look I got on the octopus hunter's boat. A long-suffering wife's scowl and we're not even married.

'I'm no fish expert. *Marbré* is what the waiter called it. A speciality around Tabarka he said.'

Just for a bit we are tourists. We are starting to stroll back to Les Mimosas. Then we turn a corner and see it. We stop and stare. It is called the Hotel de la Plage which is a lie. There is no beach. It is a block back from the roundabout with Bourguiba's statue. It's not the name that stops us in our tracks. It is the three stripes in blue chalk beside the door. It is evening and dark and we would have missed the stripes except there is a pillar made out of shells with a lamp on top. The three stripes are in the form of an arrow. They point to the hotel entrance.

Lucija tugs at my arm but I've seen him too: the policeman leaning against a wall across the street.

'The sign says *Circonscription,*' Lucija murmurs. 'Is it a police station?'

'Something to do with administration, I think.'

'Why is he standing there? What's he waiting for?'

We stay still. He is smoking a cigarette. He finishes it, flicks the butt into the gutter and moves on. We wait a minute to make sure this isn't a cop trick and then go into the hotel. The reception area is bleak. A door to the right opens to the dining room. Empty. A rotisserie is jammed against a wall, waiting for summer holiday makers. A television is playing so there must be somebody about.

I call out *'bon soir.'* No one appears. How about the handbell on the reception desk? I give that a wave in the air. Scrape of a chair and a man appears through an arch from a back room. What I notice is how his eyes drop to the floor beside us and mark there are no bags and then glance to the door where there is also no luggage.

'Is the hotel open?' I ask.

'I regret no,' he replies. Perhaps he doesn't like the kind of guests who don't have a suitcase.

'But the light outside is on.'

'The hotel is closed until the extension is finished. Perhaps you noticed the building work.'

Heaps of gravel and sand and wheelbarrows were to one side of the building. Nobody was working at that hour.

'So nobody is staying?'

'No.'

'Has anybody been staying?'

'I told you – the hotel is closed.'

'Maybe you can help us. We agreed to meet a friend in Tabarka but he didn't tell us which hotel he would stay in.'

'I regret I cannot help you, monsieur.'

Lucija knows I am getting nowhere. 'Our friend is called Matt. Perhaps he has gone to look for snow.'

Possibly he is only hotelkeeper in Tunisia who doesn't understand English. He frowns and shakes his head.

'You tell him, Baz. Snow is our safety signal.'

'*Peut-être il est allé chercher de la neige.*'

Neige unlocks a smile on the hotelkeeper's face. He holds out a hand to shake. '*Madame, monsieur, bienvenue.*'

Then there is a lot of explaining and a lot of translating.

'Your friend is a clever man. He has been staying here but he hasn't been staying here. I'll explain. Come and look.' He leads us outside and points. 'You see the shutters are open on one bedroom window. Your friend plays a trick. He explains the police are looking for him; good police and corrupt police. That is a very delicate situation to be in. The police will search all the hotels. When they come here I must tell them the hotel is closed during the building works and nobody is staying. The police have seen the open shutters of one room so they think I am lying. They demand to see the room. They go in with pistols in their hands. Nobody is there but the bed has been slept in. So I must explain someone was there until the end of the month when the hotel closed. Why has the bed not been made? Because the maid also left when the hotel closed. She will return for the high season. Then your friend says I must close the shutters because that will make the police believe I am telling a true story. Then I must take the police downstairs to look at the registry which does indeed show a German stayed in that room last month. Your friend explained that all these little things: the sheets not being changed because the maid has left, me closing the shutters, the German's name in the registry – make my story real and make the police believe they have done a good job and then they go away. That is very smart of him.'

The flow of words stops. I tell Lucija that Matt has been clever in creating his legend. The police came here and then left.

'So where did Matt sleep ?'

I translate.

'In high season,' I explain, 'the hotelkeeper puts the rotisserie outside and grills whole chickens. The smell entices holiday-makers and he employs a waiter. The waiter has a small bedroom at the back. Matt slept there. His name was not written in the registry and the police never knew.'

'I want to see the room,' Lucija says.

'The hotelkeeper insists it is just a very small room with a *clic-clac.*'

'What is a *clic-clac?* Show me.'

The hotelkeeper takes us to the back and the room is very small with a basin in one corner. A window with bars is high up so no one can see in or out. A bare bulb dangles on flex from the ceiling. The *clic-clac* is a metal bed that can be folded into a sofa. It has a blanket neatly stacked at the end as if it wasn't being used. Is this Matt trying to mislead any curious coppers that no one slept here? Lucija is staring at the pillow. It has a hollow. One head. In any case the bed is too small for two bodies. Her gaze switches to a corner.

'Those are women's clothes.'

'The maid uses this room to change into her uniform.'

'Does the maid sleep here too ?'

'Madame, I told you the hotel is closed.'

In Latvia Lucija used to work for the Citizenship Board. She weeded out people Latvia didn't want. It's where she learnt how to interrogate. Watch the eyes. Watch the hands. Watch the breathing. He's a KGB spy – get out. Red Army officer – never. Here it is more difficult. Is she questioning the hotelkeeper? Maybe she is interrogating Matt even though he's not here.

Lucija stares at the hotelkeeper. 'It is not closed for Matt,' she points out. 'Maybe it is not closed for the maid either.'

The hotelkeeper says nothing when I translate. He just shakes his head.

'How long was he here?'

'Three nights.'

'Three! But we have been in Tabarka two nights ourselves. What was he doing?'

'He was looking for the man who wants to kill him.'

'He told you this?'

'He speaks perfect German. I have worked in Germany. I was a waiter in Koblenz for three years. I was happy to speak with him one night so I do not forget the language.'

'How was he looking for this man?'

'He didn't tell me. He just came and went.

'How?'

'I show you.'

Beside the reception desk the wall has had a chunk knocked out. A heavy duty plastic sheet keeps the worst of the builders' mess from spilling into the hotel. The hotelkeeper pulls it back and we step out over rubble and spades and buckets.

'When did you last see him?'

'Yesterday. He said he was going to Tunis to get money. But you can get money here from the machine. He wouldn't use that because he said they would be certain he was in Tabarka and search everywhere for him. They would look for him hiding under every leaf, he said. Then I said to him: take a *louage* to Béja and get your money there.'

'And did he ?'

'I don't know. I haven't seen him since.'

'Did he sleep here last night?'

The hotelkeeper points to the plastic sheet guarding the hole in the wall. 'If he was quiet I wouldn't know.'

Then we hear it: the sound of a crowd, shouts, wails, cries. Whatever it is must be just round the corner. The three of us go to find out. The police are pulling a barricade across the causeway and pushing everyone behind it. A van is parked, white with script in Arabic and one big French word: AMBULANCE. Two men are carrying a stretcher across the causeway. We can't see the victim's face. No mistaking the tray resting on his chest with a scattering of necklaces and bracelets.

The crowd falls silent in the face of death.

We are back at Les Mimosas. Lucija has gone straight out onto the terrace of our room. I follow her and she is leaning over the railing like someone considering suicide.

'That man,' she says.

'Terrible. But at least the body has been found.'

'I'm not talking about him.'

She means Matt. I can't think of anything useful to say.

'Three days he's been here. Why hasn't he looked for me?'

'We're registered under my Hungarian name. He doesn't know that.'

Logic doesn't impress her.

'And the maid's clothes in that poky little room. Do you believe that hotelkeeper's story?'

'That *clic-clac* is not big enough for two people.'

'Have you never made love on the floor?'

I don't say anything.

'Baz, I want to go to bed,' she says. 'I need you. I need you now.'

CHAPTER 15

The day does not begin well. I try to ring Mary. There is no answer from the house phone. No luck with her mobile either.

I try ringing the *Old Hag*. That's what we toilers call the *Oxford Herald*. The editor is 'in conference'. Nobody goes to meetings any more. Meetings are so last century. I leave a message that someone tried to kill me but they shot the wrong man. Provincial journalist not killed in third world country – that won't even make page 13.

Hipkiss next. I greet him with a merry, 'Good day to the Panama hat. I trust it is safely on your head.'

Is he there? Finally he says, 'You haven't heard obviously.'

'What haven't I heard?'

'About Lannouz.'

'No.'

'He was shot yesterday afternoon.'

Sometimes your brain stutters to a halt. 'Dead?'

'At the Centre for Strategic Studies. In the garden. Apparently Lannouz liked to wander round smelling the roses. The cook in the kitchen heard a bang. She looked out of a window and saw a man running. The service gate to the road was unlocked.'

'Is this connected with…' I hesitate. I am using the Taxiphone but now I trust nothing.

'You're right to be careful,' Hipkiss says. 'But the answer is yes, that is the most likely reason. I had a long talk with him yesterday morning. For security I got the hell out of the embassy and I used a burner phone. You should use one too.'

Hipkiss is right. Why didn't I get a burner phone right at the start?

'Burner phones haven't reached Tabarka yet. It's the sort of place where men still hunt octopuses with a trident.'

'Is that so?' Hipkiss has the tone of voice that means he couldn't care a damn about octopuses and tridents. 'Lannouz was looking into personnel changes at their embassy and trade mission. Yes, there were changes but there is always rotation and nothing seemed out of the ordinary. Then he went on to Aeroflot's passenger lists. They don't like it, but Aeroflot has to supply details of incoming passengers. Lannouz struck lucky. There was a block booking from Moscow to Tunis. The individual names were all given and the block booking was identified as the Voronezh Chamber Quartet. A quartet is four players. There were fifteen names.'

'That was careless,' I say.

'Contact address was Hotel Pacha in Sfax. Lannouz checked. The Voronezh fifteen spent one night there then left.'

'Did they come to Tabarka?'

'Lannouz hadn't got on to that. He was checking out these Russian musicians. No idea how he did that, but two of the names checked with Federal Protective Service members; address a barracks outside Moscow.'

'Lannouz found that out? That's more than careless. That's stupid.'

'Putin doesn't see the world like we do. He's arrogant. He thinks he can get away with anything. Sometimes he actually wants you to know he's done it. His thugs are the same. They believe everybody is too afraid to go after them.'

Hipkiss is quiet. So am I.

Then he says, 'Did I hear you blowing out your breath?'

'You did. Lannouz was fitting the pieces together and now he is dead. God help us.'

'God help us? Death is certain. The existence of God is open to debate. That's my view,' Hipkiss says. 'One more thing. A detail. While Putin lives I cannot believe in a God who loves us. But there is a case to be made for a God with a sense of irony. Lannouz was shot smelling a rose. The rose was called *Peace.*'

What can I say? Nothing.

Hipkiss breaks the silence. 'I have been moved to a safe house but the Foreign Office will probably pull me out altogether. If I can't move anywhere without armed police then I can't do my job. Four of us were in that meeting room at the Centre for Strategic Studies. One is dead. I am in a safe house awaiting my evacuation orders with three armed guards for company. That leaves you and the lady. Think about it. Think very carefully.'

I do think about it. I think about it time after time but the logic never changes. Bardo has risen and risen so now he is Deputy Director of Intelligence in London. He does his job supremely well which is excellent cover for his dark side. He is Putin's man. Until Bardo is unmasked or killed Matt is not safe. Nor is Lucija. Now I am not safe either. Hipkiss is confined to a safe house. Lannouz knew the facts and he was shot. But when Bardo is dead the slate is wiped clean. Or of course when Putin is dead. That would do. Any volunteers?

I've been away an hour making phone calls. Lucija has stayed at Les Mimosas. There are two interconnecting lounges and she is sitting in the first one with a door that is always open to Reception. Her eyes are fixed on a photo on the wall. It shows a hunter posing with his rifle surrounded by twenty wild boar, maybe more. I wasn't counting.

'Do you see what I see?'

'Man with a rifle? We're next in his sights?'

She points at the photo. Beyond the dead wild boar is a drift of snow.

'Snow,' she says. 'We've got to find Matt. We can't just sit here.'

She is the one who's been sitting. I don't point this out. She's been brooding again. She's angry with Matt. It may be more than that. She may be angry with herself for being angry with Matt. Maybe she's even angry with herself for knowing she's not angry with Matt but angry with herself. And so it goes. It's complicated being with Lucija.

I tell her about Lannouz being killed. I get a nod. It doesn't hit her as hard as it hit me. She never trusted him. Being with Lucija is definitely complicated.

On with the search for Matt and Bardo and Mr Big from Gazprom and the Voronezh Chamber Quartet.

I go to Shamsi at the reception desk. If Lucija and I are looking for Mr Big from Gazprom and Bardo and a gang of Russians and maybe people from Algeria then it has to be a big villa they have rented. I ask Shamsi about estate agents and she produces a typed list of four. Why is she so quick? Many guests who stay in the hotel decide they like Tabarka, she says. They want to live here or possibly rent a house so they keep a list of recommended estate agencies. Next she produces a town plan. She points out where these agencies are. Lucija and I take two agencies each. Rendezvous in that dusty little garden we met at yesterday. It would be better if we visited the agents together because she doesn't speak French.

'I have been listening to you and I have picked up some French.'

'Well done.' I am impressed. And yet… there is something about the look on her face. 'Go on then.'

'*Bonjour. Oui. Non.*' She pauses. '*Merde.*'

'Very good.'

'You are a man. You use your French,' she says. 'I am a woman. I have a different strategy.'

She doesn't say more.

Estate agents live in a different world. This is a well-known fact. They speak a different language. A room is never small, it is perfect for a child. The kitchen is not old-fashioned and dirty, it is a space waiting for your creative vision. They smile and nod. They're eager when I say what I'm looking for. A big villa, yes, yes. A really big villa. Of course. Outside Tabarka. Hmm, yes. Ten bedrooms, silence. At least ten. Both tried to persuade me I wanted an apartment in the zone touristique. Apartments with a sea view. Balconies where I can watch the sun set over the castle. A beach right under my nose. I'm sure the beach is wonderful but I'm not looking for a beach. I asked for a big villa.

Was talking in French a man strategy? It hasn't worked. My mind drifts. I think of man strategies in history. Phillip II sends his Armada up the English Channel. Hitler invades every country he can see on a map. Napoleon marches on Moscow. Losers, the lot of them. Now it's Putin's turn. What is happening in Tabarka is part of his man strategy. I'm having these grand thoughts while I wander aimlessly.

Where am I? In a narrow street back of the centre of town. Between the houses I can see down to the harbour. Hang about - there's the Calypso. I gaze at it, willing something to happen. It doesn't move. Nobody appears. Even the seagulls are uninterested. I take a few steps and come to a halt in front of a stone-built bungalow. In the window is a hand-written notice: *Chambres à louer.*

Estate agents were no good. Time to think outside the box. Go on.

The doorknocker is a hand of Fatima. It gives a bang that frightens the pigeons. A woman about my age answers.

'Oui, monsieur?'

'Bonjour madame.'

'Et bonjour à vous.'

She is French not Tunisian. And she is dressed all in black.

'Have I come at a bad moment?'

'Why do you say that?'

'It looks as if you are in mourning.'

'I am.'

'I am very sorry. I should leave.'

'Why? You are here. You used the doorknocker. It makes a sound like a gunshot. That is how he died.' She raises a hand, two fingers extended. It makes a pistol aiming just over my shoulder. This is a woman like no other. I take a step back. 'You didn't shoot him so don't worry.'

'Who was he? The man who was killed?'

'Ibrahim.'

'Ibrahim,' I repeat.

'Everyone knows Ibrahim. Knew him, I should say. Obviously you don't. You're a stranger here. He sold souvenirs up by the Genoese fort. Also he played the drums. If your band came from, I don't know, say from Thailand without a drummer Ibrahim would step forward.'

Limp forward. I hold back from saying it. Is it just for Ibrahim that she's in mourning? She seems a tough woman. It could be something else that makes her want to talk.

'And it's his funeral today?'

'Women play little part in funerals here. But I am wearing black. Now, you knocked at my door. You came to see me.'

'You have a sign in the window that you rent rooms.'

'I do. Come inside.'

We walk straight into…what? The sitting room. It is small, made smaller by that overstuffed furniture you see in houses in rural France. I saw something like it at the Hotel Salammbo in Tunis.

'How many rooms do you have to let?'

She puts her head to one side while she considers. 'One,' she says. Why did it take so long to add up to one? 'Maybe two.'

She sees the query in my face.

'My son is fourteen. I have sent him back to France to go to school. He is at the *lycée* in Béziers. So his bedroom is free.'

'Maybe two bedrooms?'

'There is mine.'

I stare at her and she stares right back. A stupid thought pops into my head: she is included with the room. Why do men have these thoughts?

'Let me explain. Jeannot was in the army. Jeannot my husband, not my son. And he was in the French army not the Tunisian. He was sent to Mali. Mali is no longer a French colony but they still call for help when they are in trouble. Actually he was in the Foreign

Legion. The soldiers are all foreign but the officers are French. There are Islamist groups who hold bits of Mali. Jeannot and his company were sent to Timbuktu. They went to a village close to the desert. Jeannot believed a leader should lead so he was out in front and a sniper shot him. Just here.' She lays a hand on her heart.

'That is terrible, My most sincere condolences.' It sounds better in French.

'I am not Muslim but most people here are. So I am wearing black not just for Ibrahim but also for Jeannot. The custom is that a widow mourns for four months and ten days. That is very precise, isn't it? I have a calendar and I cross off the days. I am at four months and five days. After that…' She raises her eyebrows. 'Enough. About the room. Would you like to see it?'

Is it her openness? Is it the way she shares her life? Could it be the way she stares straight into my eyes? I don't know. But I need help and maybe … just maybe… she can help. See, I am thinking outside the box.

'You have one, maybe two, rooms to rent. I am looking for more, lots more. Ten, maybe twelve rooms.'

'What is it? A football team?'

'Not fun and games.' I do a bit of theatrical business, checking over each shoulder. 'The Russians are coming.'

'The Russians are coming,' she repeats. She raises her eyebrows, giving this some thought. What is going through her head? Possibly she has decided I am loopy. Maybe I am. Why am I knocking on a door in a back street of a town in Tunisia and telling a stranger the Russians are coming? But I am a newspaper man and all journalists know that sometimes it is like fly fishing and that sometimes you must cast a brightly coloured fly to tempt the prize.

Now she puts her head to one side and stares at me. Then she says, 'Tell me more. You interest me. Is this to do with that casino people talk about? The secret that isn't a secret?'

'That is what you are meant to think: a stupid casino that will never be built. No, this is serious.'

'Yes?'

Her husband was a soldier. He was killed in the service of France. This is why she will help me.

'It's to do with Russia controlling the gas for southern Europe. There is already the gas pipeline to Germany controlled by Russia. There is also the pipeline from Algeria to Italy that crosses Tunisia. Controlling that pipeline is what Putin wants. So there is this meeting to agree the plan.'

I hold her eyes and nod. I have no proof this is what the meeting is for, but it fits what I know.

'I need to find out where it is. So I said I was looking for somewhere big enough for everybody to meet and sleep.'

'You are a spy?'

'I am a journalist. And no, I don't work for *The Times*. It's just a provincial paper.'

'Maybe I've heard of it.'

'The *Oxford Herald?* I doubt you've heard of it. But this is a big story and Fleet Street will pick it up.'

'Well, all journalists are spies.' She states this as if it is a well known fact. I don't argue. I wait for her to go on. 'The Russians arrived in a private plane?'

'Yes.'

'I watched a small jet doing a lap of honour round the bay before landing.'

'That was Mr Big from Gazprom. He's in Putin's pocket.'

'Well, let's see.'

I've hooked her.

'There needs to be a room for Mr Big.' She holds up a hand and counts off a finger. 'He's bound to come with an assistant. A woman. Her job is to make him feel he is Mr Big at night too. She doesn't need a separate room. Who else?'

'Tunisian Deputy Defence Minister.'

'You are certain?'

'Yes.'

She counts off another finger.

'He'll bring a secretary, let's say two, probably male,' I say.

She counts off two more fingers.

'Deputy Director of British Intelligence.'

'Just a minute. You're not joking?'

'Don't forget I am a journalist. I know who it is.'

'Who?'

'At one time he worked at the British embassy in Tunis. Cover name Bardo.'

'More and more interesting.'

I am watching her face and see a flicker of her eyebrows and know this is not right. She wants to know who will be at this meeting. Fair enough to work out how many bedrooms are needed. But a name? No need for her to know that. She is checking how much I know. Why? She is waiting for me to go on.

'He is already here.'

She counts off another finger.

'He flew here?'

'He flew to Malta then came on the Calypso.'

'I've wondered about that boat.'

Again I pause. She is definitely checking how much I know. Do I stop here, cut my losses and leave? But I am a journalist. I go on.

'Then there will be the Algerians.'

'There'll be more than one,' she says.

'It will have to be someone with power. Plus assistants and security. I have no idea how many. You see why they need a big villa.'

She nods. She has counted off the fingers on both hands.

'You know a lot. Are you sure you're not a spy?'

'Who would I spy for?'

She opens her mouth but I'll never know her answer. She shakes her head and smiles.

'Let me see what I can do. I have certain contacts. Where are you staying?'

'Les Mimosas.'

'What room number?'

'Are you coming to see me?'

She smiles but shakes her head. 'When I telephone I won't have to give your name.'

'301.'

'Don't come back here. I'll get in touch with you.'

'I don't know your name,' I say.

'Good.'

She opens the front door and looks both ways. She's not satisfied and holds up a hand to stop me. She goes down the street to the corner with a view down to the harbour where the Calypso is anchored. She nods but I think it is to herself. She's satisfied.

'All right.' She gestures me out. 'Go.'

'Putin is a KGB man,' I say. I have already told Lucija about my strange meeting with *she who doesn't want her name known*. 'You may die of old age. You may be killed as a traitor. But you never retire from the KGB.The name changes but it is still the KGB; same aims, same killers. Putin wants to bring back Greater Russia. He wants to control the energy supply for the whole of Europe. That is the purpose of this meeting.'

'Matt believes he can stop Putin?' Lucija says. 'Truly?'

'You told me Matt wants to kill Bardo. Stopping Putin is an unintended consequence.'

The telephone rings. We both stare at it. We are in our room in Les Mimosas. Lucija is lying on the bed and the phone is on her side. She doesn't move. Who knows we are here? Abdelkader, Rym, Hipkiss, the woman with no name. Lucija gestures for me to answer. Maybe somebody has asked for the wrong room. Or maybe someone is checking to see if we are in. Remember the hotel in Tunis and how we had to run for our lives.

'Room 301,' I say in French with what I hope is a southern French accent. Pretend to be somebody else. Cause doubt. I needn't have worried.

'Don't say a word.' I recognise the voice. It is the woman with no name. 'I promised you certain information. Be patient. Finding out is taking longer than I thought. I'll be in touch. That is all.'

The phone goes dead.

Let's go out. The woman with no name has found nothing yet. Also if we go out there's the chance we'll bump into Matt.

It seems a good idea at the time.

CHAPTER 16

We're not talking. We're looking. There's the fort on the hill. There's the scrub where Ibrahim was killed because the man thought he was shooting at us. A bit closer is the old port with the souvenir stalls and somewhere in a cluster of buildings is the Hotel de la Plage.

We are walking down the drive from Les Mimosas. Spring has sprung and the oleanders have had a haircut. Shame they don't smell. Roses would be perfect. Any rose except *Peace*.

There is the new harbour with the fishing boats and pleasure craft. Where is the Calypso? We go further down the little hill and now the harbour is out of sight. We'll check on the Calypso but we'll go via the Hotel de la Plage. We walk through the centre of town. No sign of Matt.

'We should be chatting. We're on holiday.' It's something I keep saying. 'We're happy. Remember Sidi Bou Said and chatting while the motorbike cops watched? Speak to me.'

'Have you been in prison?'

'Me?' I say. 'No.'

'I have. Back in the Soviet days. I was driving down Brivibas boulevard. Those days it was named after Lenin. I stopped at a traffic light where two police were waiting. I had left the door unlocked. Stupid of me. One of them opened the door and said I was driving erratically because I was drunk. *I've had nothing to drink*, I told them. *Then have a swallow of this. He held out a bottle of vodka*. I pushed it away and he splashed it all over me. *Boris, the bitch stinks of booze, doesn't she*. Boris agrees. *Right, we're taking you in or you can pay an on the spot fine. It's thirty roubles for drunken driving.*'

'A bribe? As blatant as that?' I say.

'Bribes you got used to in the Soviet Union. That was life. That is how you got things done. Pouring vodka over me? That went too far. I'm not drunk, I told them, I wasn't driving erratically, you are liars, I'm paying nothing. All right, the alternative is we settle this on the back seat of your car.'

'Lucija, this is...'

She holds up a hand.

'You said to talk. I am telling you part of my life. I spat in his face. *Liars!* I screamed.'

This is not going to end well. I know it. I open my mouth but before I can say anything she shakes her head. 'Listen. Now we're coming to it.'

She breals off. Even after all these years it takes courage to talk of it. She glances at the tea drinkers outside a café. Do they understand what she's saying?

'In the police station I was told I stank like a whore and I must clean myself up. I was pushed into a bathroom and told to take a shower and they'd bring me clean clothes. I looked at the door: no lock. They were liars. I knew what would happen. They could smell vodka on me. I could smell the excitement on their bodies, the smell of lust. I didn't undress. I turned the shower on and stood against the wall by the door. I didn't have to wait long. The door burst open and one of the cops came in. He was already unbuckling his belt. He pulled up short. Where was I? Just behind him. He swivelled round and he got my knee in his balls. His scream brought his partner running. *Corrupt!* I yelled loud enough for the whole police station to hear. *Rapists!* More screaming while they dragged me down the corridor to a cell.'

We have come to a halt. She is panting like a dog.

'I wouldn't eat the food they brought to my cell. Most likely they'd pissed on it.' She shivers. 'They were liars. The whole system was built on lies.'

What can I say? Whatever I came out with would be trite. I put my hand on her shoulder and give it a squeeze.

'What happened?'

She shrugs. 'The ending was not heroic. It was humdrum. A lawyer got me out. Took a week.'

We walk in silence, turn a corner and then halt. Both of us put out a hand to stop the other. Just ahead is the Hotel de la Plage. Parked in front of it is a car, dun coloured.

'Is it...?' She doesn't finish the sentence but I know what she means.

Yesterday, after we'd been shot at, we walked down the hill and caught a glimpse of the car. Mostly we saw the front. We saw more when we were being paddled to safety. Now we are seeing the parked car from the rear.

'Colour of shit,' I say. 'Must be the same one.'

We step into the doorway of a shop that seems to sell chickenfeed. We wait. Not long. Less than five minutes. Two men come out. The blue shirt looks casual but seeing two together it looks like a uniform. They drive away. We wait in case it's a cop trick and they come back. No. We go into the hotel. The owner doesn't have a welcoming smile.

'Yes, the policemen have just been. Same questions. Also they wanted to know about a man and woman who were wanted for terrorism. Naturally I could not help them. If I have any news, I asked, how will I get in touch with you? His phone number seemed to be a secret. He just said they'd be back.'

'Has Matt been here?' Lucija asks.

'I don't know,' he says. 'I haven't seen him but that means nothing. There is that way in through the building works I showed you. And that little back room.'

'I want to see it again,' Lucija says.

Why? Nothing seems changed. Same unmade bed, same heap of maid's clothes.

'There,' Lucija says.

There are two blue chalk stripes on one of the *clic-clac's* metal legs. She kneels, her nose close to them. What can she smell? Matt's hand? His night with Rym? Are the chalk marks new? Were they there yesterday and we missed them? Anyway we already know Matt has been here. I thank the hotel owner and we leave.

'Now what?' Lucija says.

'Back to the hotel. We don't want to miss the woman with no name.'

A nod from Lucija. 'We'll go via the harbour. Just to check the Calypso.'

Check for what? I almost say it. But Lucija is already moving. We take the alley close to the Hotel de la Plage. It leads down to the harbour. A minute, two at the most. Look. Listen. No sign of Matt. But we can't quite see the Calypso. Go a few steps closer. There she is. Why is a boat called she? And there's a dinghy tied to the quay. Whoever was on board has come ashore.

Then it happens.

Lucija says, 'Hmmf.'

'What is it? You've seen Matt?'

'Hmmf.'

I turn my head. A man is standing behind Lucija. He's wearing a blue shirt and tan trousers. One hand grips her arm, the other is clamped over her mouth. Then fingers close round my arm. I feel a prick in the back of my neck.

A voice is soft in my ear. 'A knife is quieter than a gun. Don't be stupid.' He is speaking French so Lucija doesn't understand. But everyone understands what a knife in the neck means. Slight pressure on the knife means don't mess with me. My heart begins to stampede. Life in a newspaper office is not like this. We sit at our computers and write about kidnaps and murders. We don't live the stories.

We're pushed forward to the edge of the quay by the dinghy. The two men have a brief exchange in Arabic.

Lucija no longer has a hand clamped over her mouth. 'What are they saying?'

'No idea.'

The French speaker says to me. 'Get into the small boat. We are taking you to the Calypso. If you cause trouble we feed you to the fishes.'

Feed us to the fishes? He said that? It wasn't some kind of a joke? I search his face. It seems to have frozen and not in a smile.

I am rowing the dinghy. The thug with the knife is within stabbing distance behind me. The one who had a hand clamped round Lucija's mouth now holds a pistol. *Do something*, I order myself. This is our last chance. But do what? I wish I knew.

'Go right,' the man behind me says. 'Don't hit that anchor chain.'

I'm aiming right at that anchor chain. It'll knock both the thugs into the water.

'Go slowly.'

I heave at the oars. The knife has gone from the back of my neck. Now it rests on my throat, just above my adam's apple.

'I said *slowly*.'

The knife is sharp. I'm not James Bond. I'm a bloody journalist. No, don't think of yourself as bloody. I stop rowing. The dinghy drifts. I give one final pull on the left oar and we swing against the Calypso. It was a gentle bump but enough to make a head appear at the back of the saloon. The hair is skinhead short; a scar slices through an eyebrow, his neck is like a hippo's. He's a nightclub bouncer, a gang member at home on a Moscow street. We are meeting too many thugs. He shows no sign of recognising Lucija so he wasn't part of the reception committee for Mr Big at the airport.

The Russian and the Arabs know each other but communication is a problem. The Russian's French doesn't go much beyond *'Merde.'* The Arab has picked up Russian words from somewhere but not many. Abruptly the Russian's eyes shoot up as he understands who we are: the people Bardo has been after. He crouches down to speak right into Lucija's face. She stares back.

'All right,' the Arab says to me, 'climb on board.'

Quick glance to the left: fishing boats at anchor. To the right there is a skiff with a man rowing away from the quayside. What's the Arabic for Help? The French *Au secours* isn't urgent enough.

'No,' says a voice by my ear. 'No stupid tricks.'

At the corner of my eye I see the knife in his hand. He's twisting it.

'Go on. Move.'

The steps hooked over the Calypso are aluminium. I go up first, the French-speaking Arab follows, then it's Lucija. When she steps on the deck the Russian takes her chin in his hand. He twists her head so his face is close to hers and says something. Muscles in her cheek clench. She'd spit in his face if his fingers weren't clamping her jaw tight. He grins and pushes her away. In his other hand he holds a pistol. He's not pointing it, just holding it down by his leg. It's there, part of him, part of what he is.

The French-speaking Arab seems to be the leader. The frown on his face deepens as he tries to make the Russian understand something. I say to Lucija, 'How's your chin? Does it hurt?'

'I'm all right.'

'What did the Russian say to you?'

'It doesn't matter.'

'Lucija, the look on your face.'

'I heard the same at the airport.' She thinks how to put it. 'He said, "I haven't had a fuck all week. You're no spring chicken but you'll do."'

'Shut up,' the Russian says in English.

We're in the saloon of the Calypso. Saloon? What am I talking about? That gives entirely the wrong impression. A table with a bench and two chairs are bolted to the floor. The Calypso crossed from Gozo in a violent storm. How did they sleep? On the floor? If they slept at all. Galley corner with gas ring. A small sink is stacked with dirty plates and cups. Food? You won't starve provided you like Vache Qui Rit cheese and Hereford Corned Beef. A cardboard tray holds Celtia beer cans. No sign of vodka. A TV screen shows a Hong Kong kung-fu movie with the sound turned down. This is a boat so the toilet is the head. You must duck to go through a small door. There is no way out of here except the door we came in.

'Why are we here?' I ask the French speaker.

'You are prisoners.'

'I know we're prisoners. Why?'

No answer.

'What are we waiting for?'

'I'll speak to the boss. Tell him the good news.'

I'm scared. My hands are shaking. I press them against my legs so it doesn't show.

'Where is he? Your boss?'

He waves a hand. Out there. Mind your own business. Shut up.

I go back to studying the boat. Minimal comforts. No beds. No easy chairs. It's not for pleasure. You can transport goods. Like arms. Or drugs. Or people. Is that it? Mercenaries don't need armchairs. Could it be for the Wagner Group? They are Putin's favourite dogs of war because he denies they are anything to do with him.

The Russian has a mobile phone. I had one too but the Queen across the Water said it was insecure. The Russian makes a short call. Now there is the problem of the Russian communicating with the French-speaking Arab. The Russian is surprised to find Lucija speaks Russian and has understood his side of the phone call.

Lucija says, 'The Russian tells me his boss wants to speak with us but he's busy.'

'So we must wait?'

'You have a better idea?'

'Shut up,' the Russian says in English.

The Russian is wearing a blouson, half unzipped. He produces his pistol again and waves it in front of our noses. Point made. Lucija and I say nothing. A meaningless grin comes and goes on the Russian's face.

'Shut up,' he says again. He doesn't know any other English.

The Russian picks up a half-full beer can and has a swig. He shakes the can and decides it's not worth keeping so he finishes it. He has a belch but he masks it with a hand in front of his mouth. He grins at Lucija. *See what a gentleman I am*. His meaninglass grin lingers.

No, the grin is not meaningless. Think about it. The grin is the man. *I'm in charge*, the grin says. *I have your lives in my hands and it gives me pleasure. If the boss orders me to kill you, yes, I shoot you in an instant because that is what I do. And the woman – I'll ask what she will do to save her own life. Anything, she says. Anything? So we do it right here, on the floor, in front of those Arabs. And then I kill her.*

That is what that little grin is about.

The cabin is not big. The Arabs decide it is time to eat. Lucija and I sit on the chairs bolted to the floor on one side of the table, the others squeeze on the bench. There is a stale baguette and a tin of corned beef. The Russian pops another can of beer. The rest of us have water. But first, before anyone has a mouthful…

'Allahu akbar.' The two Arabs recite it together. *'Asshadu anna la illa ill Allah. Asshadu anna Muhammadan rasul Allah.'* Their hands are clasped in front of their chests.

There is silence. We are prisoners. How do we react? But the Russian is not a prisoner. He stares at the two men, his mouth open. He clears his throat and almost shouts, *'Na zdarovye!'* He raises his can of beer and takes a mouthful. Then he holds the can forward to the two men. Go on, have a swig of booze.

The Arabs look stunned and there is rapid chat between them. One looks as if he is about to punch the Russian and his colleague grabs his wrist. The French-speaking one turns to me.

'He is a *kaffir*. You understand? An unbeliever. He insults Mohammud by offering alcohol. He defies Allah the most merciful. We have come from Algeria and have been ordered to to stay on this boat in case we are needed. But no one can order us to witness Allah being insulted. We are leaving. We will take shelter in the mosque. After *Isha* we will return to see if there are new orders for us.'

The Algerians have pushed their way past and pause at the edge of the table when the Russian speaks. He spits the words out. There is no other way to describe it. The Algerians don't understand him. Nor do I.

'What did he say?' I ask Lucija.

'Insults.'

'Shut up,' the Russian says.

The Algerians leave. We hear their shoes on the ladder leading down to the dinghy, then the squeaking of oars. Their voices fade. Now there are two of us and only one of them. I turn my head to look at Lucija and smile. She smiles back. The Russian doesn't like this.

'Shut up.' He aims his pistol at us.

When is *Isha?* The moment the Algerians step back on the boat the odds against us go up. No, no, no, the Russian has a pistol. That is what we have against us. Do we have a plan? My eyes move to Lucija and find she is looking at me and then towards the prow. She winks. Meaning what?

She says something to the Russian. '*Nyet,*' he says. My Russian goes that far. Then he says more.

'What did you ask?'

'To go to the toilet. Maybe there's a weapon. You know, scissors. He said to piss where I am.'

'Shut up.'

The Russian points his gun at her. His finger is round the trigger. Neither of us moves. *Breathe*, I tell myself.

The Russian is tired of kung fu. He flicks between the channels. Cookery, cartoon, politician, Rambo. Hello, Sylvester Stallone is shooting with a bow and arrow. The Russian thinks it is funny. He looks at me so I nod my head and smile. Keep him in a good mood. Maybe he won't kill us. If only he'd put the pistol down.

He has invented a game to pass the time. He kicks an empty Celtia can into the sink by the cooker. Bravo, thug, well done,

The Russian freezes. Lucija and I look at each other. Yes, we both heard it. Clink of metal on metal. Definitely. Well, we think definitely. Doubt creeps in. But there was somebody. Or something. Maybe the anchor chain. Wave shifting the boat. There are no waves. We're in the harbour. Now we feel it: the boat shifts. Just a shiver of a movement. We can't all be wrong.

'Akli?' the Russian says.

Akli must be one of the Algerians. No answer. The Calypso leans a fraction to one side. Why?

'Akli, ty li eto?'

The Russian speaks more loudly. No response. He says something to Lucija. He looks at me. He frowns and points the pistol in my face.

'Shut up,' he says.

He takes a couple of steps towards the door at the back of the cabin. He listens. He pushes the door open and steps out. A passageway runs along the side of the cabin. He turns to look that way. He mutters to himself. There is something toward the bow of the boat that he doesn't like. A step, another step. Now he is out of sight. We hear his voice. I look at Lucija but she shakes her head.

'I can't make out the words,' she says.

'What did he say to you earlier? As he was leaving?'

'Don't try to escape.'

'That's all?'

'Of course not. He's Russian so there were a lot of swear words.'

There's a scream from outside. It's not surprise or fear or rage. It's horror. Lucija grabs my hand. She squeezes hard. There's another scream. Lucija squeezes harder. There is a stream of Russian. He is hysterical.

'Nyet, nyet, nyet.'

I understand that. Then words tumble out of him.

'No, don't do that,' Lucija translates. 'In God's name, somebody help.'

There's a shriek, cut short by a throaty noise. The noise stops. Silence takes over.

'Lucija, we have to.'

I don't say what we have to. We don't want to, but we have to.

We go to the open door. Nothing. We edge outside. Just to the left of us there are rungs leading to the roof of the cabin. The Russian has gone up there to find out what was causing the noise. He is sprawled on the roof, entangled in a net, a man standing over him. The man turns towards us. It is the octopus fisherman, the man who took us to safety in his skiff this morning.

'I saw the two men bring you here earlier,' the fisherman says. 'You were in trouble. I could tell. I rowed here quietly, very quietly. I waited. I waited for my chance. The two Algerians left so I climbed on board. I knew my time would come. And it did. The Russian came out to find why the boat was rocking. I was behind that radar equipment and when he came close I threw the net over him. He was my prisoner.'

He prods at the Russian with his foot, and again, until the body shifts.

'He killed Ibrahim. So I killed him.'

The octopus fisherman's trident is stuck in the Russian's throat.

'Baz, that 's not the man who shot the souvenir seller.'

'He killed the wrong bloody Russian,' I say. I take a deep breath. For us, I say to myself, he killed the right Russian.

Why didn't the Russian use his pistol? It's lying not far from his body. The net flung by the fisherman tied him down. That's all I can think. The fisherman looks as if he is going to kick the gun overboard and Lucija stops him.

'Could be useful.'

The pistol is not big and it disappears into one of her pockets.

'You know how to use it?'

'Yes.' That is all. She sees me staring at her. 'Baz, we had to fight for our independence. It needed more than sweet words to persuade the Russians to get out. Now we must deal with the body.'

I'm seeing another side to Lucija.

I talk to the fisherman. Push the bastard overboard, he says. 'There is a tide. With Allah's help it may take the body out. Maybe not. He shrugs. One thing is certain: he wants his net back. He needs it for fishing.

This is the most disgusting thing I have done in my life. I swear it is. There is blood on his throat and on his face and on his clothes and on our hands.

'Baz. This is stupid. We can just buy him a new net.'

'No. If the cops find the corpse with the net round it they'll be asking all the fishermen whose net it is.'

The net is caught up in his ears and fingers and buttons and belt. Imagine untangling that lot. We get there. Finally the three of us unroll the body and free the net. We drag the body to the side of the boat. We can't just tip it over the edge. We can't risk a big splash being heard. We have to lower it. I am at the feet, Lucija at his waist, the fisherman at his shoulders. Push a bit. Stop. Lucija grabs the belt. Half over the side. Wait. The railing is in the way. The fisherman has to get round the railing. He lets go of the body with one hand. Now the body slips, slides, out of control, our hands can't hold it and it plunges into the water anyway. We freeze. The Garde Nationale station is not far away. Anyone working a night shift? We scramble for the door into the saloon. We wait. We look at each other. We wait some more. Perhaps this is our lucky day after all.

'There is blood on the roof of the cabin,' the fisherman says. 'I'll wash it off.'

'What's he doing?' Lucija says.

'Looking for a bucket.'

'What for?'

'Blood on the cabin roof and by the railing. He's going to clean it off.'

'Leave the blood,' she says. 'It's Bardo's boat. If the police find the blood let Bardo explain it away.'

She's right. Then I think of the Algerians. They'll be back after *isha*, whenever that is. They'll find the Calypso empty and blood splashed around. What'll they do? Telephone Bardo? What can we do about that? It's a problem too far so I say nothing.

We clamber into the skiff and the octopus fisherman takes us to the quay.

CHAPTER 17

'That's twice he's saved our lives,' Lucija says.

'Deserves a bonus?'

'You British. Always a joke.' She takes a few steps. 'Matt was just the same.'

We walk on through the town centre. It's eerie how quiet it is. Just our footsteps, nothing more. My mind goes back to what she said, how Matt was no different. She said *was*, not *is*. As if Matt was history, out of her life. All right, could be I'm reading too much into one little word. And fluent as Lucija is, English is not her first language. But she was definitely…

Stop. Stop analysing what she said. Stop walking.

We have both heard it. We are on Avenue Habib Bourguiba. We know it as the main road from Tunis. But there's also a turn-off leading up into the hills. Sound of cars, more than one, in a hurry. Heading towards us. We don't discuss it. We just step off the main road into the forecourt of a big building. There's a sign in Arabic, another in French. It's a bank, flanked by oleanders. We push back branches to hide us. One, two, three, four cars. We watch them pass. The first car turns off onto the street that leads to the Calypso. The other three carry on towards the town centre. They stop in the next block and men get out. Half a dozen. Could be more.

A man is standing just behind us. Where has he come from? He's in a uniform but there's no police badge. He has a pistol in a holster, one hand resting on it. He says something in Arabic, then in French. 'Who are you?'

'We're tourists,' I say.

This doesn't impress him. 'This is a bank,' he says. 'It's not open at night. Even tourists know that. If you are tourists why are you hiding in bushes?'

'Those cars,' I say. 'We thought they were going to run us down.'

The guard doesn't like us. I pull Lucija closer.

'We have just got married. We went up to the fort because it looked romantic but it was closed.'

'Baz, what are you saying?'

'I told him we had just got married.'

'Oh.'

The security guard looks away towards the three cars. The men, whoever they are, are splitting up, going in different directions. Two are heading towards us.

'What do those two men want?' I say. 'The ones coming towards us? You've just said, the bank is not open. And all those other men, what are they doing?'

'I don't like it,' the guard says. 'It could be trouble. First you, now all those men.'

He takes the pistol out of his holster and checks the safety is off. Then he digs out his mobile phone.

'I am calling the police.'

'Monsieur, if you call the police they will think we are part of that gang and we are not. There will be shooting. We will be taken to the police station. It will be the end of our honeymoon.'

He looks at me, then at Lucija, then at me again. How to deal with honeymooners is not something he's been taught. He nods.

'All right,' he says. 'Go down that path at the side of the bank. You will come to a fence. The gate has a combination lock. 17-52-80. Repeat it to me.'

'17-52-80.'

'Go. Don't talk or those men will hear you.'

I am not good with combination locks so I am surprised when it clicks and the gate opens. We find ourselves in the kind of shadowy alley that muggers like. Our hotel is away to the left and we walk. Slowly at first. Then we hear raised voices from the bank and we walk faster.

'We can talk now, I think,' Lucija says. But she doesn't leave a gap for me to get in a word. 'Baz, you said we're married and we're not.'

'For God's sake.'

Lucija has escaped a drunken Russian with rape on his mind. Rape achieved he was going to move on to murder. Both of us. We escaped. Now we have a search party on our tail again. If they catch us, murder is back on the agenda. We have dodged the search party once and I don't want to have to do it again. And she worries that I said we were married and we're not. A detail like that? Should I make one of those little jokes that she doesn't get? Point out we are married, just not to each other? Not now. Dear God, we hear voices behind us. Has the bank guard told those men where we have gone? We were trotting before. Now we break into a run. Or try to. It's not easy because daylight is fading.

Then everything gets confused. It was already confused but this is worse. There is a bend in the path. We go round that and see the path divides. If we go left that will take us back into town and beyond that the curve of the bay to the zone touristique. We want to go straight ahead to Les Mimosas. We can see its lights are already on. We are by a hut when Lucija cries out and trips.

'Are you all right?'

'It hurts.'

'Can you go on?'

She gets up and takes a step, hobbles, then another.

'I can walk,' she says. 'I can't run.'

Walking is no good. Already the men are close.

'Look.'

I point. There is a bicycle propped against the shed. One bike, two people.

'Could be another bike in the shed.'

I try the doorhandle. The shed is locked.

'I know what,' she says.

'What?'

'Leave it to me. Hide behind the shed. Quick. *Now*. Just do it.'

It's a scramble. As I disappear I look back. Lucija is in the centre of the track holding the bicycle and blocking the way.

'Stop,' she calls out. 'Don't point that thing at me… I said put your gun down. Bloody idiot, don't you speak English?… I don't speak French… No, no, no… *Russkiy?*'

That sets them off. What is being said? Sometimes they all speak at the same time. Then Lucija speaks louder. Now it is just her voice. The other voices stop.

I hear footsteps. They have taken the path to the zone touristique.

'Safe to come out now,' Lucija says.

'What did you say?'

'It wouldn't have worked with you. You're a man and they would have shot you first and asked questions afterwards. I found out they were Russian and then it was easy. In Russia, teachers are still treated with repect so I told them I was a teacher and we were going back to the *dacha* we had rented when two people came running from town. They saw us and took the other track. Maybe they are the terrorists we have heard about. So my boyfriend – that's you – went after them on your bicycle. So the Russians went that way too.'

Easy-peasy. That's how it sounds.

Oleander bushes are our friends. They are all up the drive leading to our hotel. We stand in the bushes, half hidden, watching. Lucija shivers.

'Cold?'

'It's not that.'

'No, it's everything,' I say.

And everything is too much. We look and we listen. Nothing happens. Nobody comes to the hotel. I take Lucija's hand. I'm always doing this.

'Come on.'

It is not the nice girl Shamsi at the reception desk. A man we haven't seen before asks who we are. I tell him we're in room 301. Have there been any messages? No. Why has the woman with no name gone quiet? Why hasn't she telephoned?

The door to the lounge is open. Is the man slumped in a chair in front of the log fire security? His eyes are closed and he doesn't challenge us. Asleep? I doubt it. A fresh log has only just been put on the fire and a sleeping man doesn't do that. We climb up the curving staircase and go into our room.

'Close the door,' a voice says. 'Don't turn on the light.'

We freeze.

'Who are you?' Lucija says. 'How did you get in here?'

'I'm James Bond. I came by helicopter and landed on your terrace. I have a spare key to the French window.'

'I'm calling the police.'

'Don't be stupid. I am the police.'

'It's Abdelkader,' I tell her. 'He arrested me. Remember? He's the one who told me about the supercasino.'

'OK, let's move on. I have a lot to do and you have to escape. Arlette is sending men to kill you.'

'Who's Arlette?'

'The woman who wouldn't give you her name. She's a spy. The Russians pay her. It was the *Piscine* that warned me. *Piscine*? You know? Swimming pool in French. Last time I counted France had ten spy agencies. Maybe there are a couple of new ones I haven't heard about yet. Main one is the DGSE. Headquarters in Paris, next to a swimming pool. Everyone calls it the *Piscine*. So one day when Arlette was out I tiptoed into her house. You know that portrait of our dear leader in the front room? I put a bug behind it. That's how I know what she's up to. And everything you told her, who is coming to the big meeting. Why did you do that?'

He stares at me and I say nothing.

'Amateur. That's what you are. Amateurs always create a mess. All right, you're a journalist. I need you to go back to England and write up the story of how Putin is messing in my country. And you go with him.' He points at Lucija's jacket pocket. 'You're another amateur. You didn't even have your pistol out when you came in the room. Right, we have to get out – unless you two think you'd be more comfortable in bed.'

Abdel's hand is on the door handle. He pauses. There's a pistol in his other hand.

'I'm going first, just in case. Maybe Arlette booked a room the moment you told her you were staying here. Anyway her spying days are nearing an end. Could be a bit more information she'll let drop, I'll see. Then I'll arrest her. It's possible she'll try to resist arrest. That is usually fatal.'

Outside our room he raises a hand.

'We wait by that pillar. No trusting Arlette. She may have tricks up her sleeve.' But Abdelkader is a man who does't like waiting in silence. I think it makes him feel he's not in control.

'This afternoon I got an alert from Air Traffic Control that a flight was due from Tunis. I don't like unscheduled flights from Tunis so I went to the airport. Got there just in time. It was the Deputy Defence Minister. He didn't smile when he saw me. What was I doing there? "Just my duty, *monsieur le ministre*." He kicked the airport director out of his office and we went in there. He sat behind the big desk. I stood in front. I was a naughty schoolboy being scolded. *Now tell me what you're doing at the airport*. There are times when telling the truth is useful and I decided this was one of them. A lot of Russians have come here to Tabarka so I was seeing there was no trouble. *What do you mean trouble?* He was speaking to the third button on my chest because it was too much effort to lift his eyes to my face. All is well, I told him, there has been no trouble. *Then don't occupy yourself with Russians*. Occupy yourself, he said. Don't you love that? Then he told me to get out. I leaned over to shake his hand which gave me a view of the papers he had put down on the desk. There it was, the top sheet, headed: RDV at Ain Draham.'

* * *

'We're not taking the grand staircase,' Abdel says. 'We use the servants' way out.'

We go left. There's a door marked *No Entrance* in English, Arabic and French so we go through that. Stairs lead down. We leave the hotel building by a side entrance. There is a view of the end of a swimming pool with lights shining in the water. The gardens have lamps dotted among the palm trees. Hollywood comes to Tabarka.

'You must go,' he says. 'There's no need for me to tell you to use extreme caution. Go through these bushes down to that little road by the entrance. Cross over the road. There's a path leading down to the highway that goes to Tunis. That's the *louage* stop but there are always taxis as well. You want a taxi to Tunis airport. Don't stay in a hotel. At the airport go to…'

'But Bardo will have his men at the airport,' I say.

'Listen to me. Go to the Tunisair counter. Don't speak to the Tunisair girl. There'll be a man in a police uniform. He's one of mine. Just say "Abdel sends his good wishes." Got that? He'll take over, find you somewhere out of sight to spend the night, and tomorrow morning put you in a people carrier straight out to the Tunisair plane. No boarding pass, no passport check, no security check. You'll be on the 8.05 to Heathrow. Is that all clear?'

'You can do all this?' Lucija says.

'Yes.' He doesn't like the look on Lucija's face. 'You want to go back to your room and wait for Arlette's killers?'

'It's just I am overwhelmed.'

'So you should be. Now, Mr Journalist, I'm saving your lives and this is what you do in return. You work for *The Times*?'

'*Oxford Herald*.'

'Of course. I forgot you told Arlette that. Never heard of it, but it doesn't matter. You write the story. Put everything you know in it. The bogus story of the supercasino, the killings, Putin's geopolitical plans, the involvement of the Tunisian Deputy Defence Minister. Don't forget the lady's lover for the human interest. Everything.

When you print a story this big all the London papers will follow it up. And not just in Britain, all over the world. I want Vladimir Putin to know it. I want him to be humiliated. Tunisia is a small country but if he messes with us he'll pay for it. That's a 24-carat gold promise. Signed Abdelkader.' He turns to leave us and then turns back.

'Why are you waiting? Go.'

We make our way through the bushes. We don't meet any of Arlette's killers. We cross the road and find the path. We don't speak just concentrate on the rough path. Then we see a car coming up the road. We stop and watch it turning in to the hotel.

'Do you want to follow Abdel's escape plan?'

It's dark but I think I see her head shake.

'Ain Draham then,' I say.

CHAPTER 18

A taxi is waiting by the main road.

'We want to go to Ain Draham,' I say.

'You have a hotel?'

'Why do you ask?'

'A lot of people have gone up to Ain Draham. Maybe the hotels are full.'

'We are meeting a friend.'

'Meeting a friend,' he repeats as if that is an unlikely reason for going to Ain Draham. He nods.

And so we set off.

'How far is Ain Draham?'

'About twenty kilometres.' He takes a hand off the steering wheel and jiggles it. 'Maybe twenty-five. First we go on the Tunis highway. At the roundabout we turn right.'

The roundabout is just ahead when Lucija says 'Stop.' The taxi driver obeys. It's her tone of voice that does it. Lucija is pointing to the right. The road leading up into the hills is blocked by a police car, blue light revolving on its top. Two cops with flashlights are standing beside another car, a modest Renault that is hurting nobody. One of the cops holds a pistol, the other peers at an identity card in his hand. They're Bardo's men. I have no proof. I don't need any.

'Not that road.' I grab the driver's shoulder. 'The police will demand our passports and we left them at the hotel. They'll be angry. When we were in Tunis we saw what the police do when they are angry.'

'This is the only road to Ain Draham. Maybe…' The taxi driver rubs thumb and forefinger together.

Bribe the cops? If that doesn't work then it's double the trouble.

'Carry on along the Tunis road,' I say. 'Drive slowly.'

'Why?'

I don't answer because he'll say no. He shrugs and then gets going.

'This is the Tunis road,' Lucija says. 'What are we doing? Following Abdel's escape plan after all?'

'We're going to Ain Draham. There's this little problem at the beginning.'

I am looking back over my right shoulder until that police car is out of sight. Looking ahead our headlights pick out a breezeblock shack with a dirt track disappearing into a field.

'Turn up that track.'

'I can't drive up that.'

'A hundred dinars says you can.'

'A hundred?'

The driver rubs thumb and forefinger together again. I hand over five twenties and he turns on the interior light to inspect them. We get going again, turn off the main road by the shack and stop again. A woman has come out of the open door. When the driver lowers his window we hear the sound of a crying baby. There is a long exchange in Arabic between the woman and our driver. The woman laughs. We get going again.

'What did she say?' I ask.

'She asked why we wanted to go up the track. It doesn't go far and then it is just a field.'

'What did you say?'

'I said you were foreigners and foreigners always had crazy ideas. You thought there were wild boar here and you wanted to see them, even though it is dark. She said there were no wild boar here so we must go up to Ain Draham. So I said we can't do that because the police had blocked the road. She said to go across the field and then go left a bit until we came to a wire fence. We must follow the fence until there was a gap and if we go through that we get back on the road to Ain Draham.'

Lucija squeezes my thigh so I explain all this.

'Why did they laugh at the end?' Lucija asks. 'What's so funny?'

'The woman said we must be careful of hens' nests in the field.'

'Baz, I don't understand.'

'The woman used the French term *nids de poule*. And the driver asked if she hadn't collected the eggs yet. So it's not very funny but it's dark and we are doing crazy things because we are foreigners.'

'Baz, I still don't understand.'

'*Nids de poule* is French and it literally means hens' nests. In English we say potholes.'

'Oh.'

The dirt track has dwindled and given up. We cross a field, avoiding the hens' nests. We reach the barbed wire and turn to follow it. A line of poplars has been planted and the road to Ain Draham runs beside them. The headlights pick up a gap in the poplars. When we reach that we find the barbed wire has been folded back and the taxi can get back on the road. The taxi driver blows out a breath and mutters in Arabic.

At first the land is flat, pasture with black and white cattle. There's a half moon so I can see the cattle are standing and staring at us.

'A passing car must be a big excitement for them,' I say.

Lucija says nothing.

'I wonder if they're Friesians,' I go on.

More nothing from Lucija.

'Oh well, just a thought.'

'What are you talking about, Baz?'

'You were lost in thought. I was trying to elbow my way in so you could share your thoughts with me. Oh look, there's a house. Well, it used to be until it lost its roof. Now it's an ex-house.'

Lucija swings round. There's a bit of light from the moon and the car's dashboard. She has a face I haven't seen before. I'm lost for words. No, don't be ridiculous. I'm a reporter and newspaper hacks are never lost for words. It's as if I had seen a sudden close-up in a film, all colour drained, shocked as she realises something.

'What are we doing?'

'We're going to Ain Draham,' I say. 'Ain Draham is in the hills. The taxi is climbing now.' I gesture out of the window at a stand of trees. Maybe they're eucalyptus. The taxi goes round a corner and there's a car ahead, parked at the side of the road. Nobody about. Nothing to worry about. But why is there a car there? I worry anyway. We pass the car. No problem.

'How can you be so calm?' she asks.

I think about it. 'Numb.'

She says simply, 'I'm afraid.'

'That's natural.' What else is there to say?

I put my hand on her knee and squeeze gently. I see her head dip down, looking at my hand.

She says, 'Before when I felt afraid I also felt determined and angry, something else to hide my fear. Not now. Baz, we must tell someone where we're going. If there is a catastrophe…' She snaps her mouth shut so she can't let her fears out. She takes a breath and starts again. 'Have you spoken to your wife?'

'When has there been time? And she never answers the phone.'

'We should tell Hipkiss.'

'Or the Queen across the Water,' I say.

She looks past me out of the window. Her head shakes a little. 'We're going somewhere, we're looking for a grand villa and we don't know what to expect.'

'Lucija, we're expecting the United Nations. Bardo from London, Mr Big from Gazprom and his gang of Russians, the Deputy Defence Minister from Tunis, someone important from Algeria. Plus,' I finish, 'Matt.'

'That Matt.'

I think she is going to start again about his night with Rym but it's not that.

'I don't know what he's going to do. I don't know why it is so important that I come, following all his blue chalk marks.'

We have run out of things to say. Just for the moment. It won't last. Whenever the taxi rounds a corner its headlights sweep over dark trees. I don't know what they are. The taxi slows as the lights of Ain Draham come into view.

'Where do you want to go?' the driver asks.

We can't take the turn-off to the right. Two cars block that. They don't have police markings or revolving blue lights on their roofs.

'What's up there?' I ask.

'Important people have houses there. One of them belongs to the government. Could be someone has driven down from Tunis. They like to be private. It's our money they spend but they don't like us to know when they bring their mistress.'

I turn my head towards Lucija and see she is staring at me. I can't make out her expression but in the dim light I see she is nodding her head.

'Drop us off here,' I say.

'Here? There's nothing. I know a hotel in the town, very clean rooms.'

'Here.'

The taxi's red lights vanish into the night. Lucija and I are left alone. That hotel with very clean rooms begins to sound attractive. I put the thought in the box marked *if only I'd known.*

'These trees going up the hill,' I say, 'I've been pondering about them.'

'Pondering?'

There's a query in her voice. *Baz, what the hell are you talking about?* That's what that tone of voice means.

'They're cork oaks. I've seen them in Portugal but there they were like normal trees. Here they are twisted and evil-looking.'

'Baz, I don't understand you. Trees are trees. They're not evil.'

'These are evil. In the night they hide things.'

'Like what?' Lucija asks.

I say nothing. I point. Almost hidden in the darkness are three blue chalk marks in the form of an arrow.

'Oh.'

Beside the tree wih the blue chalk marks there is a path. Matt has gone up that so we must follow him. But first there is a stream. There's no bridge, just stepping stones. Not easy in the dark. A couple of stones are missing. First I step in the stream, then Lucija does. Now we both have sodden shoes. Stream crossed, we start on the path going up the hill.

'This can't be the usual way up,' she says. 'So what is it for?'

'Hunters? Remember that photo at Les Mimosas of a hunter standing in the middle of about twenty dead boar?'

'Correct me, aren't wild boar dangerous?'

'Everything here is dangerous.'

It's slow going up that path. It's narrow with exposed roots and fallen branches. Then I stop, Lucija bumps into me. We hear dogs barking. Dogs mean humans. We go slowly. Around a bend we come to…what? A farm? A small road from the valley – just a track really - leads up to it. What can they farm up here? Maybe he's a charcoal burner. There are two dogs and they hurl themselves against the ends of the ropes that tether them. The noise brings a woman carriyng a lantern out of the little house. She shouts at the dogs and they ignore her. She says something to us in Arabic. I ask her in French if anybody else has been up the path. She doesn't reply. I try again: is it far to the house? She shrugs. No point in trying Englsh. Or Russian. We carry on. Our path joins the track. We can walk side by side. When I stumble on a root Lucija takes my hand and we come to a halt.

The cork oaks have spread to a forest. It's darker than ever. A bit of cloud has drifted over the moon. The cork oaks are evil and twisted. I say nothing. What is she thinking about? Me? I have a memory of that first night in Les Mimosas when she came out of the shower naked and stood there and I couldn't move and she said

'Am I going to be humiliated?' Now we stand in the cork oak forest. How can we get moving again? The cloud passes on and there is a bit more moonlight. *Come on*, I tell myself.

'I was wrong,' I say. 'These oaks are not evil. They make the corks that go in wine bottles. Look.'

From the ground to above our heads the trees have had their bark stripped off. Moonlight makes the wood look white and naked. But the branches still twist at awkard angles, contorted, as if flinching from pain. Don't be stupid, I tell myself. If trees felt pain they'd flinch from a chainsaw. But deep down – beyond logic – I cling to my belief they are evil.

What has got into me? It is not knowing what faces us beyond the cork oaks.

The path leaves the cork oaks and goes through a stand of fir trees. Some have been cut and stacked. And the woodcutter has rested on the pile of logs. Did Matt come this same way? If he did, he left no blue chalk marks. There is a discarded cigarette pack, *Cristal* is the brand. Lucija and I stare at the pack as if it is a clue. It means nothing. But it does when I pick it up. It feels fresh. I don't mean tonight fresh. But it wasn't discarded long ago.

We are still climbing but gently. More cork oaks. Then Lucija grabs my arm.

'There.'

Above the cork oaks is the first glimpse of the villa, just a corner. There is a line of small windows under the roof. Servants' quarters from the days when no self-respecting millionaire's house was without live-in servants. We creep forward and come to a wooden fence but it has a gate in it. Fortune favours us and the gate is not locked. We go through and the villa reveals itself bit by bit. There are a couple of floors under the servants' quarters. No sign of Matt waving from any of the windows. Not even a French colonial would build a house so big. No, it might have been put up by some big shot businessman to boast of his success. Or it could have been a hotel at one time. Or a nursing home. Light from its windows spills onto the garden. It's night so the garden doesn't show its finer details but it seems formal with neat hedges. There are clipped shapes too. Some are just globes but there is one that looks like an overgrown pigeon. Topiary is the word I want.

'And Matt?' I say.

'Must be inside.'

Finally I snap.

'Lucija.'

She pays me no attention.

'For fuck's sake.'

I never swear except when something is monstrous. This is idiotically beyond monstrous.

'Are you saying we have to break a window, scramble in and search the rooms dodging round the dozen people there? Maybe asking if anyone has seen a stranger with a piece of blue chalk in his hand?' I pause. Lucija could say something but she holds back. So I carry on. 'Why isn't Matt waiting outside for us?' A little voice in the back of my head says we have been following blue chalk marks from Tunis all the way here but Matt doesn't know this. That's the voice of reason. I ignore that snivelly voice. So would you if you had been climbing up through evil twisted cork oaks. 'This is absolutely crazy. We don't know where Matt is. We can't spend the night out here. We'll go back down the hill and into the town and find a hotel with a room. In the morning we'll ring Abdelkader and see what news he has.'

'Baz, maybe he has been waiting.'

Lucija points at a statue in a parterre. It is in its very own beam of light from a window. Hold on. I thought it was a statue. Statues don't walk.

You'd think Lucija would rush forward to hug her lover. She takes one cautious step, two steps. She stops.

In a low voice, first cousin to a whisper, she says, 'It's not Matt.'

CHAPTER 19

I'm no expert on guns. Among Oxford dons, words are the weapons of choice. Oxford does have the occasional murder, maybe drug related. As a reporter I have a chum in the local constabulary and he'll give me a peep of the murder weapon. This is different.

The man standing in front of me holds something that glints in the moonlight. It looks like a tool a plumber might use. I've seen photos from war zones so I know better. He points it at my stomach and says something in Arabic. I don't answer. He angles the gun towards Lucija. She takes a step to the side. No idea if she is going to chance a run for it. The man lifts the gun to her face. She freezes. Now the man digs something out of his pocket. It's an old-fashioned walkie-talkie. He speaks into it and waits. A noise from the house is a door opening and another Arab joins our little group. This one is a French speaker but doesn't say much.

'Come,' he says. 'If you try to escape you will be shot. I will shoot both of you. There will be no warning. You will be dead.'

'Baz?'

'Try to escape and they'll shoot.'

'Close your mouth,' he says in French.

Or he'll shoot, I say to myself.

It's a strange room we are taken to. Five men are sitting on plastic garden chairs. They are not speaking. It could be a dentist's waiting room. Then one of them – a thug with short blond hair and a knife scar down one cheek – pushes himself to his feet. He lets out a torrent of words. Russian, I decide since he is facing Lucija. He stands close in front of her and puts his hands on her breasts. There is a grin on his face. She jerks both arms up to break his hold and then slaps his face hard, first with one hand, then the other. The grin vanishes. She spits a few words in his face. The French-speaking Arab with the rifle doesn't shoot.

'Lucija,' I say but don't get any further.

'He was one of the louts I saw at the airport. Remember? There were four of them. This is the one who said I must be desperate for it. He's just grabbed me and said *here comes tonight's entertainment.* He'll have another think about that.'

Still no reaction from the man with the gun. Suddenly shooting us seems out of season. The thing is that if you make a threat and don't make good on it then it is no longer a threat. We are worth more to them alive than dead. I take Lucija's hand and together we go to two plastic chairs against the wall. The bad thing about the chairs is that we face the five men who hold us captive.

'No blue chalk marks that I can see.' I say it just to break the silence.

'Maybe Matt did get in and is hiding.'

'And you have no idea at all what he plans to do?'

'I told you. He is going to kill Bardo. It is Bardo's life or his life. I did ask how he was going to do this and he said I'd find out.'

'You'd find out? What does that mean?'

Lucija shrugs. Then she says, 'I've thought and thought and all I can come up with is that I am involved in some way which is why I had to follow him.'

'And he involved me.'

I speak French and Lucija doesn't. Also I am a journalist. For Abdelkader that is important. I have to tell the world.

'I played some part in involving you,' she says. 'True?'

I stare at her. Is she thinking what I am thinking? Les Mimosas hotel and her coming out of the shower and standing naked in our bedroom.

There are voices outside this holding room and then the door opens. The man who comes in could be mistaken for a gentleman.

* * *

So this is the man who has caused all our troubles; the man who tried to kill Matt, the man whose gang was the cause of my wife's death, the man who probably calls Putin Vlad. There's nothing eye-catching about the charcoal grey suit; Savile Row doesn't do flashy. The tie has stripes that must mean something: London club, Cambridge college. The shoes haven't scrambled up between cork oaks. It's hard to think Bardo has crossed from Gozo in a storm.

'No introductions,' he says.'You know who I am and I know who you are. Arlette alerted me to your interest and to expect you. Also I have had reports from my people as you made your way here.'

Bardo looks pleased with himself, which no gentleman should. Perhaps he's pleased because of the two men with him. Russians by the look of them. Pistols in their hands if we want to dispute anything.

Bardo stops speaking a moment as if deciding how much he wants to say. I notice something I missed when he swept in. He has an aroma of after-shave. I'm no more of an expert on after-shaves than I am of guns but I'm sure he didn't pick this one up at a market stall. So it's early evening and he's just shaved. He wants you to know he's not like the rough boys he brings with him.

'Arlette said you knocked at her door and asked about large properties to rent – just like this one. She asked you inside while you spoke. Careless of you to trust a woman you have just met. I agree Arlette is attractive. Maybe it was that. You thought you could slip inside and enjoy a quickie. But I see you are well provided for already.'

Bardo glances at Lucija and smiles. Perhaps it is the smile that a gentleman gives a lady. I don't think Lucija is a lady. I'm proved right.

'Don't grin at me,' she says. 'I've heard enough about you to know…' Lucija pauses and lets the pause stretch out, lets Bardo wonder what comes next. 'To know you are…' Again she pauses as if she's searching for the word. A frown is growing on Bardo's face. 'You are more than a shit. You are a Putin lover. There's no forgiving that. Now take me to Matt.'

In the good old days maybe this had been a casino on the ground floor. Climb the staircase and there were bedrooms with room service of an exotic kind. Bardo leads the way, we come next, the two goons tread on our heels. Bardo unlocks a door, takes a step in but blocks the view.

'I've brought you some company.' To us he says: 'Having the three of you together makes it easier when the time comes.' He doesn't say when the time comes for what. He leaves that to our imagination because your imagination plays dirty tricks on you. 'I'll be back. I've left so the others can have their say. The big decision has been made but the little people don't like being left out. It is *politesse* to let them say their piece.'

Bardo stands aside. Lucija goes into the room and stops. I go in. The door is closed and I hear the key turn in the lock. Matt stands up.

He is naked.

I'm an intruder. I shouldn't be here. Last night Lucija and I were in bed together. That was last night. Now her life is getting back to normal. Hold it. This is not normal. It's not just that Matt is naked. He is frowning at Lucija. He hasn't hugged or kissed her. He said her name when she came in the room but nothing more. OK, I am there. Well, I can't disappear. I could hide behind the curtain but that would make it no better. Finally Lucija speaks.

'Why are you like that? Where are your clothes?'

'I tripped crossing a stream down below. I took them off here. I don't know where they are now.' Finally he looks at me. 'Thanks for coming with Luce. She has no French or Arabic and she couldn't have made it on her own.'

He calls her Luce. It makes me think of a loose woman. I'll stick with Lucija.

Then it comes, the explosion that has been building inside Lucija.

'Traitor. I should smack you in the face. How could you do that?'

'Luce, I have no idea what you're talking about.'

'That woman in Tunis. Newspaper woman. Smirk on her face when she looked at me.'

'You mean Rym.'

'Yes, that woman. You slept with her.'

They stare at each other.

'You're not denying it,' Lucija says.

'No, I'm not denying it,' Matt says. 'It was necessary.'

He's not saying anything more.

'Oh.'

Oh is what Lucija said when she realised we had to share a room at that sleazy hotel. *Oh* is all she says now.

Matt is frowning and he says, 'I can't see it.'

'See what?'

'The parcel. Don't tell me they took it from you. They could kill half of Ain Draham.'

'I don't know what you're talking about,' Lucija says.

'I had to get out of Riga in a mad dash. I told you to pick up the parcel from Andrejs. I left a message on your answerphone. Andrejs knew a defector from the Russan FSB who could get some.'

'Matt, you're not making sense. What message? I left in a hurry too. I had to catch the flight to Brussels. What parcel? What was Andrejs getting?'

'Novichok.'

I close my eyes. Sometimes you do that because when you open them again the world will have changed. That's what you hope. I screw my eyes up but the real world is still there and Novichok is still Novichok.

'The nerve agent?' I say.

Matt has forgotten I'm in the room. I get a nod so brief it is more like a twitch of his head.

'The FSB had put the Novichok in a Glade air freshener spray bottle. God knows how they did that. I was going to use it once I got in here.'

'How?'

Matt frowns at me. He doesn't like being questioned.

'That would depend on what I found when I got inside.'

I tried closing my eyes again. It still doesn't work. Matt has had no plan. And this was a man who at one time had been a British spy. Britain – be thankful he no longer is.

There is silence for a bit. We each have our own thoughts about the idiotic position we're in. Matt is the first to speak.

'Luce, I need a hug. Every time I put a blue chalk stripe on a doorpost or a rock I thought it would bring you closer.'

Did he think that? I wonder. Did he really?

'Well, you've dropped it.'

'Dropped what?' Matt says.

Lucija bends down.

'This.'

When she straightens up she is holding a piece of blue chalk in her hand. She tosses it up, not very high, just to draw attention to it.

There is no knock at the door but there is a clink. The door opens and two Arabs come in. Algerian? Tunisian? I don't know. One of them is carrying a tray, the other holds a pistol. This pistol decides it likes my face and I find I am staring down the little black hole at the end of the barrel.

'Monsieur Bardo is a kind man,' the pistol holder says in French. 'He says you must be hungry. *Bon appétit.*' The smile on his face looks as if it has been nailed on. They both leave. Scratchy noise of the lock.

My stomach says it is dinner time. There are plates with cous-cous and vegetables in a harissa-red sauce.

'Don't touch it,' Matt says. 'It's probably poisoned. Remember Bardo saying having the three of us together will make it easier.'

So we stare at the food and don't eat it. Lucija picks the tray up and puts in on the floor in a corner. She stops by the window.

'This grand villa across the road,' she says. 'It's all lit up. 'Who does it belong to?'

'Possibly the deputy defence minister,' I say. 'That's my best guess. The side road from the highway was blocked. And Abdelkader said the president told him to arrest the defence man.'

'But the deputy defence minister is here for the big pow-wow,' Matt says.

'They can't have their meeting in a government buiding. Police and soldiers will be everywhere. Portraits of the president will hide microphones. So the deputy defence minister and his mistress will sleep over there. But he'll cross the road to meet Bardo and the Russians and Algerians here.'

We are all three at the window, staring at the building opposite.

'One…two…no, three sentries I can see,' Matt says. 'So… I have an idea… half an idea… we just have to…'

Matt doesn't finish. He glances round the bedroom. There are two wardrobes. Coat hangers, nothing else. Bedside tables with empty drawers. He moves on to a metal box in a corner. Its Arabic script means nothing to us. But it also has a white lightning symbol almost as big as the door on the front. Matt pulls it open. It is a fuse box. From the number of trip switches it must be for the entire building. But it is the large switch above them that Matt points at. Next to it is another white lightning bolt. There's no missing it.

'Luce, stand at the window. Look to the right. You see the light from the windows of this building?'

'Yes.'

Matt lifts up the big switch.

We are in sudden darkness.

'The lights in the other rooms have gone off,' Lucija says.

'All of them?'

'Yes.'

'We're in business,' Matt says. He presses the master switch down.

'Lights are back on.'

'Good.'

Matt turns to speak to me. I think he's forgotten he's naked.

'The building opposite is where the government minister is staying. At this moment he is over here with his chums for a meeting. He can't have his meeting over there because it involves Russians and Algerians and Bardo and other bad people. Across the road are police, army, security, you name it. So we're going to bring them over here. Let them deal with the baddies.'

Then Matt does it. He pushes up the master switch. The lights in the entire building go out. Then he moves the master switch up and down, up and down, to send a signal: *dot dot dot, dash dash dash, dot dot dot.* He pauses. I see his lips move as he counts five to himself. Then he repeats the signal: *dot dot dot, dash dash dash, dot dot dot.* Five seconds pause. *Dot dot dot, dash dash dash, dot dot dot.*

'We think of it as SOS: *Save Our Souls.* Wrong. Nothing to do with language.' Matt's eyes are fixed on the master switch. 'It's a distress call. It's internationally recognised. Emergency. We need help.'

Dot dot dot, dash dash dash, dot dot dot.

'There's movement across the road,' Lucija says.

I stand by her and see men with guns. They don't understand what's going on here. Nor do the people at the meeting. I hear raised voices from downstairs.

'Come on you dimwits. It's an emergency. Your boss is here and something bad is happening.' *Dot dot dot, dash dash dash, dot dot dot.*

Moonlight shows men grouping over the road. Then one of them holding a flashlight darts over to our side.

Dot dot dot, dash dash dash, dot dot dot.

There's a shout outside. I don't understand what he said. I can't even tell the language. Don't be stupid. It has to be Arabic. The man who bolted across the road must have turned to face the group waiting. Then he starts it, the same as Matt. *Dot dot dot, dash dash dash, dot dot dot.* It is a signal and the men come streaming across the road. Moonlight glints off their weapons. From outside we hear a gunshot, then another. Then voices rise up inside our building.

Matt turns the lights on and leaves them on. There are more shots downstairs, not many. Screams of pain, shouts in Arabic and Russian. There is nothing we can do. We are in a locked room. Not for long. A sngle gunshot deals with the lock. A pistol edges round the doorframe. Then a figure appears and gives a swift look round the room. It is Abdelkader. He fixes his stare on Lucija.

'Yes. I thought I recognised you at the window. Why aren't you at Tunis airport? I told you to get out of the country.' His eyes move to Matt and run up and down his body. 'Why are you here? Who are you? Why are you naked?'

'My clothes were wet. They've been taken away.'

Abdel speaks to someone in the passage.

'One of the Russians will volunteer some clothes.' Abdel lifts his pistol. A good persuader. 'Well, well, you're circumcised. I say that so you know I notice things. That trick with the mains switch. How did you think of that?'

Matt shrugs. 'I was taught to think. Could have read it somewhere.'

'Not in the Bible or the Koran. Who are you?'

'Call me Matt. Since you notice things you'll see I have no papers to prove who I am.'

Abdel nods. 'But you know these two?'

'Lucija is my partner.'

'Your partner?' Abdel 's eyes move from Matt to Lucija and finally to me but he says nothing. He looks back to Matt.

'What are you doing here?'

'My business wasn't done,' Matt says.

'What business?'

'Bardo keeps trying to kill me. Wherever I go he'll track me down. I know his secrets, his links to gangs all over Europe, his connection with Putin. I'll never be safe until he's dead.'

Abdel makes a small movement with his pistol. 'A death can be arranged.' Is that all he's going to say? We stare at him. He's no better than an actor on stage, making sure he is the centre of attention.

* * *

Clothes have been found for Matt. Is some Russian now naked? Maybe they're dead man's clothes. When Matt turns round to show Lucija she puts a hand over her eyes.

'Oh.'

'Bad as that?' Matt asks.

'On your back it's printed in Russian: *Sex Instructor – first lesson free.*'

There is the siren of an approaching car. Lucija goes to the window to check. As she passes me she raises an eyebrow. What does that mean?

'It's an ambulance,' Lucija says. 'No, two, Three.'

Abdelkader has been out of the room to check on the situation downstairs. Well, he doesn't actually tell us that, he just goes. There has been no shooting for five minutes. Maybe ten. I don't know. I haven't been keeping an eye on my watch. His face looks angry when he returns. Then it changes. Now he looks as if he can't believe it, whatever it is.

'Listen to this, just listen. Four Algerians came to this big meeting, along with two or three *bints* in flashy clothes and too much perfume. They have issued a demand. Yes, a demand to me, Abdelkader. They demand to be driven to the Algerian border. At once, maybe sooner. They say they have diplomatic immunity. So if you have diplomatic immunity, show me your diplomatic passports. And their leader, or the one with the loudest mouth, says that because they have diplomatic immunity they don't have to show their passports. Unbelievable. So I told them that if they don't show me their passports I'll shoot them as illegal immigrants. I put my pistol under the chin of the loudmouth and told him I would start with him. Now they are very quiet.'

'Who are the ambulances for?' Lucija asks.

'Not for any of my men. One ambulance is for Bardo.'

'But he's alive. He doesn't need an ambulance.'

'I'm planning ahead. He will be dead. His corpse will be taken to my office. I need to get in touch with the British authorities. Not the ones here. The authorities in London. I want them to send a plane to pick up the dead Bardo. I don't want to risk the Russians pulling some kind of trick with his corpse.'

Lucija looks at me. 'The Queen across the Water?'

'Yes,' I say. 'She was Deputy Director until Bardo got her kicked out. This will be her way back. She has connections.'

'A woman.' This troubles Abdel. His face creases in a frown.

'A special kind of woman,' Lucija says. 'On the last day, after she'd been fired, she gave Bardo her knee in his balls.'

'A tough bitch,' Abdel says.

'If you meet her,' Lucija says, 'better mind your language.'

CHAPTER 20

Bardo joins our party. I wouldn't say he wants to. A cop holding a pistol in his back is a great persuader. Since we last saw him he has been roughed up a bit. He has lost his jacket and tie and he's barefoot. He doesn't look much of a gentleman now. He glances at all of us in turn and gives a nod. And now a little smile creeps over his face as his eyes rest on me.

Abdelkader takes a big breath. 'I never sent for you.'

'His wife needs to speak to him. Believe me, it is quite urgent.'

He holds out a phone to me.

'Where did you get that?' Abdelkader says. 'Your phone was taken from you.'

'One of the Russians you shot was holding it. I nudged his body and there it was.'

'Baz? Baz? Are you there?' It's on speakerphone so we can all hear. 'Speak to me.'

'Mary, are you all right?' My voice doesn't sound right to me.

'No, I'm not fucking all right, I'm tied to a chair and so are the girls. There are two men here pointing guns at us.'

'Who are they? How did they get in?'

'How did they get in? You think it's my fault? Doorbell rings, I open the door, two men say they're from the *Oxford Herald*. I say *I don't recognise you and I used to work there*. They say they're new and they have a message for you. *You and me both*, I said. *He buggers off to Tunisia with some woman…* I got no further. They pushed their way in and produced their guns. Baz, I'm telling you that you are in – bloody hell, what do think you're doing?'

'Mary? Mary? What's going on?'

Muffled voices in Oxford. In Ain Draham it's silent. Then Abdelkader takes a step forward, his pistol aiming at Bardo.

'Stop,' Bardo shouts. 'Use that gun and they'll kill one of the girls. That's the order I gave them.'

'Daddy, help. He's holding a gun to my head. Daddy, where are you?'

'For God's sake Mary,' I yell, 'what's he doing?'

'Shut up.' It's not Mary, it's Bardo who speaks. 'Tell your man with the gun in my back to get away. Go on, tell him.'

Abdelkader says something and the man takes a step back from Bardo. Abdel says something more and the man takes aother step then moves right away and stands by a wall.

'All right,' Bardo says, 'this is how it is. You have ruined this conference, so I'll leave Tunisia. This is not the end, just a hiccup. I'll be making other arrangements with Moscow. One of your men will drive me back to Tabarka and I'll take the Calypso to Algeria. If I run into any trouble my man in Oxford will shoot the girl. What's her name?'

I'm about to tell him – I've opened my mouth and taken a breath – and then I think *no, I'm not playing games with a murderer.* I shake my head.

'Don't you understand? You'll be killing your daughter.'

No. I shake my head.

'She'll be the first. Then the other girl. Then your wife. Can't you get your head round that?'

'Bardo, you are a fool,' Abdel says. 'I have a gun and you don't. I could kill you now.'

'No, you can't kill me. Use that gun and you are condemning that girl to death.'

'For God's sake,' I can't hold back, 'you can't murder a little girl. Haven't you…'

'If your daughter dies, it's your fault.'

'All right, you win,' Abdelkader says.

Can you hear silence? Abdel admitting defeat. I am too stunned to speak.

'But we've got to discuss things calmly.' Abdel goes on in a relaxed voice I've never heard before. 'I'll surrender my gun, all right? See, I'm taking my finger away from the trigger – lool, look - and I'm holding the pistol by the barrel. Now I'll drop it on the floor in front of you. You agree?'

Bardo has no time to agree. Abdel bends over to put the gun down on the floor. Except he doesn't let go of the gun. He jerks straight up, snatches the phone out of Bardo's hand and cuts the connection. Abdelkader is a big man. You wouldn't think he could move that fast.

'Idiot,' Bardo says. 'He'll ring back. Nothing has changed,'

'Then I'll be quick.' He gives an order and the cop who had the gun in Bardo's back steps forward again. 'Right, nothing has changed. I have a gun and you don't. Plus there's a gun in your back. So…'

The phone rings and Abdel answers it.

'Hello,' Abdel says. He's raised the pitch of his voice. No, it's not Bardo's voice but he only says a few words. 'Everything's OK here. Is it OK with you?'

Abdel cuts the connection again.

'Bardo, this is the truth. Just listen. I have a surprise for you.'

There's no warning. He simply aims his pistol down and shoots. It's the loudest gunshot ever. There is a hole in the wooden plank not far from Bardo's bare foot, not far at all. Bardo jerks his foot clear and the man behind him prods the pistol hard into his back. Bardo shouts something. No idea what because he's used Arabic.

'No,' Abdelkader says. 'No good asking for help. None of your men can come. They're mostly dead.' The phone rings. 'Hello. Listen, the telephone service is terrible up in the hills… yes, and your voice sounds funny too.'

Abdel cuts the connection.

'Listen, Bardo. You have to tell your men in England to untie the girl, untie both of them plus their mother. Tell your men to hand over the phone they're using. When the wife and the two girls get away they are to ring here. Got that? Suppose you don't do that. Then I'll kill you. But it won't be an easy death for you. I'll kill you toe by toe. I'll shoot your first little toe off, you'll scream for mercy. Then I'll shoot the second toe. And you'll know there is more pain to come, toe by toe. If you're still holding out I'll start shooting up your leg. I'll shatter your shin, then your knee, your hip. I'm not a patient man so if you're still being stubborn then I'll walk away.'

The phone rings.

'But you won't walk away because you'll be dead.'

Abdelkader hands the phone over to Bardo.

'This is your chance to save your life. There'll be no second chance. Look in my eyes. I'm telling the truth.'

There is a long moment while Bardot stares in Abdelkader's eyes. I don't know what is going through his brain. Is he thinking of his toe? Could he kick the pistol away? Could he drop to the floor and…and what? Could he call Abdelkader's bluff? Could he shout 'kill the girl' and move on to the next girl? That's a gamble. Would Abdelkader care? Would Abdelkader shake his head and say 'she's not my daughter – you've lost.'

Abdelkader clears his throat.

'Ten.'

What's this?

'Nine.'

Abdelkader is staring into Bardo's eyes.

'Eight.'

What's this countdown? Abdelkader never said anything about a countdown.

'Seven.'

Moscow never planned for this.

'Six.'

Is he counting down from ten because I have ten toes?

'Five.'

Would he accept money?

'Four.'

'Boss, are you all right? I keep hearing someone counting.'

'Three.'

'Boss, what's going on?'

'Two.'

No, this can't be happening.

'One.'

'Stop,' Bardo shouts. He looks in Abdelkader's face and sees his eyes drop down to the floor and the pistol aimed at his smallest toe and his mouth opens. Is he drawing in a breath? Is he going to order himself to shoot?

'I said stop.' Bardo says again. He seems to have lost his voice. It's urgent but only a whisper. Can Abdelkader hear?

'All right, Bardo. Tell your men in Oxford there's been a change of plan. Tell them to set the prisoners free. Tell them to hand over a phone and when they're safely away the prisoners are to use that phone to call us. No tricks, no double cross. If I have even a sniff of trouble I'll shoot off all ten of your toes. Look in my eyes. Do you understand?'

Bardo doesn't look in Abdelkader's eyes. His head has dropped and he is staring at his toes. He gives his head a shake, the tiniest of shakes. I think it is to himself.

'Martin,' he says, 'untie the prisoners. Let them go.'

'Boss? Really?'

'Yes.'

CHAPTER 21

I have spoken to Mary and to each of the girls. *Yes, I'm coming home. Yes, I'm all right. I've had some adventures and I'll tell you about it.*

Hm, not every detail. Definitely not.

Lucija and Matt and I are loaded into a police car. We are going to Les Mimosas. Abdelkader is going to follow. There are, he says, loose ends he needs to tie up. Maybe he's talking about the bodies. Maybe something else. When we get to the hotel we are to go to the lounge and wait for him. The lounge is in two parts so we wait in one part with the door closed. Have a drink. Maybe the hotel has champagne. Or a bottle of Scotch. Abdel says he likes whisky. Just not that camel piss made out of figs.

There is no one in the further bit of the hotel lounge so we go there to wait. Except I have something that needs doing. I find Shamsi at the reception desk.

'We need another room,' I tell her.

'Certainly sir.' She has seen us all arrive in the police car. 'What is his name?'

'It's for me.'

Shamsi looks at me and frowns.

'I was a sort of bodyguard but I'm not needed now. And could you take everything of mine out of room 301 and put it in my new room.'

Hotels are used to room swapping. That's what I tell myself.

Abdelkader arrives and his face darkens. 'What's this?' He points at the bottle on the table.

'They've run out of whisky,' Lucija says. 'They have vodka.'

Abdel picks up the bottle. He inspects the lable. 'Molotov Vodka. Molotov? Soviet foreign minister, right? Killed a few people in his time, including Russians so he wasn't all bad. Are we going to drink it neat?'

'I've heard,' Lucija says, 'that some people put a bit of toothpaste in it. Sort of a mint cocktail.'

Abdel stares at her and says nothing. Then he disappears for a minute. 'They're bringing fresh orange juice. Now about Ain Draham. The building is in a mess but it's not Abdelkader's job to clean up a mess. I have spoken to the Russian embassy in Tunis and invited them to clear up the mess. There are six Russian corpses. Two more of their citizens are in hospital.'

A waiter brings in a jug. We have glasses of vodka and orange. Abdel drinks his straight down.

'Bardo?' Matt says. He doesn't say more. He doesn't need to.

Abdel draws the pistol from his holster. He makes a performance out of sniffing the muzzle.

'Bardo resisted arrest.'

The vodka is finished. Abdel's debriefing is finished. The evening is finished. We are standing in the reception area and Shamsi has given me the key to my new room.

Lucija and Matt are going up to bed. At the turn of the stairs Lucija flips a hand behind her back. I watch something bounce right down the stairs to the bottom. I pick it up. In my hand I hold a piece of blue chalk.

What does she mean?

We'll always have Tabarka?

We'll meet again?

I look up the stairs but she has vanished.

END

About David Brierley

David Brierley was born in Durban. He moved to Canada, then England and back to South Africa all by the age of thirteen. Travel and curiosity about different countries is deep in his nature. After Oxford University, he taught at a lycée in France followed by work in London advertising agencies. Once his career as a novelist was established, he moved to France. As well as writing, he was a prison visitor. Together with his wife Jill he created a garden that won first prize in a regional competition. Now back in England, they live near Bristol in a small market town whose name – Chipping Sodbury – always raises a smile.

Safe House Books is an independent British publisher of spy fiction which is reviving quality espionage for a new audience.

Printed in Great Britain
by Amazon

62846396R00127

CONTENTS

Introduction

If you run a business, or if you are responsible for the success of a business, you know how important it is that the business continues to grow. Growth can be measured in many ways: obvious and popular metrics such as revenue, gross profit, net profit and number of locations or employees; and less common ways such as reputation, awards and other forms of social recognition.

No matter how you define it, business growth is almost always seen as a positive, something to aim for. I say "almost always" because there are businesses that are content with their results and achievements, and perhaps some that are even consciously trying to downsize. I discuss some of the perils of growth in my own chapter.

But for the most part, this book is for those business leaders who want to grow. It offers a refreshing variety of ideas for how to grow a business, and includes many proven examples and strategies that have worked for its authors. Growing our businesses has not always been smooth sailing, but we have persevered, and if you employ the lessons we have to share with you, then you too will grow your business.

As you read this book, you may encounter scenarios you recognise and challenges you have experienced yourself. You can be sure there will be more to come in the future, but we, the authors, are on your side. We want you to succeed, and we want you to do so with the least amount of stress and drama possible. Enjoy our stories and consider the advice and guidance we have put together for you. Most of all, pat yourself on the back for caring about your business and its stakeholders, and for aiming high when many others are unwilling to do what it takes. Here's to your current and future success!

Mindy Gibbins-Klein
Lead Author
Success Secrets for Business Growth

Harness Your Team's Superpowers

LEIGH ALLEN

"Everybody is a genius. But if you judge a fish by its ability to climb a tree, it will live its whole life believing that it is stupid."

Unknown

Everyone Has a Superpower

Every human that has walked on this earth is a particular combination of genetics, environment and experiences. This unique and quite frankly amazing combination means that everyone has a talent for something. This talent is their unique superpower.

To supercharge your business, you must harness everyone's unique superpowers and combine them in a way that places people at the core of your business. My own formula for achieving this is to build trustworthy systems using *faith*, *freedom* and *flow*.

Faith in this context is not religious faith, but the faith that you are a valued and integral part of something bigger than yourself. Humans have a fundamental desire to find meaning, purpose, and significance in their lives. Even in today's more secular world, people still want to believe in something bigger – to feel that they are a part of a larger community.

This sense of belonging and shared identity fulfils the human need for social connection and support, and gives people a sense of greater agency, power, and control. And if they feel empowered in this way, then they will naturally begin to express their particular talents – their superpowers.

Freedom unlocks creativity, because it allows people to explore, experiment, and feel comfortable in making their own decisions.

This autonomy allows individuals to approach problems in unique ways that align with their strengths, leading to a diverse range of novel ideas and innovative solutions. Creative diversity within teams fosters a culture of innovation, enabling teams to stay ahead of the competition and tackle complex challenges more effectively.

Teams in a state of *flow* unlock a range of benefits, including increased productivity, enhanced creativity, improved collaboration, heightened motivation, and accelerated learning – all of which contribute to the overall success of the team and the business.

Flow states are reached when an individual is able to express a high level of skill while still feeling a degree of challenge. In other words, an individual can enter a state of flow when practising their superpower in a supportive environment that allows them to push it to its limits.

Building a Team of Superpowers

To have faith, people in your organisation need to feel part of a bigger vision and mission. They must feel that everyone is going in the same direction, towards the same objective. In other words, they must have a "north star" to follow. Business vision and values need to be clear and lived, not just posters on the wall, and individuals must all align with the team ethos and the business aims and objectives. To achieve this, each member of the team will need to know their own superpower, values and beliefs.

There are several ways to identify your own or your team members' superpowers. One way is to take time to reflect on experiences, interests, and activities that bring you joy and fulfilment. Consider what activities you excel at or enjoy without feeling like they're a chore. Reflect on the moments when you feel most energised and engaged.

Consider using assessments, such as the Myers-Briggs Type Indicator or StrengthsFinder, that can provide insights into personality traits, preferences, and natural inclinations. However, I would add here that these tests are not an exact science and that you should review the results in the round, as much of this type of work can be situational.

Freedom and autonomy within teams is built by each person knowing where they fit in the bigger picture, where their boundaries are within the team, and having the right skills, tools and information to make good decisions. Polarity is also key here. The best teams have individuals that complement each other's strengths and weaknesses.

For too long, people have been told to concentrate on and develop their weaknesses. This is not the case in high-performing teams. You should develop your own strengths and rely on other members of the team to cover the areas where you are weaker. Nature is about change and polarity – the best teams are too.

And as nature is a complex adaptive system, so are teams and organisations. You can't just combine superpowers together and expect them to grow. As in nature, you need to create the right conditions for growth.

The best businesses see themselves as a "platform for growth" that enables individuals to get the best out of themselves. As with any modern platform, the best ones deliver a two-sided network effect. In other words, they allow people both to increasingly contribute and to consume, creating a continuous improvement loop and flywheel that compounds to deliver exponential growth.

Maintaining a high degree of freedom helps preserve this growth, ensuring that "everyone is responsible, and everyone has a voice", which itself ensures that any bad behaviour is obvious and rooted out early.

Business flow is about alignment, not just the individual alignment of values and beliefs with the team, but also the correct alignment of all the "cogs" of the machine. As neuroscientists are finding with the brain, it's not just endpoints that matter. The actual connection itself is a vital element; they are not just links, but bonds where trust is developed and maintained. Relationships bind teams together.

Pretty much everything in life and business is relational. For teams to have flow, not only do you need to place the right superpowers together and create the conditions for growth, you need to be aware of the relationships that make up the ecosystem of your business. Successful teams find a way to combine all these factors to create harmony. Teams in harmony can move mountains.

How Pixar Used Faith, Freedom and Flow

In 1995 Pixar released *Toy Story*, the world's first computer-animated feature film. They subsequently released many other successful films, such as *A Bug's Life*, *Toy Story 2* and *Finding Nemo*.

How did Pixar manage to create an organisation that was not only the first to achieve a Hollywood landmark, but that went on to release sequels that were as good, if not better than the original movie, all by using their own internal artists?

To answer this, I looked at their approach though the lens of my faith, freedom, and flow system.

At the core of Pixar's approach is a deep belief in their mission and their team members' abilities and potential. The leadership at Pixar demonstrates unwavering faith in their employees, empowering them to take risks, experiment, and contribute their unique talents to the creative process.

Pixar cultivates an environment where team members feel safe to share their ideas, make mistakes, and engage in open and honest dialogue. This psychological safety encourages risk-taking and creates a sense of trust within the team.

Employees at Pixar have a high degree of autonomy and creative freedom, allowing them to explore, experiment, and make their own decisions. Rather than imposing a top-down approach, Pixar encourages team members to take ownership of their work and make autonomous decisions that align with the studio's overall vision and goals.

Pixar's physical workspace is designed to foster collaboration, creativity, and a sense of community. Team members have the freedom to move between different work areas, collaborate with colleagues, and work in a way that suits their individual needs and preferences.

To encourage flow, Pixar actively cultivates alignment within its teams, allowing individuals and the collective to be fully immersed and engaged in their work. Pixar's projects are designed to present team members with challenges that are well-matched to their individual superpowers, ensuring they experience a state of optimal engagement and flow.

By seamlessly integrating faith, freedom, and flow into their team-building approach, along with creating the best environment and developing the right relationships, Pixar has consistently produced high-performing, collaborative, and innovative teams capable of delivering exceptional creative work. This holistic approach has been a key driver of Pixar's enduring success in the animation industry.

Harnessing people's superpowers in a way that develops and maintains high performing teams will supercharge your business to new heights – give it a go and watch your business achieve more than you ever thought possible!

Leigh Allen

Leigh is an experienced consultant, leadership coach, and technologist, who empowers organisations to reach new heights by creating the best environment for people to flourish.

Leigh's career in public safety includes roles in the army, police, National Crime Agency, and as an independent consultant. He is driven by a passion for keeping people safe and helping them to achieve more than they ever thought possible.

Leigh's career gives him a unique perspective on driving personal development building and maintaining high-performing teams, and creating conditions for personal and team excellence to drive business growth.

Married with four children, Leigh lives in a peaceful village in South Leicestershire, where he finds the inspiration to make a tangible difference.

www.q2m.co.uk

Control Your Focus and Thus Your Business Growth

ZAYN BLORE

My career for the last number of decades has been in IT, with side ventures into startups. I've spent quite some time being a project manager, working in the corporate space to create high-functioning teams that can deliver IT projects consistently over time.

I've been brought into a range of companies to help deliver all sorts of projects, and I've grown to understand that IT project delivery is to a large extent about people management, and the focus those people have on particular tasks and issues.

While my corporate career has progressed, I've also been involved in numerous startups, and I'm very happy to say that I've recently exited three of these successfully, with each company moving on to the next stage in its growth.

Each of these companies has had different problems moving from an idea to a fully-fledged business, and each has solved problems in its own way. However, while every company must navigate a different path to success, without a plan, any startup or business is practically guaranteed to fail.

Without a plan you cannot know when you have succeeded; even worse, you cannot break down the steps required to achieve this success. Effectively, without a plan, you don't have the focus required to move your dream into a reality.

Often people are swamped by email, interruptions and day-to-day responsibilities, rather than focusing on what is important. By having a plan, by focusing on the specific tasks you need to move your business forward, you bring about business growth. You cannot expect your business to flourish unless you have specifically targeted your key issues and resolved them. That is a fundamental rule.

One of my startups began when I was deep in the heart of a FTSE 100 company.

I was a typical office worker, who had slowly moved up the ranks until I was the team lead. I was cruising, in my comfort zone. I didn't have a plan, I certainly didn't have focus, but I knew something was missing. Something was gnawing at me.

Just before Covid, I was forced to decide whether to take a slightly different role or leave the company. Having accepted the new position, I found I had left my comfort zone and now I had to find myself. What did I want to achieve in life? What motivated me and made me tick?

I realised I wanted to start my own company and be my own boss. To make, out of nothing, something I could be proud of, that I had built with people I respected and enjoyed working with.

So along with my co-founder, that's what I did. We created a plan, formed a team around us, and began our adventure in the business world. Over time this has led to working with numerous clients and creating products and services that are respected by our partners. None of this would have been possible without our roadmap, breaking down goals into projects, projects into smaller tasks, and having the focus to deliver them.

Being proactive, understanding what is important, and breaking that down into achievable tasks each day allows you to move forward and make your business a success.

How to Focus and Grow Your Business

Focus Each Day on What Achievements Will Move You Towards Your Goals

Make a plan! You are the expert in your business, so list the key hurdles you face and break them down.

Have you identified the problems in your sales funnel or with your delivery team? Do you have a specific list of roles you need to fill, capabilities you need to achieve, and issues you need to resolve to move your business to the next level? If you don't have any of these, then how can you expect to make progress?

Now you have a list of blockers, you can work on resolving them.

Break It Down into Three Tasks (Two Business, One Personal)

Break your business's main issues into specific tasks so that you can resolve them.

That may be hiring someone or putting in place a new process. It could be performing data analysis to understand who your target market is, then breaking down step-by-step why your sales funnel isn't converting them into paying clients. It could be identifying that your delivery team is delivering sub-standard work, which is having a knock-on effect on reviews and referrals.

Regardless of what it is, you need to break down the highest priority issue into tasks on which you can make progress in a day.

I recommend three tasks. First, two business-focused tasks, one to be dealt with in the morning, one in the afternoon. Then an additional task to be performed in the evening, ideally a personal task (going for a run, cooking a healthy meal, learning a new skill).

By focusing on three tasks, you will incrementally make steady progress, every day taking steps towards your goals. And without small steps, you are just dreaming.

Block Out 45 Minutes in the Morning and Afternoon to Do Each Business Task

Dedicate your most productive time of day to moving your goals forward. Remember these tasks are your priority: everything else comes second.

If you are trying to get a company up and running but you have a day job, see if you can move meetings around so you are able to work on what's most important to you while you are at your most productive.

When the work you are doing is in alignment with your goals, I guarantee that you will be motivated, inspired, and driven to make progress on your tasks.

Focus!

Remember it's key to focus on your critical tasks exclusively. You want to put your best foot forward when you are working on achieving your goals. Close your email application. Put your phone on focus mode. Close your study door and focus. You want to achieve quality results during this time, to move that one step forward towards your goal.

Celebrate Your Achievements!

Remember that this is an ultramarathon. Business growth takes many steps, many of which end up requiring correction. Take one step each day and celebrate it! I use big green ticks on a Trello board. Other people write an affirmation journal each evening, explaining the progress they have made towards their goal.

Celebrating your progress reinforces its effectiveness and motivates you to take the next step tomorrow. Perseverance pays off. Trust me, I've run 100km races, and I started from a point where I couldn't run a kilometre. That first step is key.

Paul Shows Us How to Focus

There are many personal stories that showcase how focus and perseverance pay off: sports stars, politicians, artists, and yes, business leaders. But for me, the person who most epitomises this is one of my childhood friends, Paul Crilley.

I met Paul while I was still at school. Even then, he had one mission in life. He wanted to be a full-time author. That was his life's goal, and so he immersed himself in writing. He wrote and wrote, and occasionally he shared what he was writing. He once said to me that you have to write a full-blown book, one that will never see the light of day, before you have sufficiently honed your craft to be worthy of becoming a published author.

I can remember us gossiping about him, wondering what he would end up doing in later life. Us factory managers, IT programmers and wannabe accountants, what did we know about what it took to be a writer!

I fondly remember the day when I bought one of Paul's books (*The Invisible Order*) for my eldest son to read. He thoroughly enjoyed it, and I got to support my friend. Since then, Paul has shown repeatedly that he is a master of his craft. Not only has he now written multiple books but 27 TV shows, one of which was nominated for an Emmy.

Paul's dedication and focus on his craft and business have allowed him to be a success. Without that time-tested experience and dedication, he wouldn't be the successful author he is today. Focus is key to success in business, as in life. Without it, we'll never make progress towards our goals.

Zayn Blore

Zayn is a startup veteran, having successfully exited three businesses and been involved in numerous others. He caught the bug when he competed against Microsoft and Netscape to create the world's first web browser.

He is an expert in the delivery of projects, with a diverse range of experience earned across a long career working in FTSE 100 companies, as well as running Simplify Change, a niche consultancy focused on IT project management.

An ILM 5 certified coach, Zayn thrives when he is supporting people to make their ideas come to life through implementation, accountability and detailed planning.

Zayn loves travelling, spending time in London with his two lovely boys (now adults) and training to run his next ultra-marathon.

https://simplifystartingup.com

Trust Is the Currency of Business

JOHN BRIGHTWELL

We all know that trust is the basis of all good relationships. What is a business other than a series of relationships, with suppliers, colleagues, co-founders, directors and, of course, customers?

Trust within a relationship is not simply a question of believing in another's honesty. What I mean by trust is the belief that you have each other's best interests at heart. When your staff trust you on this level, they will work longer when needed and go the extra mile. When your customers trust you, they will not shop around for better prices or services, because they are comfortable that you will provide the best value and service. When your suppliers trust you, they know they will be paid on time and that you will deal with them fairly.

A business that runs on trust looks (and often is) something like the cliché of the family-run business where the owner knows everyone. Every customer has had some level of contact with the owner, as has every supplier, and they all feel they have a personal relationship. The staff all respect the owner and see what they do for the business through daily interactions. The business goes from strength to strength until, either through design or trading success, it becomes necessary to go to the next level.

It is as we outgrow this comfortable model that we run the most risk of losing trust. Normally at about 30-40 staff, founders are no longer able to be an ever-present in the business. A new level of management needs to be introduced, in sales, in production, and in other services, and these hirings, and the structure their roles establish, represent real and present danger to the business. Yet these disruptive changes are not only made voluntarily, but are often rushed through by founders desperate to eke out extra time for new responsibilities. I have seen good businesses devastated while trying to move to the next level. Loyal staff lose confidence and become a destructive influence; customers no longer feel the business acts in their best interest; in some cases the entire business ends up having to be rebuilt from the ground up.

All this because trusted relationships were not properly valued, and poor decisions made without giving them due respect.

I started my career nearly half a century ago at the John Lewis Partnership. As a 16-year-old trainee, two policies were particularly impactful on me: the partnership concept, the internal democratic structures, through which management had a duty to present significant policy decisions; and the "Never Knowingly Undersold" customer-facing policy, which guaranteed customers the lowest price.

Did the managers of John Lewis think their staff could run the business better than them? Did they desire to be some sort of bargain basement pound shop? Of course not, and neither of these things ever came close to happening. Both policies were about establishing and maintaining trust with both their staff and their customers.

Growing from the comfort of a family-style business to a business with more growth potential is a fiendishly hard task. You have customers you have never spoken to, let alone met, staff you did not interview, and suppliers who only exist to you as invoices. Instead of these points of contact with your business, you have investors, who represent a new type of relationship requiring your attention. Board meetings are no longer the relaxed affair they once were, requiring board packs and briefings and management reports for external directors. All of this takes you further away from the coalface and your relationships with your team and your customers.

It has long been my belief that trust is the currency of business. When I speak to a potential supplier, customer or interviewee I always ask myself the same question: "Can I develop a trust-based relationship with this person?"

So as your business grows, how do you keep trust as a core value? It is harder now; you need your staff to trust a new management team, and your customers to trust your sales and support teams. You cannot micromanage everything, but you *can* try to make good decisions using the correct criteria. Think about how you structure the company and how you recruit new people. How can you create an environment where the trust you have worked so hard to create can be maintained?

There is no simple answer that will work in every situation, but if you keep trust paramount in your mind whenever making key decisions, then you will be on the right track. Personally I am a big fan of staff share options as a reward for length of service. I have known a company who even included "Founder" in the title of staff members who were there at the start of the business.

As an example, say you are hiring a sales manager. Naturally you want someone with appropriate experience and preferably knowledge of your industry. But relationships between your new hire and existing team, customers and the rest of the management team are equally important. Can the candidate create these relationships? Existing staff in the sales team can be flashpoints, even if they did not want this management position themselves. If they liked working directly for you, and were used to certain ways of doing things, then you need to consider how any new appointment will assimilate into this existing culture. Consider how to structure this section of your enterprise so that existing relationships can all be maintained. The solution may not always be obvious, but it is worth taking time over. Getting this wrong can be hugely detrimental to your business.

I have been a senior executive in the software industry for some 35 years and have seen and helped many businesses to grow. When new people are recruited, trust is at its most precarious. Many times, I have seen the very people who helped to build the business become disillusioned, eventually leaving or getting sacked. We directors will often say something like, "They were not able to grow with the business." But this is just an excuse. I have seen many of the same people go on to achieve wonderful things elsewhere, their talents benefitting other businesses or indeed helping to build their own.

Much is said these days about company values, normally around social values, diversity, ecology, etc. All of these things are absolutely laudable, but without trust your business will never grow to a level where it can meaningfully impact any of them. But make trust your number one value, and many of the growing pains of taking your business forward will be avoided.

To close, I would like to share the story of my current company. I left the production side of software in 2020 and went to work with a company called WaveAccess, who had been supplying me with software development services for some 21 years. I met them when they first started out, when there were just 19 of them. When I joined them 21 years later, they had nearly 1,000 staff in 19 different countries. As I got my feet under the table, I was happy to discover that programmers who had worked on my projects 15 years earlier were now heading their own divisions, training and managing new people who fitted perfectly into the customer-centric ethos of the organisation. I also discovered that their customer satisfaction index was extraordinary. How, I wondered, was this achieved while experiencing such extraordinary growth?

I asked one of the founders about their customer satisfaction score, and he said, "We lose customers sometimes but we do not have unhappy ones." Indeed, like me, many customers had been with them for over a decade.

Their secret, I discovered, lay in a unique structure that creates an environment of trust and mutual respect throughout the company. WaveAccess was founded by three highly skilled technologists. Each had specialist technical education, and none had any formal business training. So as the business grew, they divided the company into three autonomous technical divisions, each run by one of the founders. Then they built shared services for marketing, HR, sales, finance, etc., and for related services like graphic design and quality assurance.

This means that every member of the production team answers to a director. Of course, there are intermediaries, such as line managers, etc., but there is always a direct line to the director they serve. Equally, while each project has its own dedicated team, it also has a director of the company who is responsible for it. Staff are happy, customers are happy, and the company has been able to grow without losing the trust-based relationships it was founded on.

I am not suggesting this structure for every business; I know it is quite unique. But if, as you grow, you consider that you got this far because of trust-based relationships, then you can develop a structure that maintains them despite the need for delegation. If you make structural and hiring decisions with such a structure in mind, then you have a good chance of achieving your goals.

John Brightwell

With 35 years at the helm of technology as a CEO and CTO, John has been at the forefront of software innovation and development. He has helped to grow numerous businesses, and as a founder he has achieved both successful exits and painful failures.

After a successful stint as a co-founder and CTO of a leading EdTech startup in the UK, John cashed out and transitioned to spearhead the UK division of WaveAccess, solidifying a long-standing partnership with the software development group.

John lives in Kent with his wife and one remaining child, three having already fled the nest. He has one beloved grandson and another on the way at the time of writing. Two dogs, two cats and a very large garden take up any time that is left over from work and family.

www.wave-access.com

https://www.linkedin.com/in/brightwelljohn

Moments of Excellence

PAUL CAMERON

When Excellence Comes, Take a Moment

As a grown-up, my most joyous memories of childhood come to life when I think of the "treehouse" my grandfather created for me. Even now, I remember just how this made me feel. My dreams became vivid, alive and animated with a sense of discovery and adventure in a wild world, bursting with colour and wonder. In reality, my treehouse was a collection of logs, homemade carpentry and aspiration, but perhaps because my grandfather had built it for me, it was everything a childhood should be: a space within which to imagine, believe and become, a time of wonder, surprise and magic.

My treehouse was a childhood "moment of excellence", one that allowed my creativity and imagination to flourish, an aesthetic experience in which my senses were operating at their peak. In my treehouse, excitement and adventure, fantasy and fun could all be expressed with wonderful confidence in my own imagination. I discovered, through imaginative play, to be curious of the world and people around me, pretending to be whatever and whoever I wished.

We all have our own childhoods, but as grown-ups, we sometimes lose the ability to be child-like. We forget our natural curiosity and instinctive aspiration. In his Ted Talk "How to Escape Education's Death Valley", Ken Robinson tells us, "Curiosity is the engine of achievement." Perhaps the true success secret to business growth is recapturing the sense of curiosity we felt in our childhood moments of excellence?

Imagination Is Your Greatest Talent

In the same Ted Talk, Ken Robinson observes that "… for most of us, the problem isn't that we aim too high and fail. It's just the opposite: we aim too low and succeed." Kids' imaginations are their greatest talents, but in the reality of the grown-up workplace, we lose this capacity. I believe that being child-like is our natural, instinctive self. When we relax, unwind and feel most grounded, how often is it that we are doing a child-like activity? Just think about how we are when we're home, when we are on holiday, when we are at the beach…

We all need passions and flights of fancy; we need make-believe, adventure, fantasy and fun. Such things not only return us to our natural child-like state, allowing us to achieve new moments of excellence: they allow our projects and businesses to flourish. Being a child is a state of fully formed dreams: "I *am* an astronaut" rather than "I *want* to be an astronaut" or "I *wish* I'd been an astronaut". The energy of such dreams empowers us to achieve our goals.

One of the child-like traits often associated with creativity is a lack of self-control. In fact, we often regard creativity and self-control as mutually exclusive: "creativity is child-like and self-control is adult-like". Consciously maintaining effortful control of ourselves, holding important things in mind, suppressing actions and thoughts that are unproductive: we believe that this is what it means to be a grown up.

Following from this assumption is the conviction that self-control is not well developed in kids. But in fact being a kid allows creativity and self-control to work in collaboration. In order to pretend, you need to hold things in mind, to inhibit reality and suppress the way you would normally behave. For your pretend superpower to work at all, you have to exercise self-control.

Why does our creativity and playful curiosity wane as we become grown-ups? One key reason is simply a lack of practice. We spend more of our time in reality and less in imagination. It is time to remember your childhood moments of excellence and find your own place to pretend.

These are not skills we need to learn. As I say, it is important to *remember*. Is it even possible to ever un-learn anything? Most of us learn how to ride a bike in our childhood, but never practise this skill as a grown-up. There can be decades in between cycling for fun during childhood and teaching your own kids. But amazingly, when that time comes, you have not un-learnt how to cycle. You might lack confidence, but it's all there: all the skills, knowledge and know how. Not only do you remember how to do it, you do it with excellence.

By excellence I mean simply getting it right. It's nothing to do with perfection. Falling short of excellence simply means falling off. As a child, you learnt how to ride a bike with excellence when you learnt how not to fall off. Years later, it's never possible to un-learn; you still do it with excellence. You have learnt the excellence and you can never un-learn it.

Grow Your Business with Moments of Excellence

The simple truth in business is to learn each moment with excellence. Learn how to get things right; learn them so that you *can't not* do them right. Instinctively, as a grown up, you teach your kids to cycle with excellence, by teaching them to stop falling off. Apply the same rule to your business, teaching your people the fundamentals of your processes so that there is no alternative to excellence.

Excellence can be a scary word, particularly because it requires some degree of aspiration. There are also contexts of elitism and privilege that can confuse the meaning. However, I advocate that the measure of excellence is that, in a particular moment, everything is right. Moments of excellence are simply times when excellence is expressed. I use the plural of moment because the magic, when practised, is to achieve a sequence of moments.

If excellence is simply getting things right, then it's achievable for each and every one of us, including in business.

As a grown-up, I thought I was immune from being 'Disney-d' at Disney Adventure Parks. But as a dad, when came the moment for me to take my children to Disney, our experience was extraordinary. The kids met Mickey Mouse – better, they *believed* in Mickey Mouse. That he was real and that they were special for being perhaps the only children who had really met him.

In that same magical moment I had a realisation: that in their search for business growth, Disney ensure that in every Disney Adventure Park throughout the world, every child meets Mickey Mouse on every trip, always. And here's the excellence: Disney make sure that no one ever sees or meets two Mickey Mouses at the same time. How tragic would that be, if whilst shaking hands with the real Mickey Mouse, another one was to walk around the corner?

These moments of excellence drive right to the heart of what makes Disney a world-class brand and experience. We were at the park for three days, but we only met Mickey Mouse once. Disney understand that the growth achieved through such moments of excellence is the growth that matters. Find one thing that makes you money; learn and discover how to do it with excellence, then repeat and replicate; work hard at getting things right and grow your business. Sometimes the simplest actions done well are the biggest money-makers.

Paul Cameron

Paul's wish is to be considered an eccentric by the time he retires, and he is very much on track: he is a session drummer who designs and builds treehouses, rope bridges and treetop walkways worldwide. Paul founded Treehouse Life, the UK's longest-standing treehouse company, and is uniquely in demand worldwide for his bespoke rope bridges. As jobs go, this might be as eccentric, eclectic and entrepreneurial as possible. It is often commented on as "the best job in the world!"

Following study at the Royal College of Music, then a period as professor of music at the Royal Military and Royal Marines Schools of Music, Paul went on to achieve a truly impressive musical career. He has been a musical director and a percussionist for the Royal National Theatre, Shakespeare's Globe Theatre, London's West End Theatre, the London Symphony Orchestra and the Royal Opera House. He performed on the Oscar-winning film soundtrack *Shakespeare in Love,* was artistic consultant to Rhythm Sticks at the South Bank Centre, an executive producer for ground-breaking collaborations, and a co-producer of a Warner Classics top five album. He has also authored a successful series of books published by Faber.

rope-bridges.com/rope-bridge-design-and-build

www.linkedin.com/in/paulcameron1

Grow a Successful Business in Just a Few Hours a Week

JAMIE CLARET

It's the summer of 2018 and I am standing in front of a boat I have just bought with my business partner. *How on earth did we get here?* I wonder to myself. We had only come out for a couple of pints!

Now, I don't want to give false advertising here. This is no billionaire superyacht, not even a regular yacht. It's what they call a cabin cruiser, and it is housed along the Grand Union Canal in Hertfordshire. I think that now would be a good time to take a few steps back to explain how, after an innocent couple of pints at a pub (ironically called The Boat), we ended up as the new owners of a boat!

It was a sunny afternoon and we had decided to take a walk along the canal to talk about work and life, etc. Naturally enough, given the setting, we were soon discussing how much we loved water and boats (we are both Pisces with the same birthday… go figure!) We were shooting the breeze about how cool it would be to have one and, if I recall correctly, at that very moment we walked past a little cruiser with a For Sale sign…

Well, we called the number, a guy came down, told us lots of things about locks and towpaths, constant cruising and fenders… basically a lot of stuff we didn't understand about boats, and that afternoon, over a handshake, we were the new proud owners, with no experience whatsoever, of the great ship *Barjoli* (we kept the name as apparently it's bad luck to change it).

I absolutely adored that boat. I used to spend days pootling up and down the canal, tinkering with the unreliable engine and sunbathing on the roof, doing a maximum of a few hours' work a week. For me it was life affirming, totally relaxing and simply good for the soul.

A few years later, I was on a Zoom call with a friend and old mentor of mine from the early days of the business (a mentor who used to patiently listen to my grumbling about being frustrated with how many hours I was working to get my venture off the ground). He highlighted that there I was, on the deck of the *Barjoli*, knowing that we had a strong and growing business, all from just a few hours a week. We had achieved what 99% of people only dream of.

Now please don't misunderstand me, I am not telling this story to brag or show off. I'm telling you this because I think it's important to understand *why* we run businesses.

It's something we often ask ourselves as we go through the pain of growing, and at such times, the answer isn't always obvious. I was like everyone else, working my butt off, doing everything that you are meant to do to grow a business, to make enough money to survive. Then something life-changing happened.

My father was diagnosed with early onset dementia at sixty-five, and then after a few short, painful years, passed away. He loved to work, loved life and it was very sad to see someone with such a zest for life pass away much too early. It is only reflecting on this now that I can see what a profound impact this had on my life.

That impact was a realisation about time and the shortness of life. It crystalised in my mind how little time we have, and that life is definitely no dress rehearsal.

His death sowed a seed, triggering a total shift in the way that I thought about work and life. My priorities had been money and growing our business; now they were about trying to get control of my time. My reasoning was that if I was to suffer the same fate as my father, which is not an unreasonable concern, then time was now my most valuable commodity.

That is the key message that I want to convey here.

As business owners we often cannot see the wood for the trees. We are too busy working "in" our business rather than "on" our business. A cliché, I know, but very true.

And the worst thing is, we don't even realise. Work grinds on, and the days, months and years tick by – until all of a sudden we are shocked out of our routine. The psychologist and writer Martha Beck often talks about a "cataclysmic event", either self-imposed or forced upon us, that is the catalyst for change. In my case it was my father's diagnosis.

I suppose as a fellow business owner I am trying to convey that of course we need to grow our businesses, of course we cannot stand still, but still we must remember sometimes to step back and evaluate *why* we are growing, and how much is being sacrificed to do so.

I consciously made the decision to spend less time working and more time living. I did of course have to ensure that our business continued to thrive, but without my being there 90% of the time.

So, without further ado, here are my three tips for reducing your workload from 100% to 10% whilst still growing and running a successful business.

Become Unavailable

I realise that this sounds provocative and possibly a little stupid – after all, it's your business! However, this is the single greatest management technique I discovered during the time of my father's illness, and I thank him for it. It never fails to surprise me how self-sufficient, how much happier and more autonomous your staff become when you are not available to them.

Simply put, an amazing thing happens when you become more "absent".

Questions and emails that ended up on your plate miraculously disappear and start to be answered themselves. Staff use their initiative, problems get resolved, and most importantly, stuff continues to get done.

An old mentor and friend of mine used to say, "Jamie, when someone dies and you must drop off the planet for a few days, the world keeps on turning, doesn't it? It hasn't ground to a halt; work continues to get done, and it's all still there when you return."

It is the same principle. Disappear, ignore and take your time to reply – you will be amazed with the results!

Maintain a Structured Time for Meetings and Updates

Of course, you cannot totally drop off the planet, but you can control when you meet, how often, and what information you need to feel comfortable that the ship (excuse the pun) is still on course.

We adopted the Traction Entrepreneurial Operating System (EOS) to manage the business. Whilst we did not stick to it religiously, it instilled in us the importance of regular heartbeat meetings every week, as well as a "scorecard" for our key KPIs.

Those regular touch points enabled us to have a much more hands-off approach to the day-to-day whilst ensuring we were always kept abreast of the important things happening in the business.

Learn How to NOT Work

The two strategies above very quickly led to my having a *lot* more time, but this bought a problem that I had not expected at all: being uncomfortable with doing nothing.

Of all the changes that occurred during this period, this was probably the hardest. We are conditioned to work harder, work more… just, well, work!

Ironically, if you achieve a position where you can spend a lot of time on a boat, people start to think you're a bit weird. It is particularly difficult when you are at a social event and people ask what you do, or if you have had a busy week.

We are all so defined by what we do and how hard we work that when we aren't doing these things, people get a little freaked out!

I will always remember one particular friend who would take the mickey out of me by half-joking (or 99% not joking), "Have you been spending all your time on the boat again, Jamie?" I think it was more of a problem for him than for me!

After a while, I am pleased to say that I very much got used to "not working" and to this day the business continues to grow and thrive. Don't get me wrong, there will always be times you need to dip in a little more than you would like. Sometimes we want to make some proactive changes that require a little more work.

But even in those times, I always keep at the forefront of my mind why I am doing this. Ultimately only you know how much, or how little, time you want to spend growing your business into a success. But I think it's important to think long and hard about what success actually means. If you remember one thing from my story it should be this: life is very short.

Ignore that email! Take that walk! Buy that boat!

Jamie Claret

Jamie Claret is an accomplished IT professional with 25 years of experience, specialising in leveraging technology for medium-sized businesses. He is the owner of Amazing Support, a multi-award-winning managed IT service provider, and the founder of Autonomate, an AI and automation business. Jamie enjoys giving talks and delivering workshops, making complex subjects easy to understand. He is passionate about helping businesses understand and integrate new technologies.

At Amazing Support, Jamie has established a customer-centric approach, emphasising exceptional customer service. Autonomate makes sense of the automation and AI revolution, guiding customers through this exciting yet daunting journey.

Outside of work, Jamie explores the world, spending time in nature, reading, and listening to podcasts and books. He lives in St Albans with his beautiful new wife and enjoys spending time with his teenage boys.

https://www.autonomate.io

www.linkedin.com/in/JamieClaret

To Grow or Not to Grow

MINDY GIBBINS-KLEIN

You may be wondering why I have called this chapter "To Grow or Not to Grow". Of course we all want to grow our businesses, right? Well… not necessarily. Business growth is a choice, and one that needs to be made very carefully and strategically.

There's a huge amount of pressure in our society to scale. Bigger is always presented as better. Sure, there are some real benefits available to bigger businesses, such as economies of scale and the ability to attract more resources, including finance, publicity, joint venture opportunities and even acquisition interest. Growth can be very exciting, creating a sense of pride for the founder or managing director, the leadership team and the entire organisation.

However, the bigger the company, the bigger the risks. There are bigger budgets that need to be balanced, and issues can escalate quickly.

In this book, you have already heard from some inspirational business leaders and read about how they and their clients have grown their businesses – many of them facing great challenges and succeeding despite those challenges.

You have heard about a diverse set of strategies, all of which can help ambitious business owners and leaders to scale their organisations to greater heights. Actual results, however, are highly dependent on choosing the correct strategy for the business. This is why I always advocate a thoughtful approach for my clients.

I have a few success stories of my own under my belt. I have grown two separate companies, having taken one of them over from a co-founder who left. However, in my new position, I made some mistakes while trying to grow the business and caused the first loss in the company's history. It took me four years to get back into profit, building the business back up and finally selling it to a competitor in the industry.

So when I say business growth is a choice, I am imploring you to make your own decisions: to decide how you want to grow your business, or even whether you want to grow it at all.

The term "lifestyle business" really bothers me. It implies that such businesses are somehow not as credible as "real" businesses. They're too small and insignificant to be taken seriously. Well, having sold one of my "real" businesses, releasing a lot of time for myself, I must say I'm really enjoying the lifestyle business I continue to run, and the lifestyle it affords me.

What's the opposite of "lifestyle" anyway? Deathstyle? For a while, when my previous business was struggling, I lost a lot of sleep due to stress. It could actually have been life-threatening if it had gone on much longer. Given the choice, I definitely prefer lifestyle!

Here's What Happened

When I became the managing director after my co-founder left, I tried to grow the business fast, to make up for what I considered to be very slow growth over the previous years. I worked with several consultants who had lots of experience with larger companies, so I thought they could help me through the process. Each consultant shared with me different options that could help us scale: partnerships and joint ventures, acquisition of another company, franchising and licensing. It was a bit overwhelming.

In my other company, I had experienced a similar kind of pressure. But here, one of the consultants I met with took a more organic approach, suggesting I build up a team of up to 100 employees. We had 10 people in the team at the time. None of them held senior leadership positions; we simply didn't have the operating budget to hire a large number of employees. So I suppose I was a bit wary, but I still wanted to grow the business.

Be Realistic about the Plan and the Finances

Around this time, while I had my eye on the prize of a multi-million-dollar enterprise that I could sell at some point in the future, various funding options were pitched to me by keen finance companies. I liked the idea of getting an investor on board, someone with a lot more experience who could help me plan and navigate the growth process. I also liked the idea of having a chunk of money to fund the growth! At this point, we had never taken on any debt to grow the business, a fact I was proud of, but I also knew that this "bootstrapping" had kept things small.

I went to a workshop about attracting investors and, together with my finance consultant, put together a new business plan and slide deck for potential investors. To my surprise, another attendee on the program knew someone who knew someone, and a conversation opened up about introducing me directly to a potential investor.

It only took a few months to put together a deal, where I agreed to part with 30 percent of our equity in exchange for their investment. Happy days! I happily paid the introducer a fee for that introduction. Except my expectations of what this investment would involve were slightly different to the reality. Whereas I was looking forward to an experienced director for my board, the investor wanted nothing to do with the business side of things. They had put their money in to defray tax on the sale of a different business and just expected me to grow the business, then sell it as per the business plan, giving us both the projected money from the exit price in that plan.

As you probably already know, projections are simply guesses, and none of us could have predicted another recession. I was myself not well prepared to run a bigger business, and while I now had the finance, I did not have the support I had expected to come with it. To make a seriously long story short (one which I am often asked to speak about in keynotes!), right after the investor came on board, the company made its first ever loss. It took four years and a lot of creativity to turn the business around. The only lucky aspect of this story is that, since the investor didn't want to be involved, they never asked how things were going, in all that time!

Once the business was turning a profit again, I was determined to grow the bottom line and sell the company. I was able to do that within another four years, but for a fraction of the pie-in-the-sky figure I had put in the plan (to which the investor had agreed).

Was it all worth it? I am a positive, optimistic person and I like to think that everything happens for a reason. I now appreciate the opportunity I had to deal with a huge business challenge (four years of losses is hard to survive, but we did it) and the sense of achievement that came from building it back up and eventually selling it.

The number of hours I put in, and the sleepless nights, I could have done without, but that is what it took to reach the goal. We got our growth, I got my exit, and I sleep a lot better now.

My Best Advice for You

I believe you know what is right for you. You just get caught up in the hype at times, and maybe even listen to the wrong people (like I did).

Consider as many business growth strategies as possible before going down a particular path. Take your time, take good notes and take a deep breath.

Get clear on your priorities. Decide what factors are most important to you: freedom of time, maximum profit, fame, grooming your business for sale, etc.

Each of these objectives has different implications. If you decide you definitely want to grow your business, everything will become more complex. You and your leadership team will need to assess current operations and processes, and you will probably need to amend them to fit a bigger organisation.

As the team grows, you may need further layers of management to manage a larger number of employees. Not only will this involve more budget, but new people come with their own personalities and issues, as well as their talents. It's not a problem, as long as you are prepared for it. I was not prepared, nor were many of my clients who have been through the growth process. You'll probably want to consider hiring an interim or virtual HR manager to help with the people side of things.

The changing nature of your business will probably mean more of your time is taken up managing the other members of your leadership team and working on the bigger stuff. If the buck stops with you, the issues are all yours. Congratulations.

Be Thoughtful

I use the word "thoughtful" very intentionally. Think long and hard about what you want to do, or what you *think* you want to do. As I've said, growth can be exciting and rewarding, but there are many factors to consider. Enjoy reading the stories and advice of my co-authors, and best of luck to you as you move forward with your business growth.

Mindy Gibbins-Klein MBA FRSA FPSA

Mindy is an international speaker and thought leadership coach. She has founded three multinational brands, which have won or been shortlisted for 19 awards. Mindy has authored and co-authored 15 books, and her clients have written and published over 1000 books.

Over the past 25 years, Mindy has presented to and coached over 50,000 business executives and entrepreneurs in 18 countries. Her TEDx talk "Sometimes You Need to Change Yourself to Be Yourself" has had nearly one million views. Mindy has been featured over 100 times in the media, and her work has been licensed and syndicated across the globe.

A native New Yorker, Mindy currently resides near London, UK, with her long-suffering husband, who is secretly proud of her entrepreneurial spirit.

www.mindygk.com

http://linktr.ee/mindygk

Customer Advocacy Is the Currency of Growth

ADRIAN HARVEY

As a poorly educated, dyslexic Gen X, I thought myself hugely fortunate to land my first serious job, aged 20, selling leasing and finance for one of Europe's largest banks. Turns out I had a knack for selling and it came easy to me.

Throughout my career I have always gravitated to sales and marketing and driving the growth of the organisation. Even when I joined British Gas as their commercial director and ultimately managing director, the narrative was always about growth.

So back in 2011, when with talented accountant Dan Gray I formed a fledgling AI business called Elephants Don't Forget, I had no qualms about business growth.

That was my super skill, while Dan could count and was good with money and all those other far less interesting things, like legal, IT, administration, policy, strategy, etc. It seemed obvious to me that we were going to succeed and would soon be supping piña coladas at the beach, basking in our success.

Oh, what a shock I got. It is all very well selling for an established brand, or indeed selling something for a start-up that your customers understand. But selling something that nobody had ever used before wasn't quite the easy life we had imagined!

After a couple of very hard years barely scraping by and living off savings, we had to consider that our strategy was wrong and that, if we continued at the pace we were currently growing, we would be bankrupt within 18 months.

Neither Dan nor I was the type of person to duck the hard truth or shirk responsibility. So we sat down and concluded that we had been focussed on the wrong thing. Quite understandably (or so we had previously thought) we had been obsessing about the financial metrics of the business: revenue, costs and profit. This manifested in chasing the next deal, sweating over pricing and managing down as much as possible our Cost to Serve (C2S).

The uncomfortable truth is, when it comes to growing a business, far too many businesses large and small fall into the same trap as we did. They focus on the wrong thing! Business is ultimately about making money, and therefore success is often measured in purely monetary terms. As a natural born capitalist, this perspective resonates with me. You can't hope to run any successful enterprise without having a keen eye on revenue, costs and profit.

But, and there is a big but, you can only have one focus (you can't focus on two objects at the same time without going cross-eyed!) and if this focus is money, then your business growth is likely to be slow and hard work. Even if you are fortunate enough to be a natural-born sales animal, or to have one on staff, you will come unstuck when your business reaches a certain scale.

Assuming you are in this for the long-term, you will grow and sustain your business fastest by cultivating exceptional customer advocacy and having your customers sell your product or service for you. It's way more fun, way cheaper from a Cost of Acquisition (COA) and C2S basis, and I firmly believe more rewarding both emotionally and financially.

The multi-million-dollar question is, of course, how you do this.

I believe you can distil the process down into three key rules, rules that as far as I can see are applicable to all types of business:

1. Focus on the value you deliver to the customer;
2. Premier League quality in everything you do;
3. Hire for attitude and train for competence.

The first rule is about value, and this should not be confused with price or how much the customer likes you. Whilst I said that you should not focus on the financial metrics, this does not mean they are not important. They are vital, both within your own business and for customers. You have a duty to ensure that your customer can themselves articulate the value your business creates for them, in a perfect world expressed in £s per annum and evidenced. If you are authentic and honest, then provided the value you deliver is a multiple of the costs of your service, and that you abide by the other two rules, you are likely not only to retain that customer but also grow their value to you and cultivate them as a vocal advocate for what you do.

This rule might at first sound flippant, and many would argue that they already provide this, it's their culture, etc. But what I have seen – and what we were ourselves guilty of in the very early days – is a propensity to compromise quality in some way because of costs. You can justify to yourself why it was acceptable to compromise on this one occasion, but you will pay dearly for that short-term saving. Make sure every single aspect of your interaction with every customer passes your own personal Premier League test. And if it doesn't, then stop, fix it and communicate the fix to your team and the customer. No element of what you do in your business "isn't important". If you do it, it must be important, and thus it must be to the highest possible standard.

I see a lot of firms hire people who are simply not good enough, and in a small business in particular this is going to retard your growth. Initially we hired for experience and apparent past success. Fortunately, we learned quickly that if you want to deliver a consistent Premier League performance, you need people who genuinely share your passion and believe in your dream. A good CV doesn't automatically translate into success; in fact, we learned that very experienced candidates were often set in their ways, and these ways were often contra to or involved lower standards than what we needed. Hire can-do, want-to-do people and train them and reward them. And harsh as it may seem, act quickly to exit candidates who, once hired, fail to meet your standards.

So if you're a money-first kind of business leader, you're going to have to change your mindset: think first about what value you will bring to this customer. Compromise on nothing, setting the very highest standards and always maintaining them. Hire can-do, want-to-do people, train them relentlessly, support them, give them the tools they need to do their job and target them on a Customer Satisfaction Score, not £ value; then trust them to deliver.

We implemented these rules, and as counterintuitive as they may sound, we have never looked back. We have a Net Promoter Score (NPS) of 67. We are world leaders in what we do. We are growing at c.40% per annum. We are profitable. We have no debt. We win awards. We have a customer base of household-name brands. We trade in 50 countries, 14 languages and have net positive churn, which means that even if we don't sign a single new customer in the next 12 months, we will still have more live user licenses then than we have today.

I think of running and growing a business as a journey, and like any journey, some experiences stick in your memory more than others. I recall signing our first customer after Dan and I had come to the agreement that we should change our strategy and focus on advocacy. We put our money where our mouth was and guaranteed to the customer that they would get what we promised or we would refund their money. Needless to say, that focussed our minds, we exceeded those promises, and that customer is still a customer to this day.

Since then we have signed lots of firms, and even more importantly, our most successful source of new customers is employees who worked at one customer, joined a new employer, then promptly called us up and said, "We need Clever Nelly," our performance-building AI. Trust me, you will never make an easier sale than this.

And now, 11 years into the journey, our customers happily go on the record saying great things about us.

They record Reels, write papers, speak at events on our behalf, and enter and win awards with us.

They attend customer gatherings and happily stand on stage, on their own, with no support or inducement from Elephants Don't Forget, sharing how they use Clever Nelly, what experiences they have and what value they harvest. They actively get involved in product development, and almost every customer willingly agrees to act as a reference for prospective customers.

And it is fun, and I get to work with lovely people who share our passion and values, and the business just keeps on growing...

Adrian Harvey

Having spent the first decade of his career working in leasing and corporate lending with ABN AMRO, BNP Paribas and GE Capital, Adrian joined the energy sector, where he was managing director of British Gas and then a division of German energy giant E.ON.

On Independence Day (July 4th) 2011, he and then E.ON financial director Dan Gray left corporate life to start Elephants Don't Forget. They have since grown it into a multi-million-pound global market leader in employee-centric artificial intelligence.

Adrian is a keen sailor and water-sports enthusiast and lives in Surrey with his twin 19-year-old sons. He enjoys keeping fit and rides his bicycle most mornings before work, regularly clocking more than 5,000 miles a year.

www.elephantsdontforget.com

Are You Truly Happy with Where Your Business Is Heading?

ADRIAN LOMAS

My guess is, the reason you're reading this book is that you want to grow your business. Perhaps you have a vision of where you'd like to be but feel frustrated by not having achieved it. You never seem to get closer to that vision, always hitting some kind of ceiling, a ceiling that stalls your performance or traps your team in a rut. Around 12% of businesses fail in their first year, with many of the remaining businesses struggling to achieve the growth their owners desire.

But did you know this is mainly down to one reason?

Leaders settle with the team they have created, often fielding a B-rate team. Sure, you may have some superstars you'd love to clone, but just not enough of them to dominate your sector, especially when you have others in the team who don't take accountability, showing up for their wages and adding nothing extra to your cause.

I spent 24 years running an eCommerce agency. I had some amazing people during those years and was super proud to achieve the coveted Investors in People Gold Standard. However, I also had some B-rate team members. Not necessarily because they were bad – they might have been superstars for other teams. Simply because they didn't align with our culture at Blueleaf.

We were busy winning awards, proud of what we were building nationally, bringing more people into the team, moving into a larger office with a meeting pod, fake grass, and a bridge (because we could). However, hubris was creeping in, a cancer that was eroding all our hard work.

What brought the stark realisation home? It was the conversation you never want to have with your accountant: "You've overtraded, you've run out of money, it's time to call in the insolvency practitioners."

This was not what I had envisioned for my life. I lived under my desk for three months, struggling to find a solution. What follows are the three key steps that enabled me to grow the business from this low point to a successful sale in 2019. All of this followed a chance encounter with the book *Traction* by Gino Wickman. This book appeared at the right time. I read it and created our new plan, following a simple yet proven process called the Entrepreneurial Operating System (EOS).

Creating a Vision That Inspires

It all started by creating a compelling vision: an inclusive, long-range vision, something for the entire team to get excited about, not just the directors. It was crucial to involve the leadership team in this exercise, which not only made the vision more comprehensive but ensured that everyone felt a sense of ownership and excitement about the future.

We made sure our vision was not just about financial targets. It included the kind of work environment we wanted to create, the impact we wanted to have on our clients, and our role in the community. Even if your ultimate vision is to sell your business, setting this as the end goal is never going to inspire the rest of your team. Why should they push themselves every day to build something just for you?

I often reflect on the inspiring speech that President John F. Kennedy made in 1962: "We choose to go to the moon in this decade, not because it's easy, but because it is hard, because that goal will serve to organise and measure the best of our energies and skills." This was a leader who set a vision that inspired a country. It's rumoured that President Kennedy visited NASA after this speech.

During his tour, he met a janitor. The president casually asked the janitor what he did for NASA, and the janitor replied, "I'm helping put a man on the moon."

Think about this. The janitor figured out something that most of us struggle with: the purpose of what he does. He kept the building clean so that the others could focus on their mission. He connected his purpose with the cause of the organisation. Together, they put a man on the moon.

What's Your Vision and, More Importantly, Why?

What is the value of values?

I love to help senior leadership teams discover their company values. The one most important thing is that these values are genuine. Integrity, Communication, Respect, Excellence… These sound great, but when you realise that the disgraced company Enron had these on their wall, it's obvious that if your values are not genuine, they won't inspire people. The senior leadership team (SLT) must always be seen to be congruent with the company values if there is any chance of the rest of the organisation following.

It's imperative that, during the discovery of your company values with your SLT, you shortlist all the values that may possibly connect your personnel. Useful questions include "Why is it that a certain superstar is so liked?" and "If you had 100 staff with a particular quality, would you smash your goals?"

Bringing the selection down to around three to five is about right, but then you need to test it. Using the People Analyzer, one of the EOS tools, list the values along the top of a page and then the names of your staff on the left.

Ask the question, do they meet each value…

- Always?
- Sometimes?
- Rarely?

This will start to give you a picture of two things: do you have the right list of values and is the person the right fit for the company?

Right People, Wrong Seat; Wrong People, Right Seat

Looking back, I have sometimes been too accepting of people's inadequacies, restricting the growth of my business. It's rare that you have staff who offer nothing, so it's easy to excuse someone's inability to deliver in their role, and to focus instead on their undoubted strengths in other areas. This is why it's crucial to make sure you have the *right people* in the *right seats.* Until this concept was made clear to me, I didn't understand its impact on my business.

Did I have the right person, only in the wrong seat? Through this framework, I could identify when I had someone who really got our culture, a solid, reliable person who ticked all the values boxes. Accordingly, if that person wasn't delivering, it was clear that they were doing a role that was not ideal for them.

Picture the scene: you decide to take on someone to do your accounts. Following your normal process, you find the perfect candidate. Meet Rita; she embodies the company values and can do her job well. Several years later, the company has grown, and the business is way more complex. Rita is struggling. She used to nail it for you but now seems to top out very easily. What's changed? Personal circumstances could be one aspect, but what about the roles of the job, the expectations? Have they changed, meaning Rita is now doing things she's not great at? This is a case of the right person (meets your values) in the wrong seat. If you have another seat in the business that Rita gets, wants, and can do, then offer that. If you don't, please don't make one for her. It's time to release Rita and find someone else for that seat.

Another example is when you have the wrong person in the right seat. Meet Bob; he's bloody good at his job, hits his numbers and seems to do what is needed. But there is an issue. No one on the team likes Bob. He just seems to work differently, in his own Bob way. In many cases, because they are good at what they do, this type of person gets promoted. Therefore, when they start to recruit, they create further divisions, as the people they hire are more likely to meet their values, not your company values.

So what do you do? Putting a spotlight on the people in your team who do not meet your values is the first step.

Doing something about them is crucial. If you have cases like the above, you *must* do something about it, otherwise you will restrict your growth by settling. How many of your team are right people in the right seat?

How Accountable Are Your People?

Leadership teams often create an organisational chart showing who reports to whom, a people-first approach. The problem with this methodology is that most of our issues come from people's suitability to their roles – not the structure that connects them.

Consider the opposite for a moment. What seats do you need in your business over the next 6-12 months, the core functions you need doing? Around four to seven is wise.

Next, what do these functions practically involve? In other words, what are the things you expect to be done, the roughly five major roles you require to execute each function?

Finally, who do you have in your team who can sit in each seat and truly own it, who meet your values, get the role, want it, and have the capacity to make it happen?

These are the three key areas that enabled me to create massive growth from a very troubled position. Have you clarified your vision, your values and created an accountability chart for growth? If not, perhaps it's time to consider it.

Adrian Lomas

Adrian Lomas is a highly respected business leader with an impressive track record. He founded Blueleaf, a creative agency based in Cheshire, which evolved into one of the UK's leading e-commerce agencies for Salesforce before being acquired by a global consultancy. Adrian's personal experience running Blueleaf on the Entrepreneurial Operating System (EOS) and his passion for helping senior leadership teams achieve what they want from their business, led him to become a professional EOS implementer.

He lives near Henley-on-Thames with his wife, Alexandra. He has three children and is often seen cycling, running, or windsurfing in the local area.

www.adrianlomas.com

www.eosworldwide.com/adrian-lomas

Be the Hero in Your Own Growth Story

BEN MAYNARD

I believe that authoring, and then telling, your own authentic story is the foundation for business growth. Success, expansion and achievement are commonly measured with numbers – percentages, sales, revenues, profits. But words drive a business forward. Telling stories is how you describe yourself, explain and differentiate your products and services, and most importantly, create connections with your customers.

A good story explains what you do and why it matters. Cutting through complexity with a narrative that is memorable, entertaining and resonates with those you need to influence ensures that you stand out from the crowd even in the most contested markets.

Don't Get Lost in Detail

The importance of storytelling is well understood in today's business environment. Humans relate to narratives that resonate with their own experience, helping them to make sense of change, and drawing them into exploring alternative paths. I won't go into the theory behind why storytelling is so compelling, there are literally hundreds of books that do that (Joseph Campbell's seminal *The Hero with a Thousand Faces* and Christopher Vogler's *The Writer's Journey* are two I'd recommend). Suffice it to say, it is clear that telling stories is deeply hardwired into our brains. Moreover, it's fundamental to establishing why your business should exist, and why customers should come to you and not someone else. The head of my old agency and luminary of the PR community, Harold Burson, famously quipped that "If you don't get out and tell your story, someone else will… And you won't like the way they tell it!"

Yet many otherwise highly successful businesspeople struggle to tell a compelling and convincing story about themselves and their business. Telling the right story, in the right way, is not simple. It takes planning, thought and practice. In over 30 years of working as a public relations consultant, I have met and coached hundreds of senior executives, entrepreneurs, leaders and inventors, all brilliant at what they do. But when it came to explaining it to the wider world, they often struggled.

Many get lost in the details and the complexity of "what" they do, losing sight of "why" they do it and for whom.

This is especially common in technology and science-based sectors, where I have spent most of my career, but it can happen to anyone. In our desire to convey the uniqueness of our proposition, we dive into the detail. If you recognise yourself in this, do not despair; it is a common trap, and one that, with some preparation, it is relatively easy to avoid.

What Makes You the Hero?

The best stories follow a well-worn path. They share the structure of the fairy stories we remember from our childhood. Someone we can empathise with, the damsel in distress, is threatened by a clear and present danger, the dragon. In rides the hero or knight in shining armour, and after a hard-fought battle, they defeat the dragon and save the damsel. They live happily ever after. Excusing the dated gender stereotypes, this format can be applied to almost every business story. The customer faces a challenge or unmet need. You offer a way to overcome that need (i.e. defeat the dragon) and everyone is better off as a result. This may seem like a simplification, but thinking about what you and your business offers along this narrative arc provides new insight and clarity as to how to express your value.

My advice to you is to start simple. Begin by building out those major story elements. Consider who is threatened and by what. Identify the urgency: why do they need help now, what will happen if they do not overcome this threat? Most importantly, consider how you will show up as the hero.

Heroes from mythology to present-day popular culture share several common traits. They usually exhibit personal courage: think Flash Gordon from the 1980s film with the Queen soundtrack ("*Just a man, with a man's courage…*") They often have some unique insight or understanding: Neo's knowledge of the true nature of the human world in *The Matrix*. And they wield a special weapon, power or other item associated with them: Thor's hammer or Harry Potter's wand.

To create your own story, with you as the hero, ask yourself these questions:

1. What do I know, or what have I spotted that allows me to tackle the clear and present danger faced by my customers?

By clearly sharing this insight, not only will you establish an important customer need, you will illustrate just how well you understand them, thus building rapport and connection. Answering this question addresses the vital "why" of any sales pitch or business case – why am I in business, who am I here to help and what will I help them overcome?

2. What unique thing do I have that will solve the issue better, faster or more completely than anyone else can?

This is your magic weapon. It is only at this point that you can get into explaining "what" your product does. Even at this point, however, consider limiting the detail to what is strictly necessary to carry the story forward. We don't need to know in depth how Thor's hammer works, only that it is an awesome and powerful way of defeating bad guys!

3. What was your courageous step?

Heroes seldom appear fully formed; they have their own journeys of development and discovery. The choices they make, the experiences they feel, all contribute to the fateful moment when they must decide to stand up and show courage. Think about how you got here – what makes you, you? Honesty and transparency build authenticity. The more "real" and three-dimensional a hero, the more we can warm to them. Highlighting the challenges that you have overcome in order to be in a position to offer assistance to your customer creates the drama in your story, building engagement and appreciation of your courage in addressing the customer's issue.

No Fate but What We Make

The heading is a line from *The Terminator 2* when, with Cyberdyne destroyed, Sarah Connor recognises that she is free from a predestined future. I use it here because it underlines the power of creating your own story as a way of shaping your future and your business growth.

Speaking of robots, although not the psycho-killer kind, I recently used this "fairy story" structure to help a London start-up to redefine their narrative. This example powerfully articulates the value of this approach in the real world. With the right story you can invent your own future.

Slamcore is an entrepreneurial business based in London with its roots in UK academic research. Using clever algorithms plus low-cost sensors, it devised a way for robots to "see" and navigate the physical world around them. The science is exceptionally complex, and with its core product being a sub-system of a complete robot, the company struggled to gain attention for its innovations.

Working with the founder and CEO, Owen Nicholson, I helped to articulate why Slamcore was the hero of the robotics sector. We started with the damsel in distress. Contrary to popular conception (and cultural references), robots often get lost. They struggle to locate themselves and navigate in situations in which even infant humans easily move from A to B. At a loss, robot manufacturers resorted to more and more sensors, adding expense, power and weight demands to their robots – but with little improvement to function. If things did not change, the promise of robots working alongside humans or taking on repetitive or dangerous tasks was at risk.

Establishing this context caught the attention of stakeholders – they recognised the threat and understood the need for action. To position Slamcore as the hero that could meet this challenge, we broke the product and the science down into a key insight and a magic weapon.

Our insight was that robots could mimic the way humans figure out where they are.

Basically, Slamcore allows robots to use two cameras and a gyroscope to locate themselves in the same way as we use our eyes and inner ears. We cut through the complexity and jargon to present an easy-to-understand insight.

Our magic weapon was the algorithm behind this process. Creating an aura of secrecy and intrigue around this helped the overall story. This was the investable value within the company, alongside the PhDs and other experts who had created it.

The courageous step was not only to position Slamcore as the plucky academic spin-out taking on larger established players, but to call for a revolution in the way the sector worked. Instead of every company working in silos and struggling to fix the same issues, why not create a market for specific solutions that could be integrated to work together?

Slamcore's new story helped secure funding, customers and growth. I have no doubt that finding and telling the right story, with you as the hero, will do the same for your business.

Ben Maynard

Ben specialises in taking complex messages and transforming them into powerful narratives that influence key audiences. He has helped global and challenger brands, member associations and numerous start-ups to navigate issues and capitalise on opportunities by finding and creating compelling stories.

With over thirty years' experience in creating communications that build understanding, change perceptions and foster growth, Ben combines deep experience of the technology industry with a well-honed sense of what makes a story. After 25 years working with some of the world's largest agencies and tech firms, he started his own business in 2018.

Ben lives in Surrey with his wife and two children. He is currently trying to rebuild the 1980s vinyl collection he wishes he'd never parted with.

Ben is founder and managing director of Story and Strategy Ltd.

www.storyandstrategy.co.uk

Authenticity

IAN MCCLEAVE

There is more to business than financial statements.

I'm not saying that successful growth doesn't require an understanding of many key factors; identifying market segments, ensuring financial readiness and operational capabilities, as well as a detailed risk management strategy are all considerations. However, a key factor that is often overlooked is the need to know your vision: *why* you started the business and turned your back on the relative security and comfort of a regular restricted income. Are you still in touch with that original purpose? Would growing the business move you closer or further away? This is particularly pertinent if a core part of your initial thinking was the wish for more time and freedom from routine. The cost of expanding your business is ultimately both financial and emotional.

For me, all these factors come down to one word: authenticity. This is a word you hear a lot right now, mostly around the importance of personal branding. But what does it really mean to be authentic?

Being authentic is about much more than differentiating yourself from the competition through branding or marketing. It is ensuring that the way you run your business is aligned with your true values, beliefs, and feelings, without succumbing to external pressures or societal expectations. It involves understanding who you are and, by extension, what your business is at its core. When you move the business forwards, are you making decisions which reflect that understanding?

My Experience

I certainly began my journey without any of this deeper understanding. I didn't set out to be an entrepreneur. I had worked successfully for a number of years, but I was suffering. I'd done lots of personal development courses, but the success that other people told me I had didn't feel real to me; my work life wasn't delivering. I had become stuck in a rut, going through the motions until I realised I needed the freedom to control my own destiny.

So I left the safety of the 9 to 5 (actually more like 7 to 9, but that's another story), only to find myself, six months down the line, still stuck going to an office every day, driven by the demands of clients, and scared to take time out because I wasn't earning. What if my clients stopped coming before I got back to the office?

Why, I asked myself, was I still sitting in an office, stuck in the same routine as I had always been, only for less money and way more stress?

We all need to earn money; the number one driver for any business is to be profitable. But there has to be more.

So I stopped!

Finding the Why

This is where authenticity came in. I think every entrepreneur needs to find their inner cause, the thing they stand for. I hadn't considered that; I'd just jumped straight into earning money, finding clients without any thought as to what my purpose was. I realised that I wasn't running a business that had a purpose and a destiny; I was simply a hired gun going from client to client for money.

That was the missing piece of the jigsaw. I had to get real; I had to sit down and get to grips with what I wanted my business to stand for, because if I couldn't get in touch with that, then my only measure of success would be the profit and loss account, and that's a wholly inadequate way to measure a life's work.

So, where did I start? Where *could* I start? This was a tough process. Self-awareness requires introspection and a willingness to explore your inner world honestly; it means talking and listening to a close friend or partner, being willing to accept how others see you, and to change what doesn't align with who you believe yourself to be. I sat down with a very close friend who also ran his own business, and we did a strengths and weaknesses exercise on each other. The results were a revelation. We don't often see ourselves through the eyes of another. I had strengths I hadn't realised, and we had a frank and honest conversation about how to maximise these whilst working on my flaws.

It takes courage to be authentic, because it often means going against the grain or facing judgment from others. Being true to yourself can involve taking risks, such as pursuing a non-traditional career, expressing unpopular opinions, or ending relationships that no longer serve you.

I want to be clear: authenticity isn't about being the same person in every situation; rather, it's about maintaining a core sense of identity while adapting to different contexts. It's the consistency of your values and character that defines your authenticity, not necessarily your behaviour in every specific circumstance. Neither does it mean imposing your views or needs on others. It involves expressing yourself truthfully while respecting the authenticity of others, creating space for diverse perspectives and experiences.

What so often happens, and I have experienced this while working alongside many business owners and changemakers, is that owners lose sight of their original purpose in the necessary pursuit of money. That's completely understandable; it is impossible to focus on your values and purpose if you're freezing and starving. But there's no reason the two have to be mutually exclusive.

So, as you think about taking that next step, moving your business to the next level, I believe it is crucial to get back in touch with your core values, your authentic self. I acknowledge that some inauthentic strategies can deliver short-term results, such as quick sales or rapid customer acquisition. However, these gains are unsustainable, as ultimately the lack of authenticity becomes apparent, in turn leading to stunted medium- to long-term growth.

An Authentic Leader

By reconnecting with your purpose, and discussing and sharing it with your team and those closest to you, a shared set of truly authentic values emerges. They haven't been dreamt up by your marketing team; they are something that you truly believe in. This belief will be something that your whole team can come together around, and that clients can identify you with; during tough times, you will have a purpose to bring people together. As your employees recognise that your ethics and values are taken seriously by the board, they will become more engaged, and this will be a crucial driver of the company's success.

Authenticity allows businesses to differentiate themselves in the market. By being true to their values and unique identities, companies can carve out a niche that resonates with their target audience. Without authenticity, businesses may fail to stand out from the competition, leading to stagnation and decline in market share.

While business ethics are concerned with a company's wider responsibility towards its community and environment, they must begin with your business itself. A period in which you plan growth is a perfect opportunity to audit your processes, procurement and company culture. It starts with the board. A healthy, open and transparent culture must be built on tangible, authentic and measurable values. They cannot be rules or promises on a policy document; they must exist as a constant part of the day-to-day business, throughout all parts of the business, both internally and externally. Remember, it's actions that matter; talk is cheap. So when you create a culture, you must ensure that it is respected, to show that you, as the business owner, believe in and are fully committed to it. The easiest way to achieve this is to be authentic and manage by values not instructions.

Authenticity is essential in leadership, as being a good leader of a team goes way beyond being good at your job. The best leaders create mutual trust; they have and communicate clear values that communicate across diverse networks, uniting a team around shared values and the trust that these leaders respect their wider community and environment. Without understanding yourself and being true to your own values consistently, you cannot expect others to follow your lead and enable you to grow your business, your team and yourself.

In essence, authenticity is essential to sustainable business growth. Get this right – and by that, I mean make it real and true to yourself – and growth will happen; it takes hard work, but it will happen. More importantly, you will have fulfilment. Because this isn't just about your business; when we live authentically, we make decisions aligned with our purpose, and we take charge of our future, and that, for me, delivers the holy grail of real freedom.

Ian McCleave is the founder of Joseph Victor, a team who believe that purpose and profitability are not mutually exclusive.

He grew up in southeast London with a severely disabled sister and father. This lived experience taught him a deep sense of social justice and how society fails to adequately value disabled people.

Ian forged a successful career but struggled to truly thrive in the culture. He started a few side businesses, some of which worked, some of which didn't. Ultimately his sense of disconnect became too much, and he very spontaneously decided he needed to find his own path.

A period of freelance work followed, before Ian met others who shared his belief that the damage being done to our environment demanded a new economic approach. Since then, Ian has worked with various organisations to develop economic and mathematical models that capture impacts on our communities and environment in credible economic terms.

www.josephvictor.co.uk

Knowing and Leveraging Your Unique Backstory Is the Secret to Your Leading Edge

EMILY RAPPITT

Often, when you shift from being a full-time employee to becoming an entrepreneur, you overlook that your unique backstory holds the key to unlocking your leading edge.

Your past is a gift, carrying a wealth of experiences, accomplishments, and vulnerabilities that can fuel your business growth and create your unique distinction.

Let's Start with My Own Backstory

When I was a little girl, my understanding of growth was simple. I knew that my body got taller – picture the marks creeping higher up the doorpost – and that flowers started as green shoots reaching for the sky before blooming. However, I didn't know you could apply the concept of growth to businesses too.

As a child, I loved creative play. I was a self-starter, highly industrious, with a vivid imagination. My passion was less "doctors and nurses" and more "business owner and staff". I dreamt of having my own business. I have no idea where this aspiration came from; I wasn't surrounded by entrepreneurs. But I had a deep-seated yearning to turn an idea into money.

I "operated" a diverse portfolio, running anything from a mud scotch egg emporium behind the shed, to Office Services Ltd using my mum's clothes-catalogue stationery packs. Even before I knew about balance sheets, P&Ls, and value propositions, I had a strong drive to run the best businesses in the neighbourhood. Take the mud scotch egg emporium: I carefully constructed semi-wet mud into egg-shaped balls; then I transformed the mud by rolling them in orange sand to mimic fried breadcrumbs.

These early traits laid the foundation for my future entrepreneurial endeavours, teaching me the importance of creativity and self-motivation in business.

In the 1980s I discovered the thrill of London. Every year, I chose a trip to the capital as my birthday treat. I adored the contrast between the fancy palaces and the gritty streets. The hustle and bustle made it feel alive, energetic, and filled with purpose – a far cry from the sleepy market town where I grew up. Growth, I realised, wasn't just about getting taller or seeing flowers bloom. It was about transformation and change, driven by passion and imagination.

Now let's wind forward to the late 1990s. At last, my dream had come true – I was living and working in London as a chartered accountant with a high-growth Big 4 firm. For most of my career thereafter, I led high-profile global white-collar crime investigations, remediations, and then transformation programs at a Swiss private bank.

In my early 40s, I noticed a shift in the office dynamic – a decline in the number of my female peers. Before long, I was often the only senior female in the room. This fuelled my passion for championing the promotion and retention of women. I led a Women in Leadership initiative and vividly recall presenting to a room of 90 men, including the CEO, about the importance of elevating the percentage of women in leadership.

Growth, I learned, also meant challenging the status quo and advocating for change.

Fast forward to today, and my second childhood dream: setting up my own business. As an adult, this desire only grew, stemming from work dissatisfaction, mixed with my perimenopausal shift and a strong desire for fulfilment.

I'm a transformation expert, focusing on transforming women leaders at critical "moments that matter" in their career, and I am now in the mid-design of my next phase to support businesses in revamping to retain female talent.

Three Prompts to Discover Your Own Backstory

So now let's discover your backstory. Dig deep into your history, and challenge yourself to find all those experiences, both as an employee and in your personal life, that you can use to sharpen your edge and grow your business.

Here are three prompts to start your reflection:

What Were the Business Growth Success Factors of Your Previous Employer(s)?

Reflect on the strategies your current or previous employers used to grow their business. Think broadly across all aspects of the business and ask yourself:

- What leadership qualities and practices drove growth?
- How did they create and nurture key relationships?
- How did they adapt to external challenges and seize new opportunities?

From my own experience, as an investigator into corporate crime, I had seen how a firm's business model might be reliant on factors outside its control: specifically in this case, external corporate wrongdoing. The growth strategies of this business, however – how it engaged with this external factor – *were* entirely within its control:

1. It invested in futureproofing skills by predicting what expertise was needed to lead the market – technology and data scientists came out on top.
2. It aimed to be on speed dial when a crisis hit by building enriched relationships with corporate executives and lawyers through regular catchups, thought leadership, and strategic partnering.
3. It deeply understood the key drivers of corporate crime by tuning into the triggers of corporate vulnerability, like interpreting how corporates might trip up if they ignored regulators closing loopholes.

What Unique Contribution Did You Make to these Successes?

While you can learn a lot from your employer's growth strategy, the valuable lesson for your own business is the unique part you played within it. This drives your differentiators and unique edge.

To make it easier to reflect on your own unique contribution, answer these three questions about the role you played in understanding:

- Why things needed to get done,

- What needed to get done,
- How to get it done.

My own reflection turned out like this:

- *Why:* I expertly turned around sub-optimal projects by digging into root causes to build back client trust.
- *What:* I adopted a holistic approach to understand what pieces of the investigation needed to fit together. From this, I built global cross-functional teams.
- *How:* I found the right resources – diverse people and skills, information, and tools – to get the job done and exceed expectations, including partnering with strategic experts.

What's Your Personal Journey?

In this era, people are captivated by personal journeys and storytelling. Be daring and identify the highs and lows of your life. Use these vulnerabilities to inspire and attract your audience on a deeper level by linking your story to your new business. Reflect on:

- What significant experiences shaped who you are today?
- How have these experiences influenced your career and business decisions?

- What personal challenges have you overcome that others can relate to?

Use my own backstory as an example. When I craft workshops or speeches, I often bring in the story of my mud scotch egg emporium to highlight my early innovation and creativity!

How My Unique Edge Grows from My Backstory

Nowadays, I continuously dip into my backstory, knowing that this is the bedrock of my future business growth. Using these three prompts set me up for the successful growth of my own business, and my mission as a transformation expert is now in full swing.

I have nurtured my business from ground zero to the fledgling enterprise it is today. Regularly, I see how my own backstory creates my unique edge and shapes my business growth.

Let me share how, in the last few months, I've been using my backstory to bring impact and value to grow my business:

- I added distinct value to a coaching client by using my corporate investigator experience. She was working in a failing business, and without her realising it, it was totally failing her. I recognised this environment and offered her my deep expertise and empathy. From this she grew the confidence to resign and is now re-positioned and content. When we parted, she gave me a card loaded with heartfelt gratitude – fuelling my passion to support the transformation of others and validating my own career pivot.

- My experience of leading global teams, and tuning into cultural sensitivities, is turning my business into a global service. Technology has made cross-border business easy.

- On International Women's Day, I proudly shared my perimenopause story on stage – with a beating drum of all things! I described how my life's rhythm got disrupted and how the newly chaotic rhythm led me to deep reflection, re-evaluation, and a transformation of my life's direction. I built deep relationships with the audience, who overwhelmingly expressed gratitude for my transparency around this taboo topic.

- Following that, I tapped into my overwhelming desire to continuously learn and qualified as a menopause coach. With this offering, I also lean into my passion for data insights and visualisation and its powerful impacts. I share a wealth of data extracted from my wearable device to graphically visualise the peaks and troughs of my hormonal shift that make the story real.

- Learning from both my childhood days of operating a "diverse portfolio", and my adult career strategically partnering with experts in corporate, I'm busy building new strategic partnerships with business networks and leadership professionals with complementary skills, knowing that this fusion of expertise adds value to clients.

By consistently leveraging your backstory, you can create an edge that sets your business apart. My own journey – from childhood entrepreneur to transformation expert – demonstrates how powerful this approach can be.

Now it's over to you – dig deep into your backstory to create your unique edge!

Emily Rappitt is a transformation expert passionate about igniting the spark in women leaders during critical moments in their life and career. She fuses her 30 years of corporate leadership with coaching qualifications, and proudly calls herself a coach, mentor, educator, consultant, workshop facilitator, keynote speaker, and illustrator.

She is also dedicated to supporting organisations rethink and redesign their strategies for retaining top female talent.

She spent 27 years at Deloitte as a chartered accountant, consulting on white-collar crime and leading high-profile investigations and transformations. Later, she served as global compliance COO at a Swiss Private Bank, leading complex cross-border transformation projects.

She loves creativity, nature, hiking, sunshine, digital art, cosiness at home, and spending time with like-minded people.

www.emilyjuliacoaching.com

www.linkedin.com/in/emilyrappitt

Building a Referral Network for Business Growth

GILL RUSSEL

The Power of a Referral Network

Building a referral network has been a game-changer for me in my career as a serial entrepreneur. I am passionate about this approach because using this growth strategy has helped me go from start-ups to building established businesses. I started to appreciate its power when I used it to launch a photography business. I realised that traditional advertising, in glossy magazines, to reach my target market was out of my budget. And so it was the referrals from my trusted network of family, friends, business colleagues and, of course, satisfied clients that truly aided my business growth.

Over the years, my knowledge has developed and allowed me to teach thousands of other business owners how to attain business growth by expanding their referral networks. I've seen how effective this strategy can be, and I am excited to share it with you.

One key lesson I've learned – and something I always stress – is that you must believe in yourself and the value you can deliver to others. Just as I needed confidence in my ability to create compelling images, you will need confidence in your offerings in order to inspire others to refer you.

Clients who were happy with their photographs naturally shared their experiences with their own network, leading to a steady stream of new bookings. This organic growth wasn't just about the quality of my work; it was also about the relationships I built with my network and the trust they had in me. Building and nurturing meaningful relationships with people, to enable them to "know, like, and trust" you, is an integral part of building a quality referral network.

Many business owners don't recognise the opportunities for building a referral network that are often right in front of them. They might have satisfied clients who would gladly refer them to others, but they haven't taken the time to ask for those referrals or maintain those relationships.

This is where I want to help you see the potential for your own business growth. By recognising the value of a referral network and taking proactive steps to build one, you can create a reliable source of new business that's both cost-effective, sustainable, and enjoyable.

Steps to Building a Successful Referral Network

In my experience, the key to success when growing a referral network is to approach it strategically, thoughtfully, honestly, and with integrity. It's not just about getting more business; its strength is in creating a community of valued, meaningful connections, including satisfied clients who are your "fans", eager to share your business with others. Here are the key steps you can take to successfully build and leverage a referral network for your business growth.

Provide Exceptional Service

The foundation of any referral network is the quality of the service or product you offer. Satisfied customers are your best advocates, so focus on exceeding their expectations. This means not only delivering what you promise but also adding a personal touch that makes the experience memorable. This level of care results in clients feeling confident in recommending your products and services to others.

Ask for Referrals

While some clients will naturally refer you to others, many won't think to do so unless prompted. Don't be shy about asking for referrals. After a successful project or sale, let your client know how much you would appreciate them spreading the word about your business. You can do this in person, via email, social media, or through a follow-up thank-you note. A simple, sincere request for referrals can often lead to new business opportunities.

The law of reciprocity, as covered by Dr Robert Cialdini in his book *Influence: the Psychology of Persuasion*, highlights how people are wired to respond to kindness with kindness, and how this can be leveraged to build strong, mutually beneficial relationships. In a business setting, if you provide exceptional service or support to a client or connection, they may feel motivated to refer you to others or offer you their own support in return.

Therefore, it is important to find out more about other businesses and how you can help them. It takes time and effort to get to "know, like and trust" them, and to understand their business and how best to refer them to others. However, becoming your network's "go to person", and recommending others you trust, is so rewarding, and it is a great way to do business, believe me!

Build Partnerships with Complementary Businesses

Another effective way to grow your referral network is by forming partnerships with businesses that offer complementary services. For instance, in my photography business, I built relationships with wedding planners, florists, and videographers. These businesses served the same target audience but offered different services, making them ideal partners for mutual referrals. Start by identifying potential partners, before reaching out with a proposal that outlines how you can both benefit from the relationship.

Please do not overlook those businesses that do not immediately spring to mind. It was a handyman/locksmith who got me introductions into the top wedding venues. He was a regular contractor for them and used his connections to get me an appointment with their wedding co-ordinator. Whether it's through an informal agreement or a more structured referral programme, these partnerships can significantly expand your reach.

Consider creating a formal referral programme that could offer incentives to those who refer new business to you, such as discounts, free services, or monetary rewards. Clearly communicate the details of the programme to your network to make it easy for them to participate. Over time, this programme can become a key driver of new business.

Nurture Relationships

Maintaining strong relationships with your connections is essential for the long-term success of your referral network. Touch base regularly, whether through personal check-ins, social media or newsletters. Thank them for their referrals and ensure they remain enthusiastic about recommending you. I would often send a handwritten thank-you note to those who referred me to others, which acknowledged their support but also strengthened our ongoing relationship.

When you focus on delivering exceptional value and maintaining strong relationships, your referral network will grow naturally, bringing new opportunities and helping your business thrive.

Realising the Benefits of a Referral Network

Once I had established my referral network, I began to fully realise and leverage the benefits it brought to my business. A well-maintained referral network resulted in more qualified leads, higher conversion rates, and lower customer acquisition costs. But the most surprising and enjoyable benefit was how referrals often led to deeper connections with those in my network.

I noticed that clients who came through referrals were not only more likely to book but also tended to spend more on additional products, such as photo albums or prints. This wasn't just about the trust factor; referred clients were often more excited and enthusiastic because they already had a positive impression of my work, thanks to the recommendation. Over time, the impact of referrals on my bottom line became clear: referred clients were more valuable, leading to more stable and predictable growth.

In addition, a strong referral network helped me build a loyal customer base. Clients who referred others to my business felt a sense of connection and loyalty, which often translated into repeat business. They saw themselves as part of my success and were more likely to return for additional services or products. This was particularly evident in my experience with family portraits; clients who referred me to their friends for weddings or other events often came back to me for future photo sessions as their families grew. This highlights the importance of customer retention, in that it is far more cost-effective to invest in and retain existing clients than to acquire new ones.

In my experience, building a referral network has been a powerful strategy for achieving business growth. By providing exceptional service, actively seeking referrals, and fostering partnerships with other businesses, I was able to create a network that continuously brought new clients to my door. But perhaps the greatest reward was the deeper relationships and loyalty that came with it. As my own story shows, the benefits of a referral network go beyond just acquiring new clients: it can lead to stronger relationships, increased loyalty and, ultimately, sustained growth for your business.

Building a referral network is beneficial for business growth, and it's not about relying on price cuts or discounts to attract new clients. The cornerstone of any successful referral network is that is requires a strategic and thoughtful approach. It's not about competing on price but on the exceptional value, quality and uniqueness of the offering you provide. Always aim to exceed client expectations by delivering outstanding service and creating memorable experiences.

When clients truly value what you offer, they're more likely to recommend your business to others. Focusing on delivering real value ensures that your referrals are based on the quality of your service, not just on price incentives.

As Porter Gale says, "Your network is your net worth."

Gill Russel

Gill is a business growth strategist with over 15 years of experience using referral network strategies. She empowers business owners to craft a business that works for them, through tailored growth strategies and by establishing effective referral networks.

As the founder of the Gill Russel Consultancy, Gill leverages her extensive experience, offering expert guidance to secure high-quality referral business. Her expertise as an iMA accredited practitioner, international speaker, and trainer has made her a sought-after consultant on business innovation and growth.

Residing on the Kent coast with her husband, Wayne, Gill is a proud mum of five children (all entrepreneurs), and nan to six wonderful grandchildren. She loves spending time with her family and their two springer spaniels, Oscar and Polly.

www.thegillrusselconsultancy.com

www.linkedin.com/in/gill-russel-2b711312

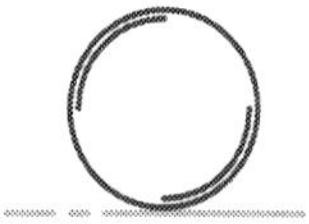

ADAPT to Flourish!

AILEEN RYAN

Thousands of businesses are launched every year – each one launched in good faith because someone believes that their product or service is something that others will want to buy.

Yet, according to various sources, 20% of businesses fail in their first 12 months, and many more fail to flourish and achieve their true potential – with market changes (shifts in market demand, competition, and industry trends) cited as a key contributor to this statistic.

In simple terms, product-market fit means that there is a match between the product you are selling and the product that your target market wants to buy. It's this match that unlocks business growth.

Despite business owners and leaders' convictions about the value they can deliver, product-market fit often remains elusive.

Your conviction alone is not sufficient! In fact, the strength of your conviction may be blinding you to valuable insights and feedback from the market.

Sometimes the market shifts and you need to adjust your product. Sometimes it may be better to change the market you're pursuing. But to make the right decisions at the right time, you must be continuously watching the marketplace.

I encourage you to weaken the strength of your convictions[1] and be ready to ADAPT depending on the evidence you uncover by using this simple framework:

- **A**sk hard questions in a structured way.
- **D**ig deeper to be sure you understand the full picture.
- **A**djust your course in response to what you hear.
- **P**ersevere with listening and gathering feedback.
- **T**ry again (rinse and repeat!)

1 https://www.linkedin.com/pulse/management-principle-2-strong-opinions-loosely-held-paraag-sarva-bkw1e/

Tips for Using the ADAPT Framework

In essence the ADAPT framework is an iterative and adaptive process, allowing you to engage broadly, spot trends early and optimise your product-market fit for success. It emphasises the importance of asking tough questions, deeply analysing and understanding the feedback, making necessary adjustments, and continuously repeating the cycle.

As a business leader it's essential that you participate in these conversations yourself so that you hear feedback from the market first-hand. However, to maximise the return on time invested, it's a good idea to have additional people from your team participate as well, as each individual may interpret responses differently.

To get truly actionable insights, you should:

- Agree in advance the target scope of your process. How many people will you interview? Have you spoken with them previously, and if so, do you need different perspectives this time? What roles and responsibilities should they have? Are there certain companies that must be in the mix?

- Design your questions so that you probe the most important angles. Ask the same questions every time in order to be better able to interpret the findings later.

- Keep good notes that can be shared and analysed later. Consider recording some of the conversations for later reference if needed.

Ask the Hard Questions

The questions you design should revolve around your value proposition and the potential match between your product and the needs of the market. These questions will yield material that can subsequently be used in developing sales and go-to-market plans. You might start by probing the potential customer's views on:

- their level of satisfaction with their current situation, the value of solving the source of any dissatisfaction, the likelihood they would actually pay for this and, if so, how much;
- if an alternative/competitive solution already exists, the value of any features this solution offers that yours doesn't, and if any of these are considered "must-have".

Both of these questions aim at establishing one crucial parameter: value.

People will often avoid giving feedback that they feel is negative, because they don't want to hurt your feelings! It's not at all uncommon to be told that your product is great and the features are fantastic, only to later discover that no one actually wants to pay for them. Try to push beyond positive feedback to get to the truth.

The adoption of any new solution is likely to cause some "pain" for the customer, so you need to clearly understand the value you offer in order to demonstrate that these benefits significantly outweigh the associated pain, both perceived and real.

Dig Deeper to Be Sure You Understand the Full Picture

Just because you can show a great value proposition does not mean that you have product-market fit. There are many additional environmental factors that influence decision-making, and you must understand these. Make sure you ask questions around:

- loyalty or lock-in to any alternative solutions or providers;
- impediments to, impacts of or risk from switching;
- what it would take for them to change from current solutions.

You may find that there are concerns around culture, language, regulation, employment law, data migration and protection, privacy or potentially even national security that massively impact the dynamics of a particular market.

Digging deeper also requires speaking with multiple people at different levels within your target customer's organisation. A direct user of your product or service may not be at the level of seniority to know the answers to some of these environmental questions. Similarly, someone in a senior management position may not understand the technical complexities associated with, for example, data migration, so it is critical to hear a range of views.

Asking the "what would it take" question serves two purposes. Firstly, it provides an opportunity to uncover anything you haven't explicitly asked about. Secondly, psychologically, it begins to transition the conversation towards an engagement opportunity.

Adjust Your Course in Response to What You Hear

Having started out with structured questions, make sure you keep records of all your conversations in a way that is easy to decode later.

When you have completed your interviews, it's time to analyse the data. Force yourself and your team to be brutally honest during this part of the process. Don't confuse what you want to hear with what you actually heard!

The data may confirm that your target market is a good fit for your product. You may identify some issues that you can overcome with product changes. You may spot opportunities for your product of which you were previously unaware. Or you may decide that there are significant concerns about your target market segment that require new thinking.

Persevere with listening and gathering feedback. Try again!

Every business environment is constantly changing. Technology, tools, customer expectations, competitors, political and legislative environments… they never stand still.

So it's crucial to remember that this process is not a one-off. You must continually engage in market discovery and regular review of product-market fit in order to spot growth opportunities that enable your business to flourish!

The ADAPT Framework in Action

I've founded, turned around and held leadership roles in several businesses over the course of my career to date, with varying degrees of success. In hindsight, it's easy to see how product-market fit and the ADAPT framework were key contributors to the outcome in each case.

Early in my career I worked with a highly experienced leader who was expert at communicating with, internalising and acting on feedback from the marketplace. Thanks to this acumen, we successfully added several new lines of business and grew to over $20M revenue per annum of business in a short time. However, we had not systematised the practice of continuously checking product-market fit, and the organisation began to falter when the leader took time out from the business. Luckily, we had "friendly" customers who advised us when the market had shifted fundamentally. We had failed to spot this. I took responsibility for the painful process of re-aligning our skills and offerings to meet the new needs of the market, and we successfully arrested and reversed the negative trend. We then systematised the ADAPT product-market analysis process, and that organisation continues to thrive today. The lessons of this experience remain with me still!

Later in my career I joined a VC-backed organisation which had a highly innovative, disruptive technology solution but very slow and challenging sales cycles. When we took a fresh and structured look at product-market fit, we realised there were adjacent markets that would benefit more from our product than our initial target market. We changed the product positioning and go-to-market approach, though the product itself remained largely the same, and quickly saw benefits in increased commercialisation!

Most recently, I co-founded a climate-tech software company. Experience had taught me the value of a systematic product-market fit process, and we diligently embarked on a series of structured interviews with our primary targets. We repeatedly heard concerns about the product being nice-to-have rather than must-have. But swayed by our unwavering belief in the benefits that our product could deliver, we ignored that feedback. For far too long, we attempted to sell into a market which is not (yet!) a good fit. Luckily, before funding became a concern, we had time to pivot to address an alternative market that our ADAPT analysis showed us has an urgent need for exactly the capabilities that our product offers, and we are now, finally, benefitting from product-market fit.

Aileen Ryan

Aileen Ryan's executive career spans software and hardware engineering, strategy and commercial operations with a variety of technology organisations. She currently serves as president and CEO of the RAIN Alliance.

Aileen was named by *Silicon Republic* as one of the top 25 Irish leaders in the Sci-Tech world, and by IT Security Guru and KPMG as one of the most inspiring women in cyber security.

She holds an MBA, an MSc in computer science, a bachelor's degree in engineering and has completed advanced executive studies at the University of Cambridge and the Stanford University Graduate School of Business.

Aileen lives in Berkshire, where she shares her passion for music and the great outdoors with her family.

in www.linkedin.com/in/aileensmithryan

Business Growth Is Actually Much Easier Than You Think

ERIK SCHWARTZ

In the world of business, growth often seems like an elusive goal, shrouded in mystery and complexity. But what if I told you that the path to business growth is simpler than most people realise? This chapter will reveal a key success secret: leveraging AI can make business growth more accessible and achievable than you might have thought possible.

With over two decades of experience in the tech sector, I've not only witnessed but actively shaped the evolution of information technology and its impact on business growth. In an era when many have started talking about generative AI, few can claim the deep, hands-on experience of building and implementing these systems across decades and diverse industries. This unique perspective allows me to cut through the hype and offer practical, proven strategies for leveraging AI to drive business growth.

My journey has taken me from pioneering roles at industry giants like Microsoft and Comcast to innovative projects at Elsevier, and now to my current position as chief AI officer (CAIO) at Tricon. Throughout this journey, I've been at the forefront of integrating AI into real-world business solutions, giving me a comprehensive understanding of both the technological and business aspects of AI-driven growth.

I've specialized in AI, information retrieval (the science of finding material of an unstructured nature), and knowledge discovery (the process of discovering useful knowledge from a collection of data). This focus has placed me at the cutting edge of integrating AI into search technologies, significantly enhancing how users access and interact with information. Whether leading initiatives at Microsoft, driving innovation at Comcast, or spearheading the Scopus AI project at Elsevier, I've consistently been involved in transforming theoretical AI concepts into practical, growth-driving business solutions.

This experience has led me to a fundamental truth that forms the core of this chapter: the key to sustainable and straightforward business growth lies in understanding and addressing real customer needs through innovative AI-driven solutions. It's a principle I've seen proven time and time again across various scales and sectors of business.

As we explore strategies for business growth, keep this central idea in mind: growth doesn't have to be complicated. It's about deeply understanding your customers' needs, identifying the right problems to solve, and leveraging technology – especially AI – as a means to that end. This approach can make business growth more accessible than you might have imagined.

While my journey provides the context and credibility for the advice that follows, the real value lies in translating this experience into actionable strategies for your own business. In the following sections, we'll bridge the gap between high-level concepts and practical implementation. I'll share specific tips and techniques that you can apply to leverage AI for business growth, regardless of your company's size or industry.

These insights aren't just theoretical – they're battle-tested strategies that I've personally seen drive significant growth and innovation. From creating highly differentiated customer experiences to unlocking new efficiencies and market opportunities, these tips represent the distilled wisdom of decades spent at the intersection of AI and business growth.

Tips for Leveraging AI in Business Growth

Identify the sweet spot between customer needs and technological solutions.

Growth isn't just about selling more. It's about finding the intersection between your customers' most pressing challenges and the solutions that technology can offer. This sweet spot is where true innovation and sustainable growth occur.

Regularly engage with your customers to understand their evolving needs. Let this ongoing dialogue inform your approach to technological innovation. Stay informed about AI advancements that could address these challenges. Keep lines of communication open and frictionless. Make it easy for customers to talk to you.

Foster a culture of innovation within your organisation. When employees at all levels are empowered to think creatively about customer challenges, you amplify your chances of truly solving the customers' problems.

Create Highly Differentiated Experiences

As products become more disposable, the experience you provide can become your most powerful differentiator. AI technologies offer unprecedented opportunities to create engaging, personalised experiences that keep your customers coming back.

Utilise AI-driven analytics to gain deep insights into customer behaviour and preferences. Really understand what they like and don't like. Double down on the areas where you create delight and eradicate those that cause friction. These insights can inform every aspect of your business, from product development to marketing strategies. Customers will stay with you as long as you keep solving their problems.

Continually refine your offerings based on real user feedback. This ongoing improvement ensures that your differentiated experiences remain relevant and valuable to your customers, driving sustained growth.

Explore the Frontiers of Customer Experience

Generative AI is opening up new possibilities in customer experience and product development.

This technology allows businesses to create content, designs, and solutions that were previously unimaginable or too resource-intensive to produce.

AI can be used to generate hyper-personalised content at scale, creating a deeply individualised experience that can be as unique as your customers are. Product experiences can be contextualised to your customers' needs and styles. Imagine a user experience that understands when you can't talk or watch a video, but can only listen, or that you are disconnected from the Internet but still want to have a deeply immersive entertainment experience.

Deliver High-Value Services with Modest Investments

AI technologies have dramatically reduced the barriers to entry for providing high-value services, and they will continue to drop in price. There are some great AI capabilities offered as a service that will allow you to prove your value for your customers without making a huge investment in customisation or hosting your own AI.

AI can be grounded with your data so that it remains reliable, telling the truth all the time and not undermining your brand. By analysing behaviour patterns, AI allow you to provide deeply engaging experiences; by providing insight into these patterns, it can help you scale your business and your reach.

And the tools keep getting better and better. After you have proven the value of your product, and have observed your customers coming back repeatedly, you can start to make deeper investments to improve the quality of your AI, or even create your own.

Act Now to Stay Ahead of the Competition

The AI revolution isn't coming – it's here. Businesses across industries are already leveraging these technologies to gain competitive advantages. Waiting to adopt AI isn't just missing an opportunity; it's risking obsolescence.

Begin with an AI readiness assessment for your business to identify immediate opportunities. Start small with pilot projects to build organisational experience and confidence with AI technologies. Invest in AI education and training for your team, building internal capabilities and fostering a culture of innovation crucial for long-term success in the AI-driven business landscape.

Remember, the key to leveraging these tips is taking action. Start small if necessary, but start now. Those who embrace AI-driven growth strategies today will be the leaders of tomorrow.

From Digital Libraries to Scopus AI: a Real-World Success Story

To illustrate how these principles play out in practice, let me share the journey of adding AI to Scopus, which provides summaries and abstracts of academic publisher Elsevier's vast library of research. In just six weeks, we incorporated a generative AI layer on top of Scopus, creating Scopus AI. This rapid development and deployment exemplified the principles discussed earlier:

- We identified a confluence of customer needs (more efficient research processes) and technological solutions (generative AI).
- We created a highly differentiated experience by integrating AI into an already powerful research tool.

- We built unique experiences that were previously unimaginable, such as AI-assisted literature reviews and research summaries.
- With a modest investment of time and resources, we significantly enhanced the value we could offer to our customers.
- We acted quickly, recognising that being the first to market with a robust solution could provide a significant competitive advantage.

The launch of Scopus AI was a resounding success, demonstrating that the principles of AI-driven business growth are not just theoretical – they're practical and achievable.

This journey, from digitising paper documents in the 90s to launching an AI-powered tool to parse and summarise dense and specialised research in 2023, illustrates the incredible pace of technological advancement. More importantly, it shows how businesses that stay at the forefront of these advancements, continuously innovating and adapting, can achieve remarkable growth and success.

As we look to the future, the potential for AI to drive business growth seems limitless. The key is to remain curious, adaptable, and willing to embrace new technologies – always with a focus on solving real problems for your customers. By understanding customer needs, leveraging cutting-edge technology, and moving quickly, you can unlock growth opportunities that may have seemed out of reach. This is the true success secret of business growth in the AI era: it's more accessible than ever before, waiting for those bold enough to seize it.

Erik Schwartz

Erik is a seasoned technology executive and entrepreneur with over two decades of experience in the tech sector, specialising in the intersection of AI, information retrieval and knowledge discovery. Over the course of his career, Erik has been at the forefront of integrating large scale platforms and integrating AI into search technologies, significantly enhancing user interaction and information accessibility.

He previously held key senior roles at Comcast, Elsevier, and Microsoft, where he led pioneering AI, search, and LLM initiatives. Erik's professional journey is marked by his dedication to innovation and his belief in the power of collaboration. He has consistently driven teams towards the swift delivery of groundbreaking solutions, firmly establishing himself as a trusted leader in the technology community.

www.triconinfotech.com

www.schwaa.uk

Optimising Growth and Reducing Risk through Strategic Market Research

ANDREW SMITH

The Biggest Risk Is Doing Nothing

Investing in growth can often feel daunting, like you are exposing your business to unnecessary risk. But once you have built a consistent revenue stream, the biggest risk to your continuing success is doing nothing, which leaves your business at the mercy of market forces, competitive activity and the potential sudden loss of core customers.

How can a business reduce the risk of investments into growth? By embracing entrepreneurial gut instinct, creativity and vision, then combining these with rigorous market research. Why would a business owner leave a growth plan, be it a new product launch, a marketing campaign, a market entry or rebrand to chance?

Market research is a vast toolbox of approaches that can be applied to the specific dynamics of your marketplace. Depending on your immediate business needs, market research can be either quantitative in nature (the numbers, the robust data), qualitative (the deeper discussions and observations, often more focused on the 'why') or a hybrid of the two approaches.

At the heart of market research is the fact that humans ultimately love to contribute. Many people yearn for a sense that, as individuals, they are making a difference. Ultimately (although many do not openly admit it) we like talking about ourselves and our particular approach to life.

Market research is about facilitating business growth. It is about informed decisions that will propel a business towards its end goal more efficiently and with greater impact. It provides businesses with the insights to engage and align internal stakeholders and investors with strategic decisions, outlining a set of priorities to manage step-changes in growth.

I'm passionate about what I do. I am not an academic researcher but operate in the real world, working with businesses ranging from start-ups to big multi-national brands. Irrespective of the size of your business or your experience of conducting market research, there are a number of recommendations that will help you optimise your growth, whilst also reducing risk.

Best Practice Market Research for the Real World

Your business's data is a potential goldmine.

I often spend time convincing brands not to invest time and money on new primary research. But why, you might ask, would I close the door on my biggest revenue driver? The simple answer is that many businesses do not realise that they are already sitting on a goldmine of data and insights.

The broader the data sets, the better. Potential repositories include web analytics, customer expenditure, registration profiles, previous research, government data and other publicly published reports. Don't stress over data silos and the fact that the data cannot be merged. It is far more important to use the individual data sets to create a narrative about what is happening in your market, with your brands and your competitors. Even if your data only provides 80% of the answer, your growth plan will already be far more informed. Then, if knowledge gaps still exist, combine the insights of your research with your sector expertise or develop a targeted research project with the money that you initially saved.

Ensure Your Market Research Is Multi-Dimensional

Whilst I would always advocate the importance of conducting market research that is focused on the core growth plan, in order to maximise return on investment, brands should also consider if there are multiple applications of their research outputs. For example, a research project may be focused on extending a brand's proposition but that journey may naturally uncover support material that can be repurposed for other functions, such as PR, thought leadership, social media content, collateral to support your sales teams, white papers, etc.

Another method that can uncover valuable insights is to combine different research, for example merging attitudinal research with real-life consumer usage habits. This is where survey responses are directly linked to customer transactions, browsing behaviour or responses to specific marketing campaigns. Combining the worlds of perceived and actual behaviour creates an enlightening window on customers, allowing brands to truly understand what is driving behaviour and to target the factors that will most likely drive revenue growth.

Embrace the Partnership of AI and HI

As Erik has just shared, artificial intelligence is evolving at an unprecedented rate, and it is now commonly incorporated into market research, tasked with the heavy lifting of data analysis, pattern recognition, scoping out themes and even predictive modelling.

However, for all of AI's advancements, a combination of AI and HI (Human Intelligence) provides businesses with the real leap forward, allowing researchers the scope to focus on getting under the skin of the stimuli created by AI.

A good researcher will cross-fertilise stimuli and teachings from other sectors, employing creativity, intuition and an understanding of cultural nuances that AI cannot currently replicate. This is particularly important for creating growth strategies and marketing campaigns that resonate emotionally with your potential customers.

HI provides the actionable insights that AI's machine-view of data or transcripts cannot. The human factor will ultimately outline strategic priorities within the context of a business's resource limits and market challenges, providing a real-world growth plan that can be both ambitious and achievable.

Market Researchers Are Your Trusted Advisors

Many business owners have coaches or mentors, and market researchers should be seen in the same advisory light. Experienced researchers are an integral part of your team; you should be 100% transparent with them and trust them to highlight the biggest growth opportunities.

It's not just anyone who can structure a survey or discussion guide to maximise insight and actionable data. The most valuable insights are often driven by cultivating a deep understanding of those motivations that customers and potential customers are not even consciously aware of themselves. Your business may need to venture beyond basic research and data analysis to utilise advanced techniques such as product-pricing sensitivity, customer segmentations, trade-off analysis or market sizing. To achieve all this, experience, independence and objectivity are essential.

Businesses should use external research agencies as partners, with both sides committed to delivering business growth. Market researchers ensure that the outputs of any research are communicated in a way that creates the maximum impact for all your stakeholders, who will see value in different aspects of the project. The output of research projects should be inspiring and challenging, promoting debate and ultimately providing the stepping stone to decisions that drive growth. Even then, businesses can look to researchers to play a vital role in guiding decision-making, moderating ideation sessions and being a "check and balance" during the implementation of the growth plan.

Growth Case Study

A B2C retailer is looking to isolate their key growth opportunities, amongst both current customers and potential customers, to drive revenue across their core markets.

Research Solution:

1. A multi-phased study across four markets: UK, France, Spain and Germany.
2. A hybrid approach incorporating internal data analysis, focus groups and a robust quantitative survey.

Research Outputs:

- A market segmentation based on behaviours and attitudes, with each of the six segments varying in size by country.
- Full insight report and recommendations presented and discussed at the board meeting:
  - drivers to increase customer expenditure and increase consideration amongst potential customers;
  - barriers restricting growth;

- advertising messages that could drive brand consideration;
- product pricing sensitivity;
- PR opportunities to position the brand as a thought leader within its sector.

- An interactive online dashboard, empowering each country's manager to interrogate their local market data.

Growth Outcome:

- The research stimulated a clear set of actions and strategic priorities to drive revenue growth, for each customer segment and local market.
- The client implemented the recommendations and has continued to record both increased market share and revenue growth.

Call to Action

Growth and market research are intrinsically linked. The outputs of any market research or data analysis must support business growth, otherwise it is a waste of time and investment. Of course, there is a cost to conducting research, but the potential ROI of market research is significant, especially when it is compared to the relatively large investments required to drive media spend or develop a sales function.

Market research is about reinforcing creativity and vision, supporting a business in making informed decisions and setting priorities. After 30 years of working in this sector, 12 of them running my own business, I still love what I do, and it's a privilege that brands trust me to join them on a journey to achieving clear and deep understanding of complex situations.

So, if you are looking to grow your business, I encourage you to go to the market, run surveys, have discussions, observe behaviour, analyse existing data, take the opportunity to ask those difficult questions and, above all, to listen.

I would urge you to embark on a journey of discovery using market research: to learn new insights, understand the implications and future challenges for your business, and ultimately to build stronger relationships with your customers. What's not to love about optimising your business growth whilst simultaneously reducing risk?

Andrew Smith

Andrew learnt his trade within media companies, conducting B2C and B2B research whilst managing centralised insight and analytics teams. In 2012, faced with redundancy, instead of diving back into the corporate world, Andrew took the opportunity to establish his own market research agency (Insight Advantage) to support businesses in building closer relationships with their customers, making informed decisions and ultimately growing their brands.

Working with start-ups through to large multi-national brands, Insight Advantage has built up a client base that spans multiple sectors. With experience spanning both quantitative and qualitative research, Andrew regularly conducts projects across global markets, helping brands power their commercial growth.

Andrew lives in West London with his wife and two daughters. When he is not researching and uncovering insights, he enjoys live music, tennis, padel and messing about on motorbikes.

https://www.linkedin.com/in/speak2andrew/

andrew@insight-advantage.co.uk